# BEYOND
# GLOBALIZATION

## NEW DIRECTIONS IN INTERNATIONAL STUDIES

### PATRICE PETRO, SERIES EDITOR

The New Directions in International Studies series focuses on transculturalism, technology, media, and representation, and features the innovative work of scholars who explore various components and consequences of globalization, such as the increasing flow of peoples, ideas, images, information, and capital across borders. Under the direction of Patrice Petro, the series is sponsored by the Center for International Education at the University of Wisconsin–Milwaukee. The Center seeks to foster interdisciplinary and collaborative research that probes the political, economic, artistic, and social processes and practices of our time.

# BEYOND GLOBALIZATION

## MAKING NEW WORLDS IN MEDIA, ART, AND SOCIAL PRACTICES

EDITED BY

**A. ANEESH, LANE HALL,** AND **PATRICE PETRO**

RUTGERS UNIVERSITY PRESS

*New Brunswick, New Jersey, and London*

Library of Congress Cataloging-in-Publication Data

Beyond globalization : making new worlds in media, art, and social practices / edited by
A. Aneesh, Lane Hall, and Patrice Petro.
    p.   cm.  —  (New directions in international studies)
   Includes bibliographical references and index.
   ISBN 978-0-8135-5153-1 (hardcover : alk. paper)
   ISBN 978-0-8135-5154-8 (pbk. : alk. paper)
   1. Mass media and culture.  2. Mass media and globalization.  3. Mass media—Social
aspects.  4. Mass media—Political aspects.  5. Mass media and art.  6. Globalization—
Social aspects.  7. Identity (Psychology) and mass media.  I. Aneesh, A. (Aneesh),
1964–    II. Hall, Lane, 1955–    III. Petro, Patrice, 1957–

  P94.6.B48 2011
  302.23—dc22

                                     2011010853

A British Cataloging-in-Publication record for this book is available from the British Library.

Visit our Web site: http://rutgerspress.rutgers.edu

Manufactured in the United States of America

# CONTENTS

# BEYOND GLOBALIZATION

# Introduction

## The Making of Worlds

## A. ANEESH, LANE HALL, AND PATRICE PETRO

Contemporary accounts of an emerging "Global Village" or "One World" system—whether in relation to economics, culture, communication, or language—may seem naïve descriptions of global integration. But discourses on globalization are perhaps not all rhetoric. To take but one example: worlds studied by anthropologists are no longer protected by geography and distance; in fact, they continue to disappear. Obstinate languages, values, norms, and practices have been either exterminated or brought out of seclusion, full of wonder and spectacle via research, representation, and multiple mediated views. Two decades ago, linguists rushed to a Turkish farming village in order to record the Ubykh language, once spoken in the northwestern Caucasus, from its last known speaker, a frail farmer whose death in 1992 also marked the death of the Ubykh language. Indeed, 90 percent of the world's languages are expected to disappear in the next one hundred years.[1] It is not surprising, then, that the unprecedented integration of the world through money, media, and communication is often experienced as disturbingly threatening and altogether "real." After all, satellites never set on the empire.

And yet, the nature of integration, captured by the term "globalization," is often poorly understood, resulting in misplaced battles over homogeneity versus heterogeneity, as if the functional expansion of markets and media could turn the world into irremediable cultural sameness.[2] Responses to an imaginary threat of homogeneity quickly lead to demonstrations of cultural distinction, such as in claims that the English spoken by Americans, Britons, Indians, and Australians (and all others) varies in each instance. One rushes to show how new diversities and cultural hybrids emerge through such integration, thus situating global integration in a positive light. Subtle differences between McDonalds in Minneapolis and Manila are explored to disprove the thesis of McDonaldization.[3] Yet such attempts to capture diversities, including the thesis of hybridity, cannot free themselves from their philosophical dependence on the notion of an original identity without which diversity or hybridity would not make sense. Thus, difference could be thought of only as difference "between" self-identical objects. Instead of looking for microscopic differences in cultural content—the diversity of various McDonalds or the Englishes spoken on different continents—this volume proposes a different measure of difference whereby the world is nothing but multiple emergences, indeed multiple worlds, under different systems of observation, always mediated by representations, artistic interventions, and social practices.

## Beyond Social Construction

For the contributors to this collection, the thesis of *worldmaking* replaces the *notion of reality* with *the making of reality* in an effort to emphasize that there is no self-identical world out there to be discovered. Instead, as the authors show, the world gets made in the very process of observation, of drawing distinctions. While culture is always already mediated by language, the increasing sophistication, multiplication, and dissemination of information nonetheless changes the experience of all culture. To confront the challenges posed by this reality, it is important to distinguish the thesis of worldmaking from two obvious, long established systems of social thought: constructionism and realism. Borrowing from both, we may indeed call our approach *constructive realism*. This is not a glibly convenient middle path, since it is developed from major theoretical developments of the last century implicitly focused on the notion of *difference*.[4]

Let us explain first why worldmaking is not simple constructionism. Constructionism in its various versions tends to evoke, perhaps mistakenly, a sense of anti-realism, idealism, or relativism, appearing to suggest that things are not real but constructed or socially made. One of the most influential works in this tradition of thought—Peter Berger and Thomas Luckmann's *The Social Construction of Reality*[5]—offers a highly sophisticated account of constructionism, explaining how everyday interactions form the basis of commonsense understanding, which over time settles into conventions, significations, and institutions, later perceived as an ordered, prearranged

reality that impinges on us. However, there are two problems with such celebrated accounts of social construction. First, they tend to privilege human
agency by tracing all domains of social reality—scientific, technological, or
legal—to original human interactions: the "social order is . . . an ongoing
human production," as Berger and Luckmann explain.[6] At the same time,
they posit a reality that is deeper than the socially constructed one, which is
temporally, ontologically, and logically dependent on what John Searle calls
"brute facts." Thus, for Searle, social constructions—like language—are epis-
temologically, not ontologically, objective.[7] Similarly, Ian Hacking[8] argues
that it is the ideas, not the objects to which the ideas correspond, that are
socially constructed. Only when ideas start interacting with and affecting
people who move in the world of objects can there be an indirect social construction of both objects and people that may be called "interactive kinds."
Thus, the "refugee" is a social construction but "quarks" are not. The refugee
interacts with things of that kind, namely people, including individual
refugees, who can become aware of how they are classified and seek to mod-
ify their behavior accordingly. Quarks, by contrast, do not form an interactive
kind; as Hacking informs us, the idea of the quark does not interact with
actual quarks; instead, they belong not to an "interactive" but to an "indif-
ferent kind."

While Berger and Luckmann argued for a slightly stronger version of constructionism, they also agreed that biology precedes the social order; "the
necessity for social order as such," they explain, "stems from man's [sic] biological equipment."[9] In this way, they implicitly agree with a hierarchical
model of reality, according to which some objects are ontologically or brutally
"real" while others are socially made or "constructed." Thus, scientific realism raises its head, stubborn and unrepentant, in the middle of construc-
tionist doctrines.

In an effort to break with this logic and approach, this volume proposes
that constructions are real and the real is constructed. The world is made and
remade through widely distributed and networked spheres of production—
across art, media, and social practices. There is no objective, universal, transcendent reality independent of all systems of observation. There is no
self-identical world out there to be discovered. Even the notion of "biological equipment" proposed by Berger and Luckmann demands revision: human
eyes may discern colors in the world, but one can never know what colors
are in themselves outside of our perception or scientific constructions of

electromagnetic frequency and wavelength. This is not philosophical ideal-ism. While there is indeed an environment without which no observation can take place, it is not possible to know this environment in its own terms because the world does not have a language of its own. And the belief that our knowledge of quarks first constructed in theory and later observed through accelerators somehow corresponds one-to-one with an identical world out there is precisely that: a belief. There is no way to confirm it. To know if it corresponds with the world is to know the world in its own terms, which is, again, an absurd proposition. This is not Kant's subject-centered transcendental idealism, which assumes the existence of an individual's mind as the condition of all understanding, a mechanism that transforms noumena into phenomena, or environmental stimulations into meaningful experiences. There are only different systems of construction without any hierarchy. Their corresponding constructions cannot be labeled as more or less real because there is no universal scale that can compare objects con-structed by an organism, for instance, with objects created by language. There is no meta-language that can compare the reality of refugees con-structed within a system of nation-states with that of quarks constructed within models of physics. One world may depend on the other for stimula-tions but it is fueled by its immanent dynamic. How else would it call itself a world? The world of art or sociology or of physics must produce its separate "self"-understanding derived from its internal order. Multiple worlds are *made* through multiple modes of construction and observation. Here we can attempt to deepen, even redirect, Appadurai's[10] emphasis on the imagina-tion as a social practice in which he combines notions of mechanically pro-duced images (the Frankfurt School), the idea of imagined communities (Benedict Anderson's[11] sense), and the French idea of the imaginary (*imagi-naire*) in the context of disjunctures among mediascapes, ethnoscapes, technoscapes, financescapes, and ideoscapes. In our thesis, the notion of imagination becomes a necessity because one loses the ability—in view of differentiated realms of art, media, or science—to *know* other realms in their original terms; one can only imagine the other and necessarily so. Indeed, the only way to conduct one's business is by reconstructing the other realm in one's own image; that is, one must imagine what is happen-ing in other spheres in the language of one's own world. It is not empty imagination, for it is not constructed from thin air, but it does owe its flight to the air of difference. Even within the cultural domain, differentiations among religion, art, and media cannot be reduced to a unity. The multiplicity of worlds comes with a multiplicity of logics, rationalities, feelings, and modes of comprehension.

## New Logics, New Multiplicities

In the sciences, aesthetic differences do not matter; for the arts, notions of verifiability or falsifiability are strange and even irrelevant concerns. The interpretive difference between aesthetic and non-aesthetic has nothing to do with that between true and false. To be sure, glossy art can enhance the appeal of scientific journals, and artists may be inspired by the truth of events. And yet scientific argument is better made without any appeal to aesthetic, economic, social, religious, or political values. Worlds of science and art may influence each other as external environments, but their peculiar production of reality is an internally developed capacity. And in our ever-expanding global systems of production, worlds continue to multiply.

Hence, if there is no one world in either art or science, how can we think critically and creatively about globalization today? Indeed, it would seem that the very idea of globalization suggests an interconnected whole, and thus, a disappearance of secluded pockets of cultures and communities, a gradual erasure of multiple worlds into media and markets. And yet the contributors to this collection suggest something very different when they evoke worldmaking as a new kind of multiplicity, based not exclusively on the logic of space, according to which cultures develop uniqueness and solidity and are safeguarded by distance and stabilized through time. Those worlds have indeed been pried open, their exclusivity rendered largely dubious. While in the past cultural dealings between socially and spatially separated groups have been sustained at great cost, information machines of our times create a new space of global exchanges that questions the stability of cultural divisions previously protected by geography.[12] Worldmaking here references multiplicity and multiple worlds, not along the old lines of cultural exclusivity and spatial separation, but along the new logics of production. And these worlds are increasingly global in their nature and effects. Hence, new questions emerge regarding how these multiple worlds interact in the age of global communication. What new forms of observation have been introduced by global systems of cultural production? Critically engaging with the widely distributed and networked sphere of global art, media, and cultural practices today, the authors whose work is included here address this question and explore the frames, functions, languages, and meaning-constituting systems that construct subjectivities and identities as well as very material experiences of space, time, and agency in our global age.

## Global Media Cultures

In his essay that opens this volume, Mark Poster makes the crucial point that "global culture can only be global media culture." For him, the question of global culture may not be raised merely in terms of its content, its homogeneity or heterogeneity, its essential sameness or enduring cultural distinction. The significant difference of the global age is instead the globality of information machines because, as he puts it, "the increasing sophistication, multiplication, and dissemination of information machines change the experience of all culture. Every cultural object now exists in a (potentially) global context." Clearly, old distinctions of culture—exotic, oriental, or western—depended on the deeply spatial character of colonial globalization when cultures were hounded out of their geographic locations and made to speak their difference in a colonial language that itself remained beyond scrutiny. But such isomorphism between space and culture is no longer so deterministic or even as important as it once was.[13] Hence, Poster turns his gaze to the observing device itself, which is no longer a colonial language stemming from the conquest of space but a global logic of information machines. In order to hear the global, Poster asks us to discern the logic of new media systems, which bring a different set of distinctions and observations into the equation.

The authors in this collection take up Poster's challenge to discern these logics and "hear the global" through new mediated information and architectural systems. In his essay included here, for instance, Fred Turner directly addresses the global reach of one of the most ubiquitous of information machines in his analysis of Google and the cultural infrastructure for new media production. His ostensible focus is Burning Man, an annual event that draws workers in computer-related industries to a celebration of art and temporary community staged in the Black Rock Desert of Nevada. As Turner points out, Burning Man had its beginnings some twenty years ago with the burning of a wooden effigy on a San Francisco beach, and later moved inland; it now boasts more than 35,000 participants each year, drawn from the ranks of programmers, marketers, and technical executives who spend a week in Nevada every August. And yet Turner is less interested in Burning Man in and of itself than in examining an affinity between the spirit of Google's corporate organization and a popular techno-culture movement, or rather, the logic behind a peer-based production ethic.

Google is an organization that resolutely stays out of content production, whose very name is pure mathematical information, a play on the word "googol," the mathematical term for a 1 followed by 100 zeros, reflecting the immense volume of information that exists, an organization whose mission is "to organize the world's information and make it universally accessible and useful." Turner does not focus on what the information machine searches and observes, or even the reality it makes; rather, he observes the reality-making device itself and uncovers the culture that animates it in the relationship between bohemian art worlds and new modes of digital manufacturing. As he explains, "Burning Man models the social structures on which manufacturing now depends and at the same time provides a place in which to work through the psychological and material constraints it imposes." Like online communities, Burning Man has become a site for both communal belonging and commercial product development. In both a structural and an ideological sense, it provides a *cultural infrastructure* for emerging forms of media manufacturing. In this way, Turner excavates the hidden language of organization that earlier remained implicit and beyond scrutiny, showing how both Google and Burning Man transform "the ideals and social structures of bohemian art worlds, their very particular ways of being 'creative,' into psychological, social, and material resources for the workers of a new, supremely fluid world of postindustrial information work."

But it is not only the fluid world of postindustrial work that is revealed in the worlds created by Google and Burning Man. Also revealed are the deep-seated anxieties about the possibilities for community within information societies, long accustomed to the belief that they have surpassed the condition of scarcity and the conflicts provoked by it. As Turner makes clear, for all the rhetoric of equality, empowerment, and voluntarism that surrounds commons-based production, technical workers remain *workers*, striving, through Burning Man, to "collectively re-imagine themselves as autonomous creators and restore to their labor, if only for a while, the sense of social value that is so often and so often falsely claimed for it by corporate marketers."

In his contribution to this volume, Peter Paik similarly explores anxieties about the promises and failures of community in multiple worlds of fact and fiction. In the wake of both information machines and the world financial crisis, Paik examines apocalyptic narratives of community in contemporary literature, comics, and film where fictional constructions appear disconcertingly real and facts of finance increasingly constructed. In an analysis that spans Cormac McCarthy's *The Road* (2006) as well as recent films such as *Children of Men* (2006) and *Blindness* (2008), Paik argues that new fictional worlds bring us face to face with possible fields of action in our elusive and transforming global context. In these apocalyptic narratives, we are confronted not only with the impossibility of community but with the reality of scarcity; characters grapple with the recognition that global society can no longer legitimate itself on the basis of the easy abundance generated by an ever-expanding market economy. Unlike earlier apocalyptic narratives, these worldmaking fictions trace not the collapse of civilization as such but rather the specter of an inexorable transition to a society characterized by markedly diminished material expectations, which even temporary communities like Burning Man tend to reflect in their focus on the limits of consumption and need for cooperation in the middle of the desert.

And yet such diminished expectations are not new to the twenty-first century, nor have they gone unchallenged by artists and technologists, as Thomas Malaby explains in his essay on two different projects of community in which urban design and the productivity of play are specific kinds of worldmaking activities. Malaby focuses his analysis on two urbanist projects: one never realized—New Babylon, the postwar unitary urbanist project of the Dutch painter Constant Nieuwenhuys, and the other host to hundreds of thousands of people today, Second Life, the virtual world made by Linden Lab of San Francisco. As he points out, architecture, design, play, and technology help us to understand the histories and ideals behind the digital architectures that increasingly mediate our everyday actions. Drawing parallels between New Babylon and Second Life, Malaby stresses the utopian rather than the dystopian impulses at work within fully automated systems of production, which aim to free individuals to fulfill their creative impulses. While providing a counterpoint to Paik's descriptions of dystopian narrative worlds, Malaby also engages with Fred Turner's ideas by providing a wider historical frame linking emerging bohemian art worlds and new modes of digital manufacturing, such as represented by Google and Burning Man. In postwar Europe and the United States, Malaby concludes, "there was a remarkable and mutually confirming combination of a deeply held skepticism toward 'top-down' decision-making—with a corresponding resistance to (and even resentment of) the institutional control of technology—and a deep faith in the ability of technology to provide solutions when made widely available." In this context, new urbanist projects imagine worlds where humans and machines interact as dynamic, collaborating elements in a fluid, socio-technical system, where control emerges not from the top-down but from the complex, and probabilistic interactions of humans, machines, and events around them.

## Media Matters

Nowhere are these new logics more visible (and audible) today than in glob-alized television formats and cinematic practices, where the stakes for sur-vival of marginalized groups have led to new modes of production, new forms of observation and engagement. Indeed, while cinema and television are often considered outmoded cultural forms, lacking the democratic potential of the internet, wedded to nationalist projects and top-down networks of pro-duction and distribution, the authors here suggest something very different in their analysis of the unique role television and cinema play in political and cultural worldmaking today.

In her contribution, for instance, Tasha Oren suggests that format tele-vision, that most conventionalized of media forms in which "contestants dance, cook, sing, redecorate, lose weight, start businesses, fall in love, or merely survive in close quarters," has indeed gone viral (in such worldwide franchises as *Idol*, *Survivor*, *The Apprentice*, *Big Brother*, and *Who Wants to be a Millionaire*). It is the format, not culture, that is increasingly global. And yet even this most standardized of products demonstrates the tension that ani-mates the space between the global medial protocol and its local content and meaning. To explore this in depth, Oren considers an Israeli television program, *Ha'shagrir/The Ambassador* (which is based on a format illicitly bor-rowed from *The Apprentice*), as a particularly telling exercise in political and cultural worldmaking. She shows how it is at once exemplary of the global format phenomena and at the same time essentially Israeli, offering a new understanding of the critical role television still plays in envisioning an interconnected world. The program clearly represents an Israeli view of the world (doubly so, as the program is about both media and political repre-sentation) as well as the possibility of intervention, or a remaking, of the world it finds. It thus partakes in a peculiarly televisual worldmaking as it articulates a unique relationship between national identity and a media-centric articulation of culture.

Yeidy Rivero similarly looks to television to discern how global formats are remade, here in the context of smaller markets in Latin America and the Spanish Caribbean. As she explains, since the late 1980s, these markets have been saturated with Mexican imports (such as the global format of the telenovela) that suggest a neutral Spanish-speaking world: neutral accents, neutral spaces, neutral expressions, and neutral moralities. Produced for the Spanish-speaking world by companies in Mexico and Miami, this putative cultural neutrality, or what one of us has elsewhere called *imperial neutrality*,[14] is more often "heard" than "seen": "the neutral accent in Spanish," Rivero writes, "is equivalent to a Mexican accent and it is utilized in the narrative to appeal to the Mexican majority that comprises the US Hispanic audience." The avoidance of cultural practices that might connect these television formats to specific countries is indeed noteworthy, but Rivero insists that we look elsewhere, specifically to Spanish Caribbean and Latin American films produced in the region, since these counter-homogenizing tendencies give voice to the plurality of immigrant stories in the Caribbean and elsewhere. As she shows, through their focus on historically situated migratory patterns, social conditions, and verbal and bodily performances, these films re-create and thus document multiple cultural worlds in the midst of globalizing media forces.

Like Rivero, Amy Villarejo underscores the multilingual compromise of global culture, seeking to account for uneven power relations, racial dynamics, and processes of transculturation that distinguish contemporary intermediality from previous modes of understanding cultural production, in this case via Brazilian television and film. As she explains, both "third world" and "third cinema" are no longer accurate descriptors of media production in Brazil, but a host of questions remain about how to "world" the world, that is, how to designate sociopolitical realities and possibilities in the wake of neoliberal reorganization and globalization. As she points out, very few Brazilians can attend the cinema, since "only about 6 percent of the population buys movie tickets each year, and the country has the second highest ratio of inhabitants to theatres in the world." Hence, while the cinema alone does not represent the underrepresented to themselves, it has become increasingly the case that television/cinema hybrids (such as the film *City of God* [2002] which has spawned the television series *City of Men*) have become the popular form of continuing a discussion about effects of globalization on the subaltern city population. These are new forms of media worldmaking that cut across markets in a commercial, narrative form that nonetheless embodies a political voice in Brazil today, circulating both intermedially and transnationally.

Finally, in her essay on the remaking of the Che Guevara myth in contemporary Latin American cinema and culture, Cristina Venegas picks up where Villarejo leaves off, showing how "third cinema" ideals have been rearticulated in the global marketplace, as revolutionary ideals now borrow from symbols rather than revolutionary concepts for reimagining the world. A new generation of Latin American filmmakers, she explains, explores the worlds of their heroes through popular culture. Walter Salles's film *Diarios de motocicleta* (*Motorcycle Diaries,* 2004), for instance, merges its interest in the historical figure of Guevara with its onscreen representative, Latin American star Gael García Bernal. As a result, "both become 'revolutionary' icons used by marketing and publicity machines, and by Bernal himself." Venegas does not bemoan this development, or see in it the triumph of global capital over local culture. Instead, she shows how it represents a pragmatic response by and to a region, seeking to reestablish its identity by capitalizing on the nostalgia of revolution, and the very real pleasures of cinematic worlds that combine the culture of consumerism with both politics and popular icons.

## Art Worlds

In the final section of this collection, three artists reflect on art practices. To practice art, they contend, is to engage in worldmaking. In his contribution, Craig Saper traces the peripatetic practice of Bob and Rose Brown, two avant-garde artists who spent much of their time traveling throughout the Amazon basin in the 1920s through the 1940s, expanding their practice of surrealist poetry to the point of categorical invisibility. Having engaged in early experiments in reading technologies, publishing pulp novels and experimental poetry, traveling to the Soviet Union, working on Hollywood movie scripts, and coauthoring cookbooks, the prolific couple's work was defined by restless creativity. As Saper explains, "The Browns' life together, lush and overgrown, reads like an epic novel; one cannot believe the scope of their interests, accomplishments, and travels." Saper goes on to detail how their travels were not merely the touristic wanderings of a privileged class, but creative journeys resulting in relational networks and aesthetic outcomes that transcended the easy categories of discernible and institutionally sanctioned art products. The Browns' "fascination with reinventing their identities through pseudonyms, collaborative work, parties, and travel" is rooted in avant-garde practice, but pushes toward a relational aesthetic that has been amplified with contemporary global media tools and technologies.

Indeed, while travel has long been intertwined as subject and process invoked by restless and wandering writers, travel as an art form itself is an interesting outcome of the avant-garde's institutional critique. If art is no longer dependent upon a received aesthetic tradition grounded in virtuosity, and is no longer entirely contextualized by an institutional apparatus of privilege and power, then art can construct a world bounded by the constraints of its own framing. Though such self-reflexivity can result in paralyzing solipsism, it also offers a rich discourse whose intentions, processes, and outcomes are in constant flux, requiring a continuous renegotiation of terms and conditions. Saper invokes Deleuze and Guattari's concept of "involution" to give critical grounding to such polymorphous practice. He uses masks and maps to explain the multiple vantage points and multidirectional flow of the Browns' "optics of fascination." Ending with the ludic quality of their work, we are reminded—as Thomas Malaby describes in his chapter on New Babylon and Second Life—that play is a large part of pleasure, and that the river traveled is at once concretely rooted in place and abstractly rooted in language.

In a more contemporary mediascape—though no less rooted in modernist avant-garde practice—Mat Rappaport writes about the collective public art organization, vib3, or "video in the built environment." Cofounded with artists Conrad Gleber and John Marshall, vib3 "sets out to explore the impact of media arts on the experience of public space" while also developing relational networks of artists interested in such practice. Rappaport offers a brief history of artistic appropriation of corporate media tools, citing such luminary figures as Nam Jun Paik, Dan Graham, Ant Farm, and TVTV. He forges a link between various inflections of the word "program," suggesting both televisual and architectural understandings. Drawing on the work of Walter Benjamin, he reminds us that film is received by a mass audience in a state of distraction. The artists working in vib3 embrace such distraction, working with the organic flow of people through dynamic yet fragmented urban spaces and exploring how the "interweaving of moving pictures into and onto the building's surface" might allow "an opportunity for artists to comment on—and shape—these environments."

In the final essay in this collection, Eduardo Kac, a pioneer in merging the discourses of technology, art, and science, describes his own worldmaking practices. In 1998, he coined the term "bio art" and in 1999 refocused the term to "transgenic art," which "describes a new art form based on the use of genetic engineering to create unique living beings." The presence of biotechnology, he contends, "will increasingly change from agricultural and pharmaceutical practices to a larger role in popular culture, just as the perception of the computer changed historically from an industrial device and military weapon to a communication, entertainment, and education tool." Kac is clear about his intentions, stating that "in my work I appropriate and subvert contemporary technologies—not to make detached comments on social change, but to *enact* critical views, to make present in the physical world invented new entities (artworks that include transgenic organisms), which seek to open a new space for both emotional and intellectual aesthetic experience." In many ways, we see an updated institutional critique initiated by the avant-garde here, although now broadened to include the art/research/science complex, where the subject matter shifts from the ontological question ("is this art?") to related, although perhaps more challenging, ethical questions posed by an interventionist activation of genetic engineering. Kac's work, like the work of the scholars included here, invites us to engage with the ethical question at the very basis of global media practices today; namely, When we make new worlds, what is our responsibility to their inhabitants?

This brings us back to the basic premise with which we started our introduction: the multiplicity of worldmaking. Transgenic art is at once science and art. At one level it must employ scientific procedures for its creation; that is, in order to come into existence it must commit itself to an empirical exercise in truth and validity. Yet, at the level of art, it cannot be judged on the basis of its successful creation or its utility. The artist cannot be suddenly transformed into an institutional scientist. Transgenic art can gain its value only through prisms of art, through internally developed criteria of what art is or can be. One can appreciate the science behind it, but its artistic endeavor lies in the field of aesthetic disturbance, which may even question, as in Kac's art, the scientific enterprise itself. Thus, science and art reflect the multiplicity of emergence that defines the global age, an age that is different from previous forms of colonial globalization that brought together geographically separate worlds. The globality of our age lies in the multiplying practices of worldmaking that are increasingly symbolic and virtual. From Poster's information machines, Turner's Google, Paik's fables of finance, Malaby's virtual worldmaking in Second Life, Oren's global formats of national identity, Rivero's globalizing media, Villarejo's and Venegas's discussion of cinema in an era of neoliberal globalization, Saper's multiple vantage points of wandering art, Rappaport's reconfiguration of public spaces, to Kac's transgenic art, it is a multiplicity of the virtual that emerges in concrete practices, a virtual that is exciting, disturbing, and global. By going beyond the logic of spatial frontiers, we hope this book is able to stretch and enhance the conceptual apparatus of our thinking about globalization.

# 1

# GLOBAL MEDIA AND CULTURE

## MARK POSTER

*The need of a constantly expanding market for its products chases the bourgeoisie over the whole surface of the globe. It must nestle everywhere, settle everywhere, establish connections everywhere.*

*The bourgeoisie has through its exploitation of the world market given a cosmopolitan character to production and consumption in every country. . . . In place of the old wants, satisfied by the production of the country, we find new wants, requiring for their satisfaction the products of distant lands and climes. . . . And as in material, so also in intellectual production. The intellectual creations of individual nations become common property.*

—Karl Marx, *The Communist Manifesto*

## Global Discourse in Question

Increasing global relations catalyze the question of culture: Are the basic conditions of culture changed, diminished, or supplemented as a result of intensified exchanges across national, ethnic, and territorial borders? What are the major discursive regimes that have emerged in connection with the phenomenon of global culture? What models of analysis are best suited to examine these exchanges—translation, transcoding, mixing, hybridity, homogenization? Do these models appear to pose the most productive questions in the present context? Do these concepts articulate the challenges and opportunities posed for culture by the rapid intensification of global exchanges? One might inquire as well, at another level, about the epistemological conditions for framing the problems of global culture. What discursive positions taken by the inquirer enable asking the question in the first place? What are the conditions of writing/speech/word processing that open a critical stance on the question of global culture? Is the subject, the "I think" of the Western Philosophical Tradition, an appropriate position of discourse in order to initialize questions about global culture? Does the fact that a large proportion of global exchanges occur only with the mediation of information machines incite a need to redefine the notion of the other, from that of personhood to that of mechanization?

## Have We Become Cosmopolitan?

Very often the figure that governs discourse about global culture is the cosmopolitan.[1] Since Immanuel Kant wrote "Idea for a Universal History from a Cosmopolitan Point of View" in 1784, the problem of global culture has been framed by the terms "universal" and "cosmopolitan."[2] Especially in recent years, major publications have addressed the emergence of a sense of the planetary, by invoking the term "cosmopolitan."[3] This recent interest in the term very often returns to Kant and his formulation of the issue. For the eighteenth-century philosopher, cosmopolitan is a determination of reason alone, requiring no practical effort of travel or acquaintance with or study of the societies of the world. By use of the term *cosmopolitan*, it is as though the human species might question its fate only from a vantage point that is not local, not rooted in a somewhere, not tied to any specific space or place, but somehow itself global, planetary, cosmopolitan; and this from Kant, who is notorious for residing almost without absence in the eighteenth-century backwater of Königsberg in eastern Prussia. Kant deploys the term *Weltbürgerlicher ansicht* (viewpoint of a citizen of the world) in a special manner. The cosmopolitan point of view for him is achieved through reason alone as it confronts the question of world peace. He writes, "The greatest problem for the human race . . . is the achievement of a universal civic society which administers law among men."[4] However well-intentioned, the problem of a global political institution is determined not by leaders of governments but by the philosopher himself. Because "universal civic society" is deemed so important, Kant finds it necessary to turn to and rely upon "a cosmopolitan point of view."

Well before neoliberal pundits proclaimed the Earth a free-trade zone, Enlightenment thinkers like Kant problematized the universal. Kant and the others easily moved from positing man as rational creature to establishing humanity as a universal species. Poststructuralists and postcolonial theorists since the 1970s have pointed out difficulties with the Enlightenment assumption of the universal.[5] The proclamation of the universality of "mankind" obviously failed to include nonwhites, women, children, non-Christians, and so forth, detracting seriously from the aspiration to a community of peoples. Religions and cosmologies of all kinds, well before the European Enlightenment, also contained elements of universality, elements that were even more limited and restricted than that of the *philosophes* since they included in the category those of other religions only if they converted or, even worse, designated the term *humanity* by the name of the tribe or ethnic grouping.

Today the question of humanity as a whole or universal takes on a new dimension: it is a practical fact that people, commodities, and cultural objects circulate around the planet and do so in an ever-increasing intensity. Humans are cosmopolitan today through their everyday actions: they emigrate, they work on products used in other countries, they consume objects manufactured elsewhere, they create and use texts, images, and sounds that are globally disseminated. One might well claim a cosmopolitan status today even if one has never left Königsberg.

But is "cosmopolitan" the best term to use in the context of present-day globalization? I think not. First, the term derives from European contexts and reflects its origins as Weltbürgerlicher ansicht. An adequate term for the phenomenon today must be determined through processes that are inclusive of heterogeneous planetary cultures. Second, the term is human, far too human. I shall argue that contemporary universality arises in practices that to a great extent rely upon information machines or media and these must be included in the formulation of the concept and the discourse of universality, just as earlier uses of the term needed to be revised to include non-Europeans, women, and children. Humans become universal only through the mediation of these machines, so they are an essential part of the picture.

If machines are partners to humans in global exchanges, do they affect the parameters of culture? The event of global culture is then immediately two-sided: first, culture is put into question by the extent and quality of global exchanges; second, these exchanges require information machines or media. Each of these problems is difficult enough. Taken together they constitute a truly complex challenge for the humanities and social sciences, in particular for critical theory and cultural studies.

## Global Media

Are there dangers in regarding information machines or media as a component of universality? The discourse on cosmopolitanism has not focused much on the media, much less global media.[6] One exception is an essay by Martin Hand and Barry Sandywell on "cosmopolis" in the special issue of *Theory, Culture and Society*. Unfortunately, it illustrates some of the limited directions that can be taken when confronting the question of global media. Hand and Sandywell argue that all global media are equally complicit with the forces of neoliberal transnational capitalism. Their Marxist framework leads them to emphasize the control of all planetary media by capitalist corporations. Perhaps broadcast media like radio, film, and television may be fruitfully examined exclusively from this perspective since, at least historically, these media are few-to-many systems of communication, requiring large capital investments available only to the few. Scholars committed to cultural studies, especially of the Birmingham School variety, might dispute the degree of control of media by the culture industry by pointing to the creative and resistive response of audiences to media programming.[7] This critique can be extended in accordance with constructive realism. Media constructions may be prompted by profit motives but such motives do not determine the content. The audiences are not lured by money into watching a show. The content must be natively "interesting" irrespective of profit motives. Failure to connect with the audience—whose tastes may indeed have been cultivated over time by the media—would result in a commercial loss. So the profit motive alone cannot guarantee the success of a show; or else, there would be no flops or failed shows at all. While economic and media domains do affect each other, they do not share the same internal logic for constructing their respective worlds. Nonetheless, radio, film, and television do present restrictions on positions of speech and enunciation that have been deeply shaped by advertisers, investors, and the other actors within the capitalist class.

One might argue differently for new media, digital technologies, and networked computing. Some scholars such as Manuel Castells have done just that.[8] But Hand and Sandywell will have none of it. For them, "The Web is no more than a new culture industry elevated by corporate market powers into a position of global hegemony."[9] The fact that the internet is architecturally different from broadcast media does not dissuade them from their critical position. Yet one may readily show that the internet multiplies voices so that every node in the network is a position of speech, that digital formats of texts, images, and sounds render cultural objects easy to alter, store, reproduce, and disseminate, bringing to fruition the dream that all consumers might become at the same time producers, that national borders almost disappear in internet exchanges, and that the technology of networked computing when compared to producing and transmitting television and radio shows, or making and distributing films in the analogue era, is so affordable to the degree that by 2005 well over one billion people had regular access to it (imagine if all of them were producing television, film, and radio shows). These indications that something new may be at hand in the field of media are summarily dismissed by Hand and Sandywell in favor of the old questions: ". . . the critical questions about the new digital capitalism remain: who *controls* the global media infrastructures of the information age? Who decides the form and content of the new media industries? Who will police the Net? Who, in short, will benefit in material terms from the information revolution?"[10] While the opening of networked computing media toward more democratic global communications is uncertain, these are open political questions that call for active engagement rather than the paralyzing rhetoric that discovers capitalist machinations in every nook and cranny. Indeed, capitalistic practices—such as global finance—themselves change through information machines, challenging the argument of linear or hierarchical determinations.

But the most important point I would like to raise concerning global media is that networked computing places in the hands of the general population information machines that are linked to their existences in fundamental ways. Regardless of the efforts of the capitalist class (as well as those of the nation-state), the assemblage of human and information machine must be accounted for as a phenomenon unprecedented in the array of media technologies, an innovation that is drastically changing the character of culture. For the human/information machine link introduces new configurations of the binaries of space and time, body and mind, subject and object, producer and consumer, indeed all the constituents that form cultures. While the economic questions raised by Hand and Sandywell are valid and exigent, they do not account for the potentials of change and resistance at stake in networked computing. They do not address the politics of culture in a manner that opens both sides of the question: the new aspects of surveillance and control by established political orders and economic interests but also the practices that fall outside these initiatives and portend great trouble for them.

Hand and Sandywell, along with so many other scholars who come to similar conclusions, are aware of these potential risks and affordances. They raise the specter of cosmopolitanism as global citizenship: ". . . digitalized capitalism promises a reconstruction of the polity as an electronic global village, inaugurating processes of civic renewal, raising us into the era of *global citizenship.*"[11] But they are too quick to dismiss such rosy outcomes as when they write: "*Cyberculture* . . . simply builds upon and further deepens the chronic social inequalities of class, gender and race created by the course of modern capitalism."[12] If there is to be a global (or cosmopolitan) culture, it will surely engage the internet in crucial ways.

In addition to the internet itself, there is another aspect of the relation of globalization to media. Satellite technology—distinct from but connected with the internet—takes the planet as its target of communications. This system of information machines, Lisa Parks informs us, significantly shapes ". . . the spheres of cultural and economic activity that constitute what we know as 'the global'."[13] Like the internet, communications satellites connect cultures across national and traditional boundaries, but they lend themselves to different sorts of exchanges. These technologies easily transmit broadcasts (television and radio) over very wide footprints, promoting continuous connections, say of migrants with their cultures of origin. They also enable geographic location devices to pinpoint relatively small objects and humans, a boon for surveillance practices of many kinds. Populating the skies with ever-increasing density, communications satellites lend themselves to global cultural dissemination but also to close control by extant powers. They are double-edged media, allowing greater freedom for individuals and groups and greater control by dominant institutions. In this respect, similar to the internet as Wendy Chun discloses, satellite media are therefore open to vastly divergent political uses.[14] They may solidify modern institutions but also may lead to new directions of global political culture.

## Analogue and Digital Culture

Global media are now digital and this technological change significantly influences the development of global culture. The shift from analogue to digital technology alters the basic features of the production, storage, reproduction, and dissemination of culture. Understanding these changes is essential to the future of culture especially in its global spread. Some view the changes as entirely progressive while others rue them as the end of civilization. Both of these positions are beside the point and lead down fruitless lines of inquiry. The fact is we are now faced with digital forms of culture and must attempt to develop them in the most beneficial and creative directions. Social institutions, especially the nation-state and the corporation, have begun to recognize the change in culture from analogue to digital and have mobilized to adapt the newer technologies to their own ends. It is incumbent upon university researchers and teachers, as well as cultural workers in all fields, to come to terms with the emergence of digital culture and attempt to shape its practical forms in ways that best further the deepening of human freedom, ways that to a large extent are in conflict with the tendencies of the nation-state and the corporation.[15] The fate of global culture is currently at a significant stage and the political alternatives are stark. If the nation-state has its way, American forms of copyright will prevail globally, and if the transnational corporation succeeds in its aims, culture will be increasingly commodified. The introduction of digital technologies, however, facilitates alternative models of global culture, and the university, a key developer of these technologies, must play a major role in resisting the other forces and offering less constraining cultural practices, ones that preserve the vital premise of the free exchange of all cultural forms.

Analogue technologies of culture have served well the development of modern society. First book production, then film and radio, then the telephone and television have all extended cultural forms to most levels of society. For Theodor Adorno and Max Horkheimer, this phenomenon has massified society, undoing the dialectic of class struggle and distracting the critical attention of the oppressed.[16] For others, such as Walter Benjamin, analogue technologies like film have brought the masses closer to critical thinking and opened new forms of political opposition.[17] Many have argued that even the most benighted of analogue cultural technologies, television, has enabled national cultures to subsist even in highly populated and dispersed nations like the United States. Benedict Anderson's important contribution, in this context, was to articulate the salient role of the analogue technology of print in the formation of the nation.[18] And Michael Warner pointed to the importance of print newspapers in opening the cultural space for democracy by positioning ordinary individuals as contributors to public thinking.[19]

These analogue techno-cultures formed practices of reading, writing, viewing, and listening that are specific and far from amorphous. As Marshall McLuhan urged, the medium is the message.[20] In the case of analogue technologies of culture, the medium creates what I call fixed cultural objects: texts, images, and sounds that may be widely disseminated and effectively stored (books, celluloid films, long-playing records, etc.) but are not easily altered by the consumer of culture. What you see on the printed page is what everyone else with a copy also sees. If you scribble on your page, only your copy is affected. Analogue media resist alteration once they are reproduced. They encourage the value of the original, the privileged position of the author or creator, the remunerated role of the reproducer since material costs are not negligible, and a sharp distinction between the producer and the consumer of culture. In fact, practices of consuming analogue culture promote celebrity of authors and fan appreciation among consumers, two vastly different positions and practices. In the modern period of analogue cultural production, theorists have rebelled at such constraints,[21] and authors from Lawrence Sterne to the Oulipo group and more recently Mark Danielewski[22] have wrestled with loosening the limits of analogue texts. Cultural Studies scholars have disputed the tyranny of analogue authors arguing for the creativity of readers.[23] And finally historians of print, like Adrian Johns, have shown how the vaunted stability and fixity of the analogue book is often overstated. Johns admits however that intellectuals from John Locke, to Denis Diderot, Antoine-Nicolas de Condorcet, Immanuel Kant, and Johann Herder imagined print as essential to human progress because it materialized writing in a relatively permanent form.[24]

And yet there are significant differences with digital cultural production. Digital cultural objects have a material support that unifies them.[25] Instead of paper, vinyl, and celluloid, texts, sounds, and images are embedded in computer machine code and even further in a binary logic of on/off or zero and one, or pulse and lack of pulse. This means that the medium plays a more leading role than in analogue culture in defining the material nature of the cultural object. All cultural objects now may be produced, reproduced, stored, and disseminated in networked computers, in the same information machine. Compare the material resources required for printing presses, movie production, and television transmissions to that of the networked computer and it is apparent that a vast dissemination of cultural production is well under way, with fully one sixth of the human population in a position to do what it took armies of cultural creators and producers to do in the modern period of analogue culture.

Most crucially, instead of fixity, digital technology gives us fluidity of text, image, and sound. These cultural objects are opened on a PC by programs that almost always enable the user to alter them, store the altered file, copy it, and distribute it. And in this respect, digital texts, images, and sounds differ from analogue. Perhaps hypertext was the earliest instance of this. New cultural practices have developed and continue to be developed that start with the changeability of the computer file to create new cultural objects and then to distribute them in new ways. The consumer has become a user, maker, and/or creator. Examples of such practices are YouTube, MySpace, and Second Life. In each case, the provider of content, the old cultural industry, is now the ordinary individual coupled with a networked computer. In the case of YouTube, some sixty-five thousand cultural objects are uploaded for sharing every day. Cultural production has clearly shifted from an elite system with major capital resources and heavy editing or gate-keeping functions to a bottom-up, mass movement. We cannot argue that the result is always excellent in quality—whatever that might mean—but we can say that a very different set of practices has emerged and continues to develop, a non-exclusive system that encourages anyone who wants to participate. In this sense, the new cultural practices are oriented to a global media culture even when older forms of controls are imposed on them. The argument here is not that digital culture is free from threats of control; rather, the contention is that the digital allows a new set of possibilities previously unavailable in analogue systems.

The basic structure of YouTube and the other sites mentioned above is peer-to-peer file-sharing. Although YouTube follows the web-based client-server architecture instead of direct file transfers, I consider it as a peer-based production and file-sharing system. Anyone can upload content and anyone can download it. Each user is in that sense a peer. This digital technology is embedded in the architecture of the internet and is difficult to eliminate. Its most notorious and celebrated use has been sharing of content that falls under existing copyright laws. Billions of texts, images, and sounds have been shared in direct transgression of these statutes. Neither the corporation nor the state has been able to prevent such "infringement." File-sharing has confounded the culture industry, especially the RIAA and the MPAA. The way it works is this: indexing sites inform sharers of what is available and client programs search the hard disks of other users to obtain copies. The information goes from peer to peer. Only the abrogation of the first amendment of the U.S. Constitution would allow corporations to stop this from happening. Thus far, a good deal of digital culture has remained outside the commodity system.

Peer-to-peer architecture is fundamental to and inseparable from the internet.[26] It facilitates a structure of communication that is as difficult to monitor as face-to-face speech, although it relies upon a highly complex technological infrastructure. What is more, it promotes the user's invention of new applications of the technology so that much of what we find on the net is not the product of large industry but of inventive individuals and groups often with few resources beyond their programming skills and their imaginations. The history of technology, especially media technology, is strewn with examples of promising innovations that are soon domesticated by corporations and turned into popular but by no means resistant uses. It remains to be seen if the same fate will befall the internet. One of the reasons for hope is the very global nature of the medium, with the resulting difficulty of any nation, even a behemoth like the United States, to determine its nature. One does not have to be a futurist or a zealous technophile to realize the potentials for deepening global freedom intimately associated with net-worked computing.[27]

The U.S. government has attempted to end peer-to-peer file-sharing by including U.S. copyright law in trade agreements of the World Trade Organization. It wants to globalize American law. Yet in China and much of Asia, DVDs of better quality than those sold in U.S. markets are available for fifty cents. And when the U.S. government attempted to get the Swedish government to close down an indexing site (The Pirate Bay) in 2006, they were met with resistance and failed. In 2009, the site was finally asked to stop operations by a Swedish court; in response, the site moved its servers from Sweden to another country (possibly Ukraine), and has continued to work at the time this essay was written. One result of the court's action was to increase the popularity of the site, the same outcome that met the recording industry when it sued Napster and threatened lawsuits against file sharers. Digital cultural distribution obviously requires a complete revamping of copyright law, a change that no doubt will have dire consequences for the relation of culture to the economy. But for our purposes, the following conclusion is likely: digital production and distribution of texts, images, and sounds promotes a worldwide process of culture to a degree far in excess of the analogue. The technological architecture of networked computing, as Manuel Castells argues, promotes a global media culture to an extent impossible before.[28] Cultural practice is becoming planetary, and the shape it may take can only be imagined.

## Global Culture

Anticipations of global culture are no doubt contemporary with culture itself. But as the twentieth century wore on, more and more cultural works, at the time embedded in analogue media, began to be distributed globally and to mix art practices from cultures around the planet. As the flow of texts, images, and sounds around the world increases exponentially, the question of global culture becomes more and more exigent. Perhaps the leading polemic about it remains the (usually) unwanted prospect of homogenization: looming on the horizon is a world with one culture, one type of voice, one vision of reality. But this position ignores several factors: that diversity of languages persists and new languages (global English) arise; that "foreign" cultures are integrated with local cultures in inventive hybrids; that new local cultures arise among subgroups, increasing diversity not homogeneity; that the homogeneity thesis ignores problems of translation and trans-coding; the mixtures of cultures at the global level are infinitely varied.[29]

The issue of translation and transcoding itself is highly complex. Clearly a translation is not isomorphic with the original. Languages do not overlap one-to-one. If that were the case, translation software would already have developed perfect algorithms for the task. Anyone who has either attempted a translation or used one of these programs knows all too well the difficulties entailed in the work. Walter Benjamin's argument must also be taken into account: on which side does the brunt of the translation fall—the language translated or the language into which the translation is made?[30] This seemingly paradoxical question is developed by Rey Chow into a fascinating analysis of the export of Chinese films to the United States[31] and Asian literature translations in the West.[32] The translator is illuminated about his or her own language by the translation and this "original" is altered in the process. As Chinese cinema develops, Chow argues, it looks at itself in new ways, incorporating the position of the foreigner who will view the film and thereby practicing ethnography upon itself.[33] The original—the Chinese culture that is the subject of the film—is produced anew in the process. The problem of translation in the context of global culture, then, she concludes, implies "a thorough dismantling of *both* the notion of origin and the notion of alterity as we know them today" (emphasis in original).[34] The development of global culture then must be seen not as the negotiation between fixed cultures in competition for hegemony (which language will become the new lingua franca?), but an entirely new scene of cultural configurations whose outlines can certainly not be discerned today. Global culture is a new project for humanity. It will mix relations of forces with creativity before anything like a temporary stasis emerges.

With the question of global culture in mind, we must ask if a new cultural politics is possible, required, or emerging. Kevin Robins argues that migrants, at least in Europe, no longer accept the assimilationist model of identity whereby the nation remains a homogeneous cultural unity.[35] Contemporary migrants maintain multiple, partial commitments to their adopted location but also to the land of their origins. They are able to sustain this complex of attachments in part through cheap transport systems and also through new media: the internet for email and web sites, communication satellites for television shows from back home. The European Union has, as a result, changed its policy from insisting on the dominance of the main culture to recognizing a positive value for diversity in culture. Global culture thus surpasses postcolonial hybridity in recognizing the heterogeneity of migrant identities instead of insisting on the relative unity even of hybrid selves. Global cultural politics, in a similar tendency to creative industries, loosens the grip of the nation as a cultural center toward a more individualizing, multiple figure of the self. Similar tendencies are evident in the United States with Latino/Latina migrants sustaining deep relations with their Latin American place of origin and many Asian migrants engaging in similar connections back home.[36] This emerging global culture has by no means eliminated older forms of nationality but has become an increasingly common part of the current landscape of cultural politics. Predictions about future global cultures are not appropriate or even possible today. Yet the trend of a new direction is clear. After all, national cultures themselves are historical formations, won at the cost of thousands of local cultures that were actively destroyed in the process. It is hardly impossible to imagine new connections between culture and location as globalism becomes more and more dominant. In Robins's words, ". . . the old and assumed isomorphism between culture, polity, and territory is no longer to be taken as given. The fundamental

principle upon which national cultures and communities have been predicated has been called into question."[37]

It appears that a new politics of culture and a new cultural politics are on
the horizon. None of this has elicited or given rise to corresponding political
and cultural organizations and practices.[38] One finds no global imagined
communities, to paraphrase Benedict Anderson, in current discursive
regimes. Instead, there are adaptations of the capitalist corporation and
nation-state to the new phenomena, alterations that at bottom are attempts
to preserve modern institutions in an increasingly hostile or antagonistic
environment. What is called for then are cognitive experiments or imaginary
flights that attempt to outline new directions for institutional and practical
reorganization in order to make the most of a future in which global culture
is not grudgingly recognized but celebrated and embraced. The key to such
discursive innovations, I believe, is the full acknowledgment of the assemblage of humans and information machines.

## Global Media Culture

For global culture can only be global media culture. From underwater telephone cables to communications satellites and the internet, human beings
across the planet are able, with exponentially increasing frequency, to send,
to receive, to store, and to distribute texts, images, and sounds. One may
argue that culture is always already mediated (by language). But the increasing sophistication, multiplication, and dissemination of information
machines changes the experience of all culture. Every cultural object now
exists in a (potentially) global context.

These information machines are also changing so rapidly that modern
institutions have difficulty keeping pace with their development. The culture
industries have clearly been unable to integrate new media entirely within
their commodity forms. The music industry has globalized through mergers
and acquisitions, reducing to a handful the number of major players (80 percent of CD sales are controlled by four or five companies).[39] But new media
technologies enable anyone to start their own "culture industry," and this
has become an emerging trend in music production. While the RIAA, after it
belatedly awakened to peer-to-peer file-sharing, has made great efforts to
curtail what they call "piracy," every new attempt (lawsuits against down-
loaders and related software companies) is met with increased awareness of
file-sharing and expanded ranks of "pirates." Efforts to extend American

copyright law to all nations have been at best only partially successful. Since President Clinton, every U.S. administration has pressured other nations to conform to outdated copyright law, disregarding the benefits to innovation new media promote.[40] The Clinton administration also attempted to control the flow of information on the internet, recognizing that national boundaries are out of synchronization with its basic architecture.[41] Nations are less and less able to monitor and to control the global flow of cultural objects.[42] There is less and less of a match or overlap between territorial demarcations of the nation and exchanges between individuals and groups.

Are we then at the point of emergence of a new cosmopolitan culture?[43] Is global media culture "cosmopolitan?" Certainly, scholars like Robins are discovering far more extensive global cultural practices than one might expect. Lisa Parks reported on the Australian Aboriginal use of satellite technology to broadcast television across the large southern continent. The culture they transmitted was selected by the Aboriginals and most often produced by them as well. Parks's argument is that Aboriginals' use of Western technology was not another case of imperialism but an adaptation of the media that promoted the interests of the non-Western group. The Aboriginal uses of satellite media, she writes, "challenge critical assumptions that satellite television works *only* as an agent of Western cultural imperialism and neocolonial control."[44] The Inuit, like the Aboriginals, successfully adapt satellite technology to enhance their culture with global knowledge and to preserve their own practices and beliefs.[45] Similar findings are widely evident in the literature of global media culture. There exists a myriad of local adaptations of new media that promote combinations of cultural parts in infinite varieties. Ien Ang warns, however, that the spread of popular cultures between and across ethnic identities might have more to do with corporate control of culture than with free dissemination of images and sounds.[46] If the figure of the cosmopolitan suggests an upper- or middle-class liberal persona, then the recent articulations of global culture are well beyond those relatively restricted limits, extending the imagined community of participants quite broadly across the planet and throughout all social strata.

The subject who, like myself, writes and thinks about global media culture does not resemble the cosmopolitan of the past, for the epistemological position of contemporary students of global media are linked to different information machines from the cosmopolitans of earlier epochs. Not analogue print and perhaps photograph culture, but digital networked computing alters the relation of the writer to his native land, ethnicity, and gender. Writers like myself are connected to the world immediately, through the fiber optic cables and communication satellites that cross and envelop the earth. This deterritorialization of the critic changes his or her position of speech and relation to cultures everywhere. Peer-to-peer media technologies (file-sharing, Wikipedia, MySpace, YouTube, massively multiple online gaming, and the rest) partially detach the body from its location in space, loosening the binds to the local, and connect the writer with global culture. This shift involves an "intimacy" with information machines that cannot be ignored. Everyone now potentially participates in the cyborg experience, which can be interpreted as the basis for a new species with its own commonalities and conflicts.

What today might be called "global culture" is quite distinct from the planetary borrowings of earlier centuries, even granting their extent and importance. One new aspect of the current configuration of global culture is its heavy reliance on highly complex media technologies. As we begin to study and to learn about contemporary global culture we need to pay close attention to its dependence on information machines, to the intricate, heterogeneous, and varied assemblages that are invented and practiced by users across the globe. This is perhaps one of the great challenges for scholars and intellectuals in the present. The current global media culture is multicentered; its voices, practitioners, and inventors deriving from all corners of the earth, violating assumptions about center and periphery, North and South, first and third worlds, Western and non-Western, imperial and subaltern, colonizer and colonized. This perhaps fragile global culture is not endorsed, backed, or promoted by the great powers-that-be. It requires a new political theory and new political practices that might promote its expansion. Twenty-first-century global culture might or might not conflict with national and ethnic cultures of the past, but it is certainly different from them. It might constitute a counterforce against the major powers that quite naturally seek nothing more than their persistence. If the tendency of neoliberal, transnational corporations has been and continues to be to globalize the planet with their habits and ways of doing things, then the task confronting global culture is to promote something different, something that might extend democracy in unforeseen and unforeseeable directions.

# 2

# Burning Man at Google

## A Cultural Infrastructure for New Media Production

### Fred Turner

To anyone accustomed to visiting the main offices of industrial-era information technology powerhouses such as IBM or AT&T, a stop in the lobby of Building 43, Google's Mountain View, California, headquarters, presents something of a shock. The cool blonde wood and carefully recessed lighting that have marked the power of industrial firms for decades have disappeared. In their place, plain white walls are posted with some two dozen unframed photographs of massive sculptures set out in a flat, white desert, and of fireworks exploding over the head of a giant neon stick figure. On the floor above, another thirty images line the hallways and overlook an in-house café and pool table. In these pictures, shirtless men in pantaloons spin fire-tipped batons in the dark. A tiny clapboard house with a bicycle out front stands alone on an empty plain, while a two-story-tall chandelier lies crashed to the ground, baking under the sun.

To the thousands of San Francisco Bay–area programmers, marketers, and technical executives who spend a week there every August, these images are instantly recognizable. They depict Burning Man, an annual celebration of art and temporary community staged in the Black Rock Desert of Nevada. Begun some twenty years ago with the burning of a wooden effigy on a San Francisco beach, and later moved inland, Burning Man now draws more than 35,000 participants each year.[1] A great many come from the San Francisco Bay area and work in the region's high technology industries.[2] In the last week of August, they pile into everything from ancient Honda Civics to 32-foot RV's and drive out into an alkali desert, a dusty plain completely devoid of water, where daytime temperatures can reach 110 degrees and nights can near the freezing mark. They set up geodesic domes and tent cities, pirate radio stations, elaborate computer networks, and huge, if temporary, dance clubs. They hold lectures, throw parties, and traverse the desert in what passes for public transportation: some 500 art cars rigged to look like everything from furry mushrooms to fire-breathing dragons. And on the next to the last night of the week, they burn a forty-foot-tall effigy of a man.

The question is: Why? What does Burning Man offer to workers in computer-related industries that justifies their often extraordinary efforts to participate in it? Over the years, Burning Man has often been depicted in the popular media as a desert bacchanal, rife with public nudity and drug use. On the scholarly side, it has been studied largely as an example of a new social form, one that incorporates the syncretic religious impulses historically common to West Coast countercultures and the pro-art, anti-consumerist sentiments of contemporary DIY culture.[3] Both of these accounts are true enough, but neither explains Burning Man's appeal to technologists. Since statistics on the employment patterns of Burning Man attendees have never been kept, it is impossible to determine precisely what proportion of Burning Man attendees work in high-technology industries. Yet, both journalists and scholars have long pointed to a very high contingent of technical workers and information industry professionals among Burners.[4] Burning Man's links to Google have been particularly visible. In 1999, for instance, Google's founders, Larry Page and Sergey Brin, decorated Google's home page with a Burning Man logo to alert users that they and most of their staff would be going to the festival. Both have attended regularly since then. In 2001, they hired Eric Schmidt as Google's CEO in part because he too attended Burning Man.[5] In recent years, Google employees have attended company parties in Burning Man–derived costumes, maintained internal e-mail lists devoted to the festival, and, in 2007, even produced a 37-minute online video on how to cook during the event.[6]

But why? How is it that New Age religious inclinations, a celebration of amateur art, and a rejection of consumerism should so appeal to the computer programmers and software engineers of Google? And what can that appeal tell us about the relationship between bohemian art worlds and new modes of digital manufacturing?

In recent years, a number of scholars have pointed to an entangling of bohemian idealism and high-tech industry.[7] Perhaps most visibly, Richard

Florida has mapped the co-location of bohemian social worlds and knowledge-based manufacturing, suggesting that they emerged side by side in a joint celebration of "creativity."[8] This chapter will draw on a mix of archival research, interviews, and participant observation to explore the social mechanics of that emergence in the San Francisco area.[9] It will not, however, take creativity as a property somehow native to both art worlds and high technology manufacturing. Rather, it will analyze the social work that goes into defining new media labor as creative in an artistic sense. As a number of scholars have noted, a new mode of hypersocialized manufacturing has recently grown up alongside digital media in both proprietary and nonproprietary settings.[10] My research suggests that for those who work in this new mode, Burning Man models the social structures on which manufacturing now depends and at the same time provides a place in which to work through the psychological and material constraints it imposes. My research also shows that, like numerous online communities, Burning Man has become a site for commercial product development. In both a structural and an ideological sense, Burning Man provides what I will call a *cultural infrastructure* for emerging forms of new media manufacturing. As once, more than a century ago, churches translated Max Weber's Protestant ethic into a lived experience for congregations of industrial workers, so today Burning Man transforms the ideals and social structures of bohemian art worlds, their very particular ways of being "creative," into psychological, social, and material resources for the workers of a new, supremely fluid world of post-industrial information work.

## The Socialization of Technical Production

Before we can explain the appeal of Burning Man to the workers of Silicon Valley, we need to acknowledge that in recent years, a dramatic socialization of technical labor has taken place. Two accounts of this process have emerged, one focused on the rise of the internet and online collaboration, and the other focused on the development of networked modes of doing business within and between firms. Though they are rarely linked, when told together, they suggest that the manufacture of information and information technologies is becoming increasingly entwined with the making of social worlds—inside, outside, and in-between the boundaries of firms.

Since the World Wide Web first came online in the early 1990s, scholars and pundits alike have suggested that networked information technologies have been reworking social and economic relations in their own image. Most recently, analysts have begun to argue that online social networks constitute a new site for the production of cultural goods and perhaps of other kinds of goods as well.[11] In contrast to industrial-era factories, these scholars argue, computer networks give rise to a new kind of collective work space, a site for the making of information goods that exists only in the wires, so to speak. These sites in turn allow for what legal scholar Yochai Benkler has called "commons-based peer production."[12]

Setting aside the question of whether this shift is largely a benevolent one, as many believe it is, we need to note that commons-based peer production depends on a particular structural and ideological scaffolding. Structurally, such work requires a *commons*, a shared space that in most internet-driven accounts consists of digital messages, but that could as easily be located in some single geographical space. In these arenas, members of diverse social worlds can gather and collaborate toward some end. The commons in turn affords them *visibility*. Being able to be seen by one another makes it possible for workers to find one another, to select projects, and to build and maintain reputations.

In addition, online commons-based peer production depends on the interaction of some sort of communal ethos and multiple, non-monetary forms of compensation.[13] In the open-source software community, for instance, programmers often think of themselves as warriors fighting the dark forces of Microsoft, a firm they imagine to be hierarchical and closed.[14] In other settings, such as the Wikipedia project, collaborative news production ventures, or even parts of e-Bay, a rhetoric of community often pervades production processes.[15] To make valuable information goods is to give "gifts" to the "community." This shift in rhetorical frame from factory and market to gift and community in turn legitimates the multiple systems of reward actually in play. Because they are explicitly removed from systems of market exchange, gifts can come back to participants not as money, but as reputation, artistic pleasure, or friendship—or all three. At the same time, rhetorics of mission and community allow collaborators to imagine that all participants, regardless of actual standing, are in fact social and ethical peers. In any online production community, some participants have greater intellectual, social, financial, or reputational capital than others, and thus, the wherewithal to more easily monetize the group's work in other settings. In terms of the ethical frameworks established by the rhetoric of community or of the battle against the dark forces of Microsoft, however, they can be imagined as peers devoted to a collective mission.

Though scholars have generally ascribed the rise of commons-based peer production primarily to the diffusion of the internet, it also represents the latest stage in an ongoing transformation of white-collar labor. The last thirty years have seen a dramatic shift in the landscape of manufacturing across a number of industries and numerous attempts to imbue the factory with features of the wider social world. Beginning in the early 1980s, as Walter Powell has shown, the sharp divisions of labor, the job security, and even the geographic stability that characterized many mid-twentieth-century industrial firms began to erode.[16] For many workers, and particularly for the workers of Silicon Valley, job turnover became so frequent that maintaining rich social networks became a key factor in sustaining one's employability.[17]

At virtually the same time, managers began to look to corporate cultures as sources of motivation and control for rapidly changing firms. In the early 1980s, many in the corporate world feared that Japanese firms had begun to outstrip their American competitors. This fear in turn led to a revival of the study of corporate culture.[18] Managers who turned to books like *In Search of Excellence* (1982) and *Theory Z: How American Business Can Meet the Japanese Challenge* (1981) learned that culture was a key to corporate success.[19] To many, it began to seem that embedding labor within the norms and values of everyday life, as well as within the rule-managed sanctions and rewards of conventional bureaucracy, could increase profit, innovation, and worker loyalty. A decade later, the managers of digital start-ups from San Francisco to Manhattan embraced this turn, sometimes to excess. For companies ranging from Cisco to Razorfish, the cultivation of the corporate workspace as a home-away-from-home, of the high-tech worker as a playful, emotionally integrated hipster, and the corporate team as a cross between a family and a rock band became commonplace.[20]

## Commons-Based Peer Production at Google

Today, few firms have taken more aggressive advantage of the integration of culture and labor than Google. Founded in 1998 by two Stanford graduate students, the company has developed not only its ubiquitous search engine, but a variety of search-related services in arenas ranging from news to mapping to shopping to scholarship.[21] Like Silicon Valley predecessors such as Apple and Hewlett-Packard, it has proven to be extremely nimble at building alliances, making acquisitions, and developing new and very popular products. Though its rapid growth, its lack of layoffs, and its enormous profits make Google atypical within its industry, its reliance on elements of commons-based peer production does not. At Google, as at other firms, managers have developed a set of both electronic and material commons within which to organize work and have created a culture in which multiple reward systems are in play. Unlike those of many other firms, Google's managers have also subsidized the individual intellectual explorations of their engineers and administrators, and they have relentlessly promulgated an ethos of benevolent peer production among them.

In the fall of 2005, Douglas Merrill, at that time a Senior Director for Information Technology at Google, tried to explain to an audience of information technology executives from around the country how the firm had grown so quickly.[22] He noted that Google, like many other firms, maintained a relatively flat management structure. He also suggested that the firm maintained several types of commons. These included databases of ideas that could be accessed by anyone in the firm, e-mail lists that were likewise very open, though not necessarily to the whole firm, and various physical spaces inside Google's Mountain View, California, headquarters in which teams could meet and collaborate. In this setting, he argued, data could drive decision-making—since it could be made visible to everyone—and individuals could pursue reputations on the basis of ideas that could be presented to and tested by all. "Everything is a 360 [degree] public discussion," he said.[23]

In addition to building both electronic and material commons inside the firm, Google creates temporary commons via the web and e-mail within which its customers can act as testers for beta versions of its products. As Marissa Mayer, Vice President of Search Products and User Experience, told an audience at Stanford University in May 2006, "we expect everyone to have ideas. Some come from our engineers. Some come from our customers."[24]

Google also explicitly subsidizes the individual development efforts of its employees by asking that every engineer spend 20 percent of their working time on projects of their own choosing. Such projects can range very widely and, officially at least, need not contribute directly or indirectly to Google's bottom line. Yet, according to Mayer, this subsidy has important material and ideological benefits for the firm. In an internal survey in early 2006, Mayer and her colleagues discovered that fully 50 percent of the products Google launched in the second half of 2005 were created out of projects developed in "20% time." The power of subsidy, she points out, is not so much in the time it frees up, but in the ways that it enlists the emotions of employees:

> The key isn't the 20%. . . . I think that our engineers and product developers see that and realize this is a company that really trusts them and that really wants them to be creative, that really wants them to explore whatever it is they want to explore. And it's that license to do whatever they want that ultimately fuels a huge amount of creativity and a huge amount of innovation.[25]

In this sense, subsidy does for Google's engineers what it does for those who participate in online commons-based peer production: by granting them limited powers of choice over their activities, it simultaneously engages their individual creative interests and encourages them to re-imagine their workspace as a congenial, high-trust environment. It also blurs the line between workers' social and professional worlds in ways that are highly advantageous to the firm. Within their 20 percent time, at least, the subsidy suggests that engineers should stop thinking of working for Google as just a job and re-imagine it as a way to pursue individual growth.

Like the builders of Linux or contributors to Wikipedia, then, many Google engineers contribute to multiple projects over time, do so in ways that are performance driven and highly visible to the production community as a whole, and do so, at least in part, under conditions of subsidy. Though at the middle and upper levels they are well paid, many also accrue substantial rewards in non-monetary terms. Moreover, since its earliest days, Google leaders have sought to infuse their company's work with an ideology of social benevolence. Under the banner "Don't be evil," Brin, Page, and Schmidt have encouraged their employees to aim to serve users first and to allow profits to grow from rather than drive that process. Some might question the firm's allegiance to that model in the wake of some of its corporate choices, but inside the firm, the argument that Google is changing the world and changing it for the better encourages employees to align their sense of personal mission with that of the company.

This fusion of the social and the professional, of personal growth and product development, has substantial manufacturing power, as a brief example should demonstrate. In the wake of the 9/11 attacks, a Google engineer named Krishna Bharat had been searching the web for news. Realizing that he could automate the process, Bharat wrote a script that visited his fifteen favorite news sites, gathered the news they reported, and clustered it in patterns according to his interests. As Marissa Mayer later told the story, Bharat "mailed [his script] out to the company [on an internal e-mail list] and said, 'Hey, I use this to read my news; maybe some of you would find it helpful.' A lot of us saw that and said, 'Hey, this isn't just a tool to help Krishna read his news better, this could help a lot of people read their news better'."[26] Within months, the company had formed a development team and launched a new product, Google News.[27]

Set against contemporary accounts of online peer production, the story of Google News serves as a reminder that commons-based production, overlaid with an ethos of sociability and peer relations, can very much be a form of for-profit, proprietary manufacturing as well. Though he was employed by Google, Bharat in fact wrote his script on his "own" time—that is, on time made free by his salary, including its 20 percent subsidy for exploration. He gave it to his colleagues as a gift, in the spirit of community, with an eye toward performing a social service. He did so using an electronic commons— the internal e-mail list—and when he entered that commons, so to speak, he and his product were observed, evaluated, and, ultimately, celebrated. Through his efforts, Bharat enhanced both his own reputation and Google's product line.

### Burning Man and the Theater of Peer Production

If the workers of the industrial factory found themselves laboring in an iron cage, the workers of many of today's postindustrial information firms often find themselves inhabiting a velvet gold mine—a workplace in which the pursuit of self-fulfillment, of reputation and community identity, of interpersonal relationships and intellectual pleasure help drive the production of new media goods. At Google, the fusion of the social and the productive has been both profitable for the firm and appealing to potential workers. In 2006, the firm received more than 1,000,000 applications for the more than 2,000 jobs it added that year.[28] However, outside Google, commons-based production has done little to reduce the transience of employment, the mobility of workers, or the importance of social networks to employment. As workers from Manhattan's Silicon Alley to San Francisco discovered in the wake of the dot.com boom, even the coolest jobs can vanish in an instant. And even when jobs remain, frequent job-hopping has been a constant in the technology sector for more than twenty years. In Silicon Valley, for instance, recent survey data suggest that approximately 2.5 percent of college-educated males working in the computer industry change jobs in any given month—substantially more often than workers in other industries, and somewhat more often than computer workers in other regions.[29] Moreover, as they have become more common, neither the practices nor the ideology of peer production have lessened the actual power of managers to hire and fire, nor that of customers to make demands for particular products. For all the rhetoric of equality, empowerment, and voluntarism that surrounds commons-based production and new media labor more generally, technical workers remain *workers.*

With this in mind, we can begin to appreciate the appeal of Burning Man for the developers of computer hardware and software. Over the last two decades, Burning Man's founders and participants have transformed the explicitly artistic, bohemian traditions of festal gathering and the co-creation of art and theater into the organizing principles of a temporary town they call Black Rock City. The city in turn has spawned social networks, mailing lists, party circuits, and building projects that extend across the year and around the globe. Following the lead of its founders and participants, scholars have generally depicted Black Rock City as a sacred place for the celebration of art and creativity and the enacting of New Age religious rituals.[30] Yet, for the thousands of engineers who attend, Black Rock City also serves as a massive example of the fusion of the social and the productive around which so much of their everyday employment is now organized. For one week each year, Black Rock City becomes a commons. It is inhabited by individuals and teams devoted to launching small technical projects for artistic purposes and to organizing community building and individual identity work around those projects. It is a place where engineers can both celebrate the ideals of collaborative peer-production and work through the contradictions it entails and obscures, especially in corporate settings. And after the weeklong gathering dissolves, it becomes a symbolic touchstone and a source of social connections that can help sustain participants throughout the year.

Though it has since developed a substantial organizational infrastructure, Burning Man began as an offhand artistic gesture. In the summer of 1986, Larry Harvey, a landscaper, and his friend Jerry James, a homebuilder, took an eight-foot-tall wooden statue of a man to San Francisco's Baker Beach and burned it. As the Man burned, a small group of spectators gathered around. Harvey later recalled, "We were inspired by the sudden society of strangers we had created" and over the following three years, Harvey and James returned to the beach each summer, burning a man and drawing ever-larger crowds.[31] In 1990, after crowds had grown into the hundreds, the San Francisco police asked them to leave before they could burn the Man. Harvey and his fellow burners joined up with San Francisco–based members of the Cacophony Society—a network of artists and activists devoted to staging random, Dada-esque pranks and performances—and at their instigation, Harvey and some-where between sixty and eighty friends drove out into the Black Rock desert of Nevada for the burn itself. From 1991 on, the entire event has been held in Nevada.

For the first few years in the desert, Burning Man remained an anarchic, unregulated get-together with a heavy emphasis on performance art and pyrotechnics. Each year attendance more or less doubled, growing from 250 in 1991, to 4,000 in 1995.[32] Campers were individually responsible for bring-ing everything they needed to survive into the desert with them, but when they arrived, they grouped themselves in a circle around the then-forty-foot tall man. One visitor in 1995 described the scene thus:

> There are all sorts here, a living, breathing encyclopedia of subcultures: desert survivalists, urban primitives, artists, rocketeers, hippies, Dead-heads, queers, pyromaniacs, cybernauts, musicians, ranters, eco-freaks, acidheads, breeders, punks, gun lovers, dancers, S/M and bondage enthusiasts, nudists, refugees from the men's movement, anarchists, ravers, transgender types, and New Age spiritualists.[33]

That same year, some participants organized themselves into "theme camps." With names like Tiki Camp, Algonquin Roundtable Camp, and Croquet Camp, these were clusters of tents and vehicles and people who worked together to put on a performance, create a work of art, or provide some serv-ice to the City as a whole. Finally, in the wide-open expanse of the desert itself, individual artists and various groups built several very large art works.

By 1995, then, Black Rock City had begun to develop several of the key fea-tures of commons-based peer production. Its citizens had established a com-mons; they had created temporary project teams for the building of art and theme camps; they had used the desert plane to make themselves extraordi-narily visible to one another; and they had subsidized this entire system with earnings from other parts of their lives. There was a strong technological bent to many of the art works they created—particularly those dealing with fire—but the event's principles were not aimed toward the emerging corpo-rate world of the dot.com boom. On the contrary, in 1996, when Burning Man organizers assigned the event its first theme, they chose "The Inferno (a.k.a., HelCo)." In this elaborate collective fantasy, acted out in various ad hoc settings across the city, a multinational conglomerate attempted to take over Burning Man and was rebuffed. Anti-corporate themes have persisted in years since. In 2000, for example, a group of artists built a perfect replica of a corporate cubicle, complete with desk, chair, filing cabinet, Post-It Notes, and "Success" poster on the desert's open plain.[34] Another artist wore a three-piece suit and carried a briefcase as he dodged from person to person, saying "Excuse me gentlemen!" and rushing on his way.[35]

Yet even as Burning Man's artists began to mock corporate America, Bay Area technologists began to join the event in force. Many had heard about the festival on the nascent World Wide Web; others had heard about it from friends or colleagues. When they arrived in the desert, they found a world that organizers and visitors alike described as a mirror of the internet itself. As Larry Harvey told an interviewer in 1999:

> I gradually realized that this environment that we've created is a physical analog of the internet. It's radically democratic. It allows people to conjure up entire worlds—like websites—voila! out of nothing. The internet is a populist medium which has a unique way of empowering every individual. And it's an interactive medium—unlike TV—which allows people to connect with other people and out of that precipitate new forms of community. And that's what we are.[36]

The notion that Burning Man was both visible on the internet and somehow *like* the internet drew technologists in droves. In 1996, science fiction writer Bruce Sterling visited Black Rock City for *Wired* magazine. Very soon, Burning Man was playing host to computer industry luminaries such as Jeff Bezos, founder of Amazon.com, John Gilmore, a co-founder of the Electronic Frontier Foundation, Brian Behlendorf, a key figure in the open-source movement, and Sergey Brin and Larry Page of Google.[37] By the year 2000, when overall attendance reached 23,400, Burning Man had become a highly visible ritual in Bay Area tech culture. "So embedded, so accepted has Burning Man become in parts of tech culture," wrote reporter Vanessa Hua at the time, "that the event alters work rhythms, shows up on resumes, is even a sanctioned form of professional development."[38]

Today, Burning Man is if anything larger and more thoroughly integrated into Bay Area technical culture. Black Rock City has become a well-organized, horseshoe-shaped town, nine blocks deep all along its length in 2006, whose two ends, about a mile and a half apart, open on to an art-filled expanse of playa and the statue of the Man himself. The original group of friends who founded Burning Man has spawned a Limited Liability Corporation (Black Rock City LLC), which in turn manages a small paid staff and hundreds of volunteers. Together, paid staffers and volunteers lay out the city each year, manage its Department of Public Works, its medical services, and its toilets. Though solid statistics are very hard to come by, the vast majority of Burners seem to be white adults, heavily though not exclusively concentrated in their late 20s through their late 40s. Few lack financial or social resources: each has paid between $175 and $250 for their entrance tickets alone, as well as hundreds and often thousands of dollars in travel expenses.[39] The ticket fees in turn help defray the more than $5 million in annual expenses accrued by the organizers for everything from environmental protection to art grants to payroll, printing, insurance, and medical supplies.[40]

As Burning Man's organizational infrastructure has grown, its ethos has become increasingly codified. A quick visit to the Burning Man Web site acquaints new participants not only with the long list of things they will need to bring with them to survive in the desert, but the organization's mission statement and its "10 Principles."[41] For many participants the 10 Principles serve as an informal social contract. At the top of the list is "radical inclusion"—which is to say, that anyone can join the event. Numbers two and three are "gifting" and "decommodification." Despite the extensive consumption required to get there, Black Rock City aims to be an anti-consumerist world, one in which individuals retreat from the money economy toward interaction, participation, and the giving of performances, objects, and goods that help sustain communal bonds. "Radical self-reliance" and "Radical self-expression" in turn suggest the libertarian undertone of the communal work: it is through the sustenance and display of the individual self that the community as a whole will be born. Subsequent principles stress the need for all to participate and to celebrate immediate experience, for each individual to be responsible to a civic whole, and for the citizens of Black Rock City to "leave no trace" on the desert floor when they leave.

For many Burners, these principles have taken on a spiritual cast. But in order to see how Burning Man's culture intersects with Bay Area techno-culture, and how its particular spiritual orientation helps sustain technical production, it is important to remember that the festival grew up alongside both the fading of the social contract that once governed manufacturing and the increased socialization of technical work. In the late 1990s, the dot.com set may have come to Burning Man in part because they believed it resembled the internet. Yet, the principles they encountered there resembled those of their professional worlds. At Burning Man, "radical self-reliance" meant remembering to bring sufficient food, water, and shelter for yourself and your friends. In the start-up frenzy of the late 1990s, as in the broader context of an industrial world from which job security had begun to vanish, radical self-reliance also neatly described the mindset proper to every technical worker. Gift-giving likewise spoke to the increasing importance of social networks to employment and production. Though at Burning Man, gift-giving was explicitly proposed as a benevolent alternative to market exchange and a way to push back against the encroachment of capitalism on everyday life, as early as the late 1980s, gift-giving had also come to be a key principle behind emerging forms of commercial manufacturing. In a professional world that depended on social networks as both sites and engines of production, as the Bay Area's did from the mid-1980s onward, gift-giving provided an important way to cement the social ties that bound individuals and firms to one another.[42]

## Silicon Pentecostalism, or, The Pursuit of Vocational Ecstasy

On the playa in August it is the fusion of Burning Man's self-centered spiritualism, the collaborative habits of the art world, and the material conditions of contemporary technical production that sustain Black Rock City. Burning Man's founders and evangelists tout the week in the desert as a personally transformative experience of noncommercial community and as an encounter with radically public art. They also tend to downplay the moral diversity of the community and its willingness to embrace sexual fetishists, Ecstasy eaters, motorcycle crazies, and alcoholics. Given the vast range of potentially self-destructive behavior at Burning Man, and given the desert conditions in which it takes place, it seems likely that Black Rock City should have disintegrated by now rather than grown. Yet, at Burning Man, the collaborative creation of art works and the individual performance of self become for many participants one and the same. Together, they become the basis for the organization of the commons that is Black Rock City, and for the feeling of community that permeates it.

The work of building that community begins for most participants well before August. While some participants simply hear about Burning Man, buy a ticket, and go, most seem to learn about the festival and attend it with members of social or socioprofessional networks. For many participants, though, "attend" is the wrong verb: the ethic of participation that permeates Burning Man (and is its ninth principle) means that many come to the playa as part of a social unit devoted to doing work or creating a project in the desert. They may be attached to a theme camp; they may be part of a group devoted to constructing a particular art work; or they may have volunteered for one of the groups responsible for managing the event's infrastructure, such as the Black Rock Rangers (something like a gentle police force) or the Lamplighters (who light the lamps that lead to the Man each evening).

Tim Black, for instance, is an embedded computing systems engineer in Silicon Valley and a leader of a group called the "Mad Scientists." Black has been coming to Burning Man since 1998 and has built or helped build a number of major art installations on the playa, many of them with the Mad Scientists (for examples, see Black's personal Web page http://www.quantalink .com/artindex.html). During the year, the Mad Scientists include what Black calls a "core" of 10-12 people, almost all engineers, and a "cloud" of 100 or so who come and go. Black's house becomes a factory, particularly in the spring and summer months, as together, he and the Mad Scientists meet and build. As Black puts it, the group is "mostly pretty hard core geeks."[43] The Mad Scientists themselves, though, are a "collective" and a "meritocracy," he says. They are open to new members and when a potential member exhibits a skill, they are quick to exploit it. They are also a first-rate technical production team. In 2006, they received a grant from Burning Man organizers to build the L3K light system, a ring of plastic-encased LED lights running through the sand around the Man. Though the process involved sophisticated wiring, plastics molding, and the transport of hundreds of pounds of gear, Black and the Mad Scientists managed to carry out virtually all of the manufacturing at his suburban home. When the project ran almost $20,000 over budget, members of the team made up the difference—just as they would have if they had been a Silicon Valley engineering firm working for a commercial client.

Yet, for all its resemblance to the stages of commons-based manufacturing in other settings, the work of participants like the Mad Scientists is explicitly aimed at the production of art—within the official ethos of the festival at least, the antithesis of a consumer good. It is done not for profit, but with an eye to helping build a noncommercial community—ostensibly,

though as we've seen in the case of Google, not always actually—the antithesis of the corporation. This re-articulation of the practices that increasingly define project-based commercial labor in the high-tech world within an
anti-corporate ideological register in turn transforms the work of engineering into a spiritual task, and, for some on the playa at least, the pursuit of a
kind of vocational ecstasy.

In a 2006 interview, Larry Harvey explained that the world outside Black
Rock City was "based on separating people in order to market to them." At
Burning Man, he argued, participants would encounter the "immediacy" of
art, and through it, ecstatic feelings of community.[44] In that sense, he
implied that Burning Man would offer its participants the feeling of "effer-
vescence" and "social solidarity" that Durkheim long ago argued formed the
basis of religious feeling.[45] In Harvey's account, Burning Man and its art play
similar roles. Gathered in the desert, participants in the festival can feel an
electric sense of personal and collective transformation.[46] The sacred
emblem of that transformation is the Man—a single, neon figure, apparently
genderless, set at the center of Black Rock City.

For many of the participants, their desert rituals blur the line between the
sacred and profane. Greg MacNicol, for example, is a 55-year-old computer
animator who has attended Burning Man for nearly a decade. In 2006, he
joined a team to develop a pyrotechnic event for that year's Black Rock City.
Part of the project's appeal, he later recalled, came simply from designing and
building the pyrotechnics: "Part of the fun is having a dream about something, building it, seeing it work. Seeing it work is just a real high." So, too,
though, was the work itself. The pyrotechnic team, he explained, "were
people like me . . . very focused, very few words, open to anything . . . no egos.
We worked very tightly as a team [and we were] open to very intense focused
energy in the whole team."[47] MacNicol loved the "feeling of flow" on the
team, which he described as an extended, ecstatic feeling of interpersonal
unity and timelessness during the project's construction. At the same time,
he acknowledged that working on pyrotechnics at Black Rock City felt a lot
like working as a computer animator on a Hollywood film crew. It was "obses-
sive . . . exciting . . . [and you were] not taking care of your physical needs."
What was different about Burning Man, he said, was that he was in charge.

Such autonomy has long been one of the promises of the socialized workplace. So, too, has the notion that team-based labor leads to the building of
community. At Burning Man, those promises come true. As they engage in

making art, individuals begin to see and feel the manufacturing potential of collective, commons-based labor. Tom Gruber, for example, is a long-time Burner, a photographer, and the Chief Technology Officer at RealTravel, an online start-up headquartered in Silicon Valley. Alongside the pleasures of flow, he explains that the art at Burning Man demonstrates that "collaboration is power. . . . Nobody could build a temple in a week by themselves with the same fidelity and beauty you'd have in a Hollywood film. It destroys the myth that you need Microsoft's money to make stuff happen."[48]

As Gruber implies, it is partly because this work is not being done for money, but rather is being subsidized by Burners themselves, that participants can re-read it as a species of collaborative social action. Yet, even as they specifically place such work outside the money economy, Burners enjoy many of the rewards of proprietary forms of commons-based peer production. Not unlike the meeting rooms or e-mail lists of Google, the desert floor of Burning Man renders participants highly visible. This in turn allows them to transform their projects into temporary celebrity. Waldemar Horwat, a senior programmer at Google who has become an accomplished fire spinner, explains that "programming things tends to be very subtle and hard to see. When you prove a mathematical theorem it can be very beautiful but only for a few mathematicians. At Burning Man just about everybody can see what you're doing." Moreover, he argues that Burning Man is "very much a meritocracy. If you do something cool you'll be known for that. It will open a lot of doors."[49]

With its emphasis on teamwork, flow, peer production, meritocracy, and reputation building, Burning Man's culture clearly celebrates values and practices common to high-tech production. At the same time, it transforms them from a means of pursuing profit into tools for individual and collective change. Computer and software engineers in the San Francisco region and elsewhere work in an industry whose products are steadily marketed as tools with which to free the individual worker, link the world in a web of communication, and ultimately, change life as we know it. Yet, the daily experience of producing information goods can be far less inspiring. Greg MacNicol, for instance, recalls that working at Disney was "Really grim. . . . They're in control. You're not allowed to have an opinion. You're not allowed to do anything creative. You're told to follow directions, period."[50] Eric Payoul, a software engineer, reports that, "my regular work has no meaning to me. I mean, writing a piece of software is useless, it's not going to change anything. . . . My work at Burning Man has more meaning than my work in the real world."[51]

By reframing technological work as a species of artistic creativity, by restating its goals as those of community building rather than profit seeking, the citizens of Black Rock City can collectively re-imagine themselves as autonomous creators and restore to their labor, if only for a while, the sense of social value that is so often falsely claimed for it by corporate marketers. That is, at Burning Man, they can engage in many of the same practices that drive software engineering, they can acknowledge the failure of those practices to live up to marketers' and managers' claims in the day-to-day factory, and at the same time, they can replace that failure with a lived experience of the ideal itself: the making of multimedia products that, on the playa at least, can indeed be shown to be changing the world.

## The Festival Becomes the Factory

At the end of the week, of course, it all comes down. On the Saturday night of the event's last weekend, the citizens of Black Rock City gather around the Man and watch as it becomes a giant bonfire. Thousands shout and dance around the blaze. The next night, the last of the event, a quieter crowd gathers around the temple, a place where many have written messages on the walls across the week, especially to friends and family members who have died, and watch it burn as well. During the final day, Burners gradually take down their tents, pack up their performance gear, dismantle (or burn) their statues, and drive off. Six weeks later, thanks to the efforts of a stay-behind clean-up crew, the desert is empty again; no sign of the city, not even tiny scraps of litter, remains.

In Burning Man's list of principles, leaving no trace is an ecological ideal. It also hints at an almost Buddhist understanding of the temporariness of experience and, with it, the importance of paying attention to the immediate present. Yet, the social networks formed before and during Burning Man linger throughout the year. For some in Silicon Valley, they provide sources of employment. For others, they provide a shared language for gathering in online social networks, for meeting in parties, and increasingly, for forming Burning Man–related events in an ever-widening array of cities in the United States and abroad.[52]

Even as it extends its social and symbolic reach, however, Black Rock City—like various online game worlds, like the Linux project, or even like

Wikipedia—is also becoming a setting for commercial product development. In 2006, a team of city designers and programmers who had long been core members of the Burning Man community began collaborating with Google on the creation of Burning Man Earth. Since about 2000, a Scottish-born painter named Andy Johnstone had been building what he called the "Virtual Playa." Using a Microsoft flight simulator, he had created a virtual model of the city through which visitors could fly. In 2006, Rod Garrett, the person responsible for laying out the city on the playa every summer, began playing with Google Earth maps. He approached both Johnstone and Google to see if the projects could be fused. In the summer of 2006, Google sent an airplane and a photographer out over the Black Rock desert; today, the images he created are part of Google Earth.[53] Since then, Garrett, Johnstone, and programmers Michael Favor and Zhahai Stewart have worked with the Google Earth team to develop what they hope will be both a digital portal to Black Rock City and a beta space for developing new tools for Google Earth.

So far, no money has changed hands. "We're working in the spirit of co-operation and comradeship and good faith, and I don't see any reason to change that," explained Rod Garrett in the fall of 2006. "That's the spirit of Burning Man and much of Google also. It's not being handled with lawyers and accountants."[54] Michael Favor agreed. "The power of Google is that they don't do all the work," he said. "People posting content do. The same is true here at Burning Man. Citizens create the vast majority of things."[55] Over time, Favor and other long-time Burners hope that Burning Man Earth will allow virtual visitors to fly into a model of the actual Black Rock City, learn about its art works, and, via avatars, meet their creators and their neighbors. They also hope to transform Black Rock City's citizens into a development team for Google. As Andy Johnstone explained, they expect Google to "use our piece of desert as a Petri dish." Once Burning Man participants "start hacking [Burning Man Earth]," he said, Google will "get content they'd never dream up in a thousand sushi power breakfasts."[56]

## Conclusion

In the nineteenth century, the commanders of emerging industries turned to the arts to legitimate their positions. They built museums, commissioned paintings, took themselves to concerts and balls.[57] For the Brahmins of Boston and other industrial-era elites, the factory existed in order to provide the material basis to support the higher arts. Contemporary scholarship on the "creative class" has observed a similar distinction: for these workers, as Richard Florida has suggested, the arts are important evidence of social standing and of the values on behalf of which these workers labor.[58]

Burning Man, however, suggests that artistic and new media production may be becoming entangled in new and important ways. After all, the Burning Man festival not only legitimates emerging high-tech forms of wealth creation; it actively helps drive them. It does so in two ways, one ideological and the other, structural. For seven days in the desert, Burning Man provides a living model of commons-based peer production carried out for non-monetary purposes. Black Rock City presents an idealized commons, one in which project-based labor is subsidized, made visible, and transformed into the basis of individual reputations and of communal intimacy. For one week at least, its citizens build a utopian world driven by the pursuit of self-realization, project engineering, and communication. This world in turn both models the many claims made by marketers of information technology and, by explicitly disowning the marketplace, lets participants redeem its failures. It provides a ritual space in which the same sorts of engineering projects that organize participants' work lives in the everyday, secular world induce feelings of effervescent, even sacred community. In the process, it suggests to its participants that engineering can remake the world for the better.

For contemporary information workers, that belief alone has substantial value. As Lilly Irani, an interface designer at Google, put it, "We need to hang on to the idea that we are here to make the world a better place. If we don't keep that in mind, then we don't have anything but the bottom line to come to work for."[59] At the same time though, as the Burning Man Earth project suggests, the festival is not only a ritual space, but a potential factory. Like multiplayer online role-playing games or open-source projects in various fields, Burning Man is becoming a site at which the traditional features of artistic bohemias—collaborative commons, visibility, subsidy, project labor, and the fused pursuit of self-improvement, craft, and reputation—help structure the manufacture of new information goods. In the nineteenth century, at the height of the industrial era, the celebration of art provided an occasion for the display of wealth; in the twenty-first century, under conditions of commons-based peer production, it has become an occasion for its creation.

# 3

# APOCALYPSE BY SUBTRACTION

## LATE CAPITALISM AND THE TRAUMA OF SCARCITY

PETER Y. PAIK

*How sad to see great nations begging for a little extra future!*
—E. M. Cioran

### Expansion or Death

The comics series *Fables*, written by Bill Willingham and published by the Vertigo imprint of DC Comics, concerns a community of refugees in New York that is composed of familiar characters from fairy tales and nursery rhymes. Beloved as well as infamous figures from European folklore and legend, such as Snow White, Prince Charming, Pinocchio, Cinderella, Bluebeard, Boy Blue, the Frog Prince, Beauty and the Beast, the Black Forest Witch, and the Big Bad Wolf all live undercover on a single city block in Manhattan known as Fabletown, having been forced to flee from their magical homelands by the invading armies of a shadowy figure known only as the Adversary. Having left behind their wealth and possessions in the old world, the members of this invisible diaspora, who call themselves "Fables," form a new society under a covenant that grants them immunity from prosecution for any crimes they committed in the past before their arrival in the mundane world. Thus, the Big Bad Wolf, having taken human form, is in charge of security in the highrise where most of the Fables rent apartments. The Black Forest Witch, best known for nearly having made a meal out of Hansel and Gretel, now provides an indispensable service to the community by using her magic to help keep Fabletown concealed in plain sight from the ordinary residents of the city, whom the Fables call "mundanes," or "mundys" for short. Though the Fables regard themselves as members of a closed, traditional ethnic community, they for the most part lead lives of anonymous toil, their daily activities being little different from the everyday experience of ordinary mortals. For the dull and disenchanted world where these virtually immortal beings have taken refuge seems to be the only realm that the mysterious Adversary has shown no inclination to conquer.

The reprieve enjoyed by the Fables from the depredations of their enemy comes to an abrupt end when a detachment of animate wooden soldiers arrives from the fairy tale homelands to demand their surrender.[1] The Fables defeat these troops in the ensuing battle, but not before these formidable warriors, who are immune to pain and do not eat or sleep, inflict heavy losses on the community of exiles. In response to this attack, the intrepid Boy Blue undertakes a secret mission that sends him back to the homelands with the objective of uncovering the identity of the Adversary.[2] Traversing the myriad magical realms that have been united under the Adversary's rule, Boy Blue eventually reaches the imperial capital, where he uses his enchanted sword to decapitate the emperor, a terrifyingly powerful giant who has led the armies that have conquered and subjugated thousands of worlds. Taken prisoner after seemingly accomplishing his task, Boy Blue learns that the real power in the empire is wielded by the humble woodcarver, Geppetto, whose wooden soldiers comprise an elite caste charged with carrying out the most important administrative as well as military assignments in the realms. Held captive in Geppetto's modest workshop, Boy Blue promises to restore to the craftsman his eldest son, Pinocchio, if he will reveal how a lowly woodcarver in a distant and insignificant land came to build a vast empire, crushing countless lives and taking over innumerable kingdoms and principalities in the process.

The political significance of *Fables* as an act of literary worldmaking arises from the reflections it provokes regarding the nature of imperial expansion and the fate that this path sets in motion. The empire it portrays, to be sure, is one that possesses a medieval caste hierarchy composed of humble peasants, haughty landlords, rapacious soldiers, and supercilious administrators. The comic depicts moreover not a historical medieval world, but the one found in contemporary fantasy narratives, in which magic is an accepted reality of everyday life. Yet, the narrative manages to convey with considerable forcefulness the way in which empire provides a seductive solution to problems that might otherwise be arduous, if not altogether unsolvable, in a system of values that seeks to promote both freedom and equality. Empire, not least in the U.S. context, permits a rising standard of living by opening up new markets for domestic goods, creates opportunities for advancement for those of humble origins (fostering or preserving thereby belief in the equality of opportunity), and provides ideological cohesion for a diverse and pluralistic society. Expansion, as thinkers since Machiavelli have recognized, mitigates and redirects the internal tensions that would otherwise explode into class warfare and civil strife between various groups within a state. Expansion assures sociopolitical harmony by giving those at the lower end of the socioeconomic ladder a sphere in which to pursue their ambitions and to acquire wealth. As historian William Appleman Williams points out, in the context of the United States, the conquest and incorporation of the lands along the frontier were regarded from the earliest days of the republic as essential for making good on the promise of liberty and equality for all its citizens. Whether it took the form of seizing the lands inhabited by Native Americans or opening up overseas markets for American goods, expansion was recognized as vital to the well-being of the nation. Only expansion could "stifle unrest, preserve democracy, and restore prosperity."[3]

### Rescued by Empire

Given the prevalence of anti-imperial discourses in Anglophone Cultural Studies, in which modern empires are reflexively condemned for oppressing and exploiting subject populations, it can be somewhat startling to take note of the fact that overseas expansion was embraced by a broad and approving majority in the United States during the economic crisis of the 1890s. As Williams notes, liberals and conservatives, Democrats and Republicans, and even large numbers of radicals were united in looking to an expansionist foreign policy as the means for recovering from the severe economic downturn and for preventing future crises. The fateful step toward empire for the United States—its decision to go to war with Spain over its inability to govern Cuba—was taken not as a "blind and irrational outburst of patriotic or ideological fervor," but rather came about as the outcome of a "conscious exercise in considering alternatives."[4] A series of violent strikes by coal-miners and railway workers, along with an unemployment rate that had risen by some estimates to above 18 percent, served to convince many Americans that new markets for American exports were necessary to forestall the eruption of chaos and upheaval. An expansionist foreign policy was not a nefarious plot foisted upon an unsuspecting public by bankers and industrialists, but was actively embraced by labor and farm leaders such as Samuel Gompers and Jerry Simpson, who saw the opening of overseas markets as crucial for improving the lives of factory workers and farmers. In the words of Wisconsin Senator James Doolittle, the absorption and integration of the lands inhabited by Native Americans "will postpone for centuries, if not forever, all serious conflict between capital and labor."[5] Thus, the well-being of the American economy came to be intertwined with the creation of "new frontier[s] of exports."[6] Indeed, many of the Founding Fathers themselves held the project of imperial expansion to be vital for sustaining their version of democratic republicanism. In the view of James Madison, the system of checks and balances on its own was not adequate to prevent the formation of factions that would threaten the stability of the republic. Something more was needed to defuse the inevitable economic conflicts that would arise in a society organized around commerce. Thus, a policy of expansion came to be regarded as indispensable for a thriving democracy. Madison, for his part, was far less sanguine about the eventual fate of the fledgling republic. Given the reality that land and resources are finite, he concluded that the United States would one day be forced to relinquish this most dependable method of neutralizing internal discord. Having run out of space in which to grow and develop, the United States would become a monarchy, a shift that Madison saw as taking place at the end of the 1920s.[7]

Williams, an anti-capitalist critic of the New Deal, which he regarded as an effort to save corporate capitalism through subsidies provided by lower- and middle-income taxpayers, argues that Madison was not wrong if one understands by monarchy a "highly centralized and consolidated central government."[8] For Williams, the defining achievement of the presidency of Franklin Delano Roosevelt was its renewal of the Open Door policy and its repackaging of the imperial endeavor of achieving global supremacy into a "vision of progress for everyone" in an age of mass ideological politics.[9] Williams's criticisms of FDR draw attention to some disconcerting realities. For as much as the kinds of violence and oppression that have accompanied imperial expansion—the annihilation of native populations, the use of slave labor, and the expropriation of raw materials—are now objects of universal censure and moral condemnation, it nevertheless remains quite difficult, especially for those living in the United States, to contemplate or even imagine a way of life not centered on some form of expansion. Indeed, while

Anglophone cultural and postcolonial studies has dedicated itself to exposing and denouncing the crimes of Western imperialism and the prejudices
that gave them legitimacy, there is far less reflection accorded to the question of what it would mean for the globe's dominant power to break from its
tried and true path to security, unity, and prosperity.

For it is apparent that the undeniable social progress, racial equality, and
political stability that the United States has been able to attain—indeed the
qualities and achievements for which the nation is widely admired throughout the world—are deeply entwined with an emphatically expansionist conception of its historical destiny. The United States, after all, has shown far
greater willingness than most other advanced industrial nations in accepting
and absorbing immigrants, and in allowing them to rise to positions of
leadership in business, education, and politics. As Andrew Bacevich argues in
*The Limits of Power*, the success of the civil rights movement in overturning
racially discriminatory laws and the emergence of other groups, like women
and gays, engaged in the struggle for equality owed much to the prosperity
generated by the postwar economic boom. While the "circle of freedom"
would not have "widened appreciably" without the work and sacrifices of
progressive activists, nevertheless, the condition of abundance cannot be
discounted as a crucial factor in these far-reaching social transformations: "It
does not diminish the credit due to those who engineered this achievement
[of greater social equality] to note that their success stemmed, in part, from
the fact that the United States was simultaneously asserting its claim to
unquestioned global preeminence."[10] The postwar American empire thus
acquired its legitimacy from the "widespread perception that power was
being exercised abroad to facilitate the creation of a more perfect union at
home." The pursuit of "more power abroad" produced "greater abundance at
home," which then "paved the way for greater freedom" for American society. Thus, as Morris Berman concludes, the rampant consumerism and imperial foreign policy of the United States are inextricable from its "tradition of
political democracy and civil liberties, including its willingness to provide
asylum to millions of immigrants and refugees seeking the 'good life.'"[11]

The critique of empire undertaken by Bacevich and Berman thus returns
us to Madison's bleak prophecy. Can liberty be preserved in the United States
in the absence of ceaseless economic growth and an ever-increasing standard
of living? Or has the way of life permitted by its imperialist expansion become
so deeply rooted in American society as to render its democracy unthinkable

apart from the promise of wealth accumulation? And what of the mechanisms of self-correction that are vital to the well-being of both its democratic institutions and its economic prosperity—might the pursuit of abundance, taken beyond a vital point, come to corrode these attitudes and dispositions as well? Such questions generally do not emerge, or appear reassuringly counterfactual, when the expansionist ventures of the United States meet with success and when there are accordingly few doubts concerning its status as the world's preeminent power. As Williams forcefully argues, empire allows the avoidance of moral and political choice—it constitutes the denial of the "essence of politics" as "the process of defining and choosing between alternatives."[12] Any alternative to imperial expansion is rejected from the outset as "anti-American." The United States had thus far been able to escape the burden of real choice, which is in any case not to be confused with the unthinking and ubiquitous invocation of "freedom" in American political discourse, thanks to a combination of might and luck, whereby it has been able to continue in its pursuit of power and abundance for over half a century without encountering any serious reversals, whether a crushing defeat in war, or the fate of being invaded or occupied by an enemy.[13]

But the impasse in which the United States currently finds itself would indicate that the long-deferred day of reckoning has arrived. Ensnared by fighting interminable insurgencies in Afghanistan and Iraq, trapped by ballooning levels of debt to foreign lenders, and burdened with a political system in which the force of corporate power and entrenched interests stifles efforts at substantive reform, the United States has reached the point at which it cannot sustain the ideology of expansion without suffering grave political or economic harm. As Bacevich notes, "Iraq has revealed the futility of counting on military power to sustain our habits of profligacy."[14] Indeed, the cluster of assumptions whereby "expansionism, abundance, and freedom" reinforce each other has become untenable, as expansionism now "squanders American wealth and power, while putting freedom at risk."[15] But the prospect of breaking with the attitudes, habits, and expectations that date back to the founding of the nation appears nothing short of traumatic. Indeed, it is perhaps no exaggeration to say such a development typically evokes a sense of dread and alarm that the peoples of other countries would associate with the fate of being conquered and occupied by a foreign power, a tribulation from which the United States has been notably spared. The fact that it is the lack of restraint, the inability to master one's desires, and, as

Williams emphasizes, the refusal to live within one's means, rather than foreign overlords with a superior military force, that are the primary factors behind this predicament does little to make it any less shattering.[16]

## States of Mainstream Nature

While the political class has stumbled on in a state of denial, at least before the public, concerning these dire and inescapable realities, invoking the familiar bromides of American exceptionalism and promising the return of prosperity, the prevalence and popularity of postapocalyptic themes in films, novels, and video games bears out the fact that fears of an uncertain future, in which one's way of life will be irrevocably transformed, have become at present quite widespread and keenly felt. But the blockbuster action and disaster films involving doomsday scenarios are largely exercises in special effects, aimed at satisfying the conventional appetite for violence and spectacle, rather than efforts to grapple with the root causes behind the entwined crises that have the United States in their grip. While it is unrealistic to expect most commercial films to engage in such meaningful social and political inquiry—horror movies such as *28 Weeks Later* (2007) and *The Land of the Dead* (2005) stand out as commendable exceptions—what is noteworthy about these disaster and action blockbusters is how they license a further retreat into fantasy within the framework of some universal calamity.

For example, while the climate catastrophe film *The Day After Tomorrow* (2004) received praise for spreading awareness of the destructive consequences of global warming, the film does not merely exaggerate the impact of climate disasters (such as giant hailstones, rapid freezing of an entire continent) to show off the virtuosity of its technical effects. It also concludes with a fraudulent political fantasy that shows the American survivors of the climate catastrophe finding refuge in the poorer countries of the global South, as though the governments of these countries would have remained entirely oblivious to the barriers and mechanisms employed by wealthy countries to keep out or control flows of migrants from the developing world. In typical Hollywood fashion, the characters chosen for the audience to care about find safety in refugee camps at the end of the film, while millions of others perish. A chastened U.S. Vice President, clearly modeled on Dick Cheney, apologizes for his earlier skepticism regarding climate change and expresses gratitude for the hospitality shown by countries like Mexico to refugees from the United States. One might argue that a truly interesting and politically salutary narrative would commence at the exact point where the film ends, with an assortment of characters accustomed to prosperity and abundance forced to endure confinement in a grim and squalid refugee camp, deprived of the comforts and services that they formerly took for granted. But to tell that story (which is told well by J. G. Ballard in his novel of the Second World War, *Empire of the Sun*) would violate the therapeutic denial of reality that has played a significant role in generating the crisis in the first place.

Capitalist society has thus far found it quite easy to reject the difficult measures that would enable it to avoid worse predicaments in the future. This denial of catastrophic threat and imminent danger carries over into the realm of culture as a crisis in cinematic and literary representation. Here, the sense of fatalism and resignation find their correlative in narratives that portray not the descent of the social order into the state of nature but are instead already set in the state of nature, rendering the breakdown of civilization as a foregone conclusion. Thus, reflection upon human fallibility can be dispensed with in favor of a standard action adventure narrative that pits the agents of good, usually those who stand for freedom and dignity, against the forces of darkness, who seek to enslave and exploit the former to enhance their own chances of survival. This facile ethical vision, which belongs to the universe of the morality tale, unfortunately mars the most highly praised contemporary postapocalyptic literary narrative, *The Road* by Cormac McCarthy (2006). The novel portrays the journey of a father and son through a shattered and burned-out landscape toward the hope of a distant refuge in the south. The cataclysm that has destroyed not only civilization but also nature itself goes unnamed, while the novel immerses itself in the struggle of the protagonists to survive in a despoiled and gruesome world "populated by men who would eat your children in front of your eyes."[17] The pair search for food, find shelter in abandoned houses, and hide from vicious gangs of roving marauders.

The novel has been widely acclaimed for its vivid evocation of physical detail as well as its lyrical descriptions, enunciated in a loftily archaic diction, of a nightmarish postnuclear wasteland. Even most colors have leached away from an utterly desolate nature, leaving shades of ash and the blackness of charred matter, while the brightness of blood fades rapidly into rust: "On the far side of the river valley the road passed through a stark black burn. Ash moving over the road and the sagging hands of blind wire strung from the blackened lightpoles whining thinly in the wind. A burned house in a clearing and beyond that a reach of meadowlands stark and gray and a raw red mudbank where a roadworks lay abandoned."[18] The father and son are constantly cold, hungry, and anxiously watchful, as most of the human beings they encounter have resorted to cannibalism to perpetuate their physical existence in a world deprived of the capacity to nourish life. But the immersion of the narrative in the ruined environment of the postapocalyptic world not only arises as a symptom of its indifference to the social and political factors that have set in motion the universal catastrophe, but also reveals the novel's deeply ideological character. The overriding focus of McCarthy's novel is on the father's concern for the survival of his child in the face of such lurid and grotesque threats as cannibals who take fellow humans captive, and butcher their victims one limb at a time. Any concern with the causes of the calamity, whether spiritual or economic, is cast aside in favor of a demonology in which vulnerable innocence must be protected against the eminently representable threat posed by an externalized evil. Thus, the organized bands of cannibals who roam about the ruins of civilization in search of food and tools remain unknowable ciphers, their perspectives left entirely blank.

One might argue that the primary defect of the novel is its failure to humanize the inhuman. McCarthy, in leaving the interiority of these admittedly minor characters unexplored, flattens them into one-dimensional threats, placing them on the same order of natural dangers like giant man-eating sharks or lethal microbes. The novel thereby not only abdicates much of its claim to literary seriousness, but also falls short of the complexity and nuance of even the pulp narratives invoked by its very premise. To invoke a more literary example, one of the most chilling anecdotes related by Tadeusz Borowski in his stories about the real-life horror of the Nazi concentration camps occurs in a brief tale titled "Supper." A group of Russian prisoners is executed by the SS. After the firing squad departs, the narrator witnesses a group of inmates "burst into a shrieking roar" and "swarm" over the fallen bodies like an "avalanche."[19] The crowd is broken up by the prisoners in charge of the barracks, who force them to return to their blocks. It is not until the following day that an explanation is given for why the prisoners piled onto the corpses. The narrator finds himself working alongside a "Muslim-ized" prisoner, a man reduced to the condition of bare survival, who spends much of the time trying to persuade him that human brains are "so tender you can eat them absolutely raw."[20]

In this exchange one encounters a disconcerting mixture of yearnings and intentions—there is the desire of the prisoner to receive exculpation from his interlocutor, as well as his hope that the narrator will likewise repudiate elementary human restraints and avail himself of the same nourishment. Borowski evokes thereby a most unsettling and unwanted sort of intimacy, in which one character displays an utter lack of shame in order to convince the other to discard a fundamental human taboo. Such an instance casts us onto a threshold in which the human and the inhuman, sociability and abandon, are rent apart and then stitched together in horrifying and unexpected ways. The horror arises not from the act of consuming human flesh, which has become in recent decades a stock theme in popular entertainment, but rather from the peaceful and nonviolent efforts of the cannibal to convince the still civilized other of the advantages of his ways. These kinds of exchanges are absent from *The Road*, which makes McCarthy's novel memorable solely on the basis of its lapidary style, rather than for its thematic complexity or its insights into human character under the pressure of extreme situations. Indeed, even the vicious marauders in the now-archetypal postapocalyptic film *Mad Max 2* (1981, released in the United States as *The Road Warrior*), intent on brutalizing a group of peaceful settlers and seizing their oil, console each other with the memories of their deceased loved ones in order to prepare themselves psychically to slaughter and pillage their victims.

Of course, it could be argued that *The Road* evokes a world in which the bonds and structures of civilized life have dissolved altogether so as to render irrelevant the order of more complex concerns regarding social conditions. Yet, the novel's refusal to ascribe a sense of interiority to the figures who threaten the protagonists corresponds to what Williams regards as a hallmark of the imperial worldview in the U.S. context: the tendency to externalize evil. *The Road* accordingly emerges as a deeply ideological attempt to reassert the image of an "embattled and beleaguered" community, in which the subjective position of the adversary simply does not matter beyond posing a danger to what is rightful and legitimate.[21] On the other hand, despair and futility from which such an apocalyptic vision is suspended reflects the plight of a modern industrial society as it finds itself forced to deal with the reality of scarcity and grapple with the recognition that it can no longer legitimate itself on the basis of the easy abundance generated by an ever-expanding market economy. One suspects that the real object of the fear behind the proliferation of mainstream apocalyptic narratives is not the utter collapse of civilization as such but rather the specter of an inexorable transition to a society characterized by markedly diminished material expectations.

## Imagining Scarcity

Such a prospect is particularly daunting with respect to the United States. As George Kennan noted, the decisive role of geographic and economic expansion in American political life had left Americans with scant experience of the "deeper dilemmas in the predicament of man as a member of a crowded and inescapable political community."[22] Though the adjustments necessitated by environmental crises and by the depletion of key resources might be more fittingly described as moderate rather than cataclysmic when considered against the broad sweep of history (e.g., the fall of Rome or the French Revolution), Kennan points out that the political culture of American democracy, in which elected officials have little incentive to raise unsettling truths with voters and are routinely punished for doing so, lacks the capacity for coping with the limits of expansion and the emergence of scarcity as a major factor in economic life:

> Like many other Americans, I never ceased to ponder, in these first years of renewed confrontation with the American scene, the phenomena which the diary notes cited above so depressingly reflect: the obvious deterioration in the quality both of American life itself and of the natural environment in which it had its being, under the impact of a headlong overpopulation, industrialization, commercialization and urbanization of society. And I came up, invariably, before the dilemma which these tendencies presented. Allowed to proceed unchecked, they spelled—it was plain—only failure and disaster. But what of the conceivable correctives? If these were to have any chance of being effective, would they not have to be so drastic, so unusual, so far-reaching in the demands they placed on governmental authority and society, that they would greatly exceed both the intellectual horizons of the American electorate and the existing constitutional and traditional powers in the United States? Would they not involve hardships and sacrifices most unlikely to be acceptable to any democratic electorate? Would they not come into the sharpest sort of conflict with commercial interests? Would their implementation not require governmental powers which, as of the middle of the twentieth century, simply did not exist, and which no one as yet—least of all either of the two great political parties— had the faintest intention of creating?[23]

Writing in the early 1960s, Kennan recognized that the United States would eventually come up against arduous dilemmas for which its political system would be wholly unprepared, predicaments that would reveal the deep-seated inadequacy of existing sociopolitical arrangements. Kennan looked with grave dismay at the rise of the automobile as the dominant mode of transportation in the postwar era and the dependencies it would create. Indeed, the present-day crises of resource depletion and catastrophic climate change raise fundamental doubts about the continued viability of the capitalist system itself. The economic system that promises limitless accumulation and unending growth requires access to cheap petroleum, stocks of which are being rapidly depleted because of the continued rise of worldwide demand.

The increasing demand for energy has led to efforts to extract oil from such alternative sources as shale through costly methods that are themselves energy-intensive, while the burning of coal exacerbates the levels of carbon emissions trapped in the atmosphere, accelerating the process of global warming. The global economy's dependence on fossil fuels would work to ensure a grim future of climate disasters and environmental destruction, in which millions face the prospect of being uprooted by rising sea levels and of suffering famines triggered by the disruption of rainfall patterns. The rapid rise, moreover, of the economies of Brazil, China, and India has exacerbated the competition for oil, natural gas, and other vital resources. Although the emergence of these nations as economic powerhouses has succeeded in lifting millions out of poverty, the world's energy output must, according to Michael Klare, "increase by 57% over the next twenty-five years," a highly optimistic prospect, to avoid the onset of a severe global recession or depression.[24] The increased demand for hydrocarbons has revived the "great game" between the major powers for the vast energy resources of Central Asia, as the United States jockeys with China and Russia for favors from the corrupt oligarchs who control the region.[25] The dominant forces in the global economy create the conditions not only for environmental disaster but also embroil the major powers into conflict as they compete against one another for increasingly scarce resources.

The problems of global warming and resource scarcity present a crisis that capitalism may not be able to withstand, since the world cannot maintain an economy based on limitless accumulation and rising standards of living without inviting cataclysmic disaster. Yet, the growing awareness of the

destructive and unsustainable course of industrial capitalism has not translated into a significant rise in support for socialism or any other alternative
economic model. The opponents of capitalism, for example, have not been
able to exploit the crises of climate change and resource depletion to make
credible the prospect of radical sociopolitical change. As Imre Szeman notes,
the "very possibility of a disaster on the scale of the end of oil seems, on its
own, not to be able to generate the kind of social transformation one might
expect would be needed in order to head off a crisis that would be felt at
every level—including that of capital accumulation and reproduction."[26]
Why is it that this stunning reversal of fortunes for the neoliberal right has
not worked to the benefit of the socialist left? The persistent inability of the
left to exploit the weaknesses of its rival arises from the fact that the former's
programs for economic redistribution are likewise premised upon growth
and thus deny the problem of scarcity. The "Left discourse" that has emerged
to critique the unsustainable course of late capitalism, Szeman points out,
fails to move beyond an "eco-apocalypticism" which is characterized by resignation to environmental disaster as a kind of fate.[27] That is to say, there is
no hope that the transition from liberal capitalism toward some new type of
economic and political order will take an incremental form and represent an
unambiguous improvement over the status quo. Instead, the movement away
from capitalism will involve some kind of trauma, and the consequences are
likely to disappoint both those seeking to protect an unsustainable status
quo and those struggling to create a more egalitarian sociopolitical order.

The sense of this trauma altogether escapes postapocalyptic narratives
like *The Road*—the destruction of civilization in these instances merely sets
the stage for predictable narratives arousing rather conventional emotions.
On the other hand, one finds a more inventive and fruitful approach to examining these transformed realities in speculative narratives that register the
shock of scarcity and the demise of progress by portraying a fictional world in
which some vital aspect of everyday life has been removed. In the film *Children of Men*, as well as in the novel on which it is based, human beings have
for some unexplained reason ceased to bear children, with no new children
having come into the world for the past eighteen years. In José Saramago's
novel *Blindness*, a mysterious epidemic robs people of their sight, eventually
striking blind nearly the whole of humankind. The comic *Y: The Last Man*
commences with a mysterious plague that takes the life of every male mam-
mal on the planet except for the protagonist and his pet capuchin monkey.

On a comic note, intelligence is the element that goes missing in the future world portrayed by the satire *Idiocracy*, in which a soldier of average intelligence and a prostitute awaken after 500 years spent in cryogenic sleep to find themselves the most intelligent people on the planet. All four works register the trauma of historical change in a manner akin to the amputation of a limb from the body of deeply rooted, if tacitly cherished, social and economic expectations.

In all these narratives, there is a large-scale breakdown of the mechanisms of government, as the state becomes overwhelmed by a cascading series of problems that it cannot handle. In *Y: The Last Man*, the world is thrown into disarray by the sudden annihilation of the males of the species, and in the chaotic aftermath of the plague, those nations in which the greatest number of women could exercise political power and engage in military service, such as Israel and Australia, find themselves with an overwhelming strategic advantage over their counterparts in which traditional gender roles prevailed. *Idiocracy* is set in a United States on the brink of famine because the semi-illiterate population, having become utterly dependent on automated devices, no longer recalls how to make crops grow. The crisis of universal infertility in *Children of Men* leads to the collapse of governments across the globe. The only state left relatively intact is the United Kingdom, which is accordingly flooded by refugees fleeing the nightmarish chaos that has overtaken the rest of the world. The refugees, or "fugees," as they are called, are herded into detention facilities by the military. These internment camps are not prisons actively maintained and administered by the state but rather lawless zones where black markets flourish and armed militias hold sway. Although British soldiers regularly enter the camp to terrorize the migrants or to profit from the contraband trade in weapons and drugs, the government nevertheless holds back from imposing complete control over the facility, since to do so would tax the resources of the state. Instead, the detainees, while exposed to constant danger at the hands of British forces, are nevertheless able to carve out territories and settlements for themselves based on national origin or religious affiliation—the film shows a group of Muslim militants marching with machine guns and shouting "God is great" as well as a militia united under the French tricolor.

Similarly, those who lose their sight at the beginning of *Blindness* must contend with degrading and inhuman conditions thanks to the malign neglect displayed by the government with regard to the crisis. As in *Children of*

*Men*, the authorities respond to what they consider an insoluble problem by confining those infected by the malady to a walled-off site, the grounds of a disused mental hospital, and forbidding them from leaving this space. A stern voice coming out over a loudspeaker informs the internees of the services they are provided and the rules they must follow: the lights in the building will be kept on at all times; each ward is supplied a telephone with which to request toiletries and other items to maintain hygiene and cleanliness; the internees are to wash and sanitize their clothes by hand; each ward should elect a representative; containers of food for the interned will be left at the main entrance to the facility.[28] The further stipulations that the patients must burn their leftovers as well as all containers, plates, and utensils, and that they will not receive help from the fire department should these blazes go out of control, foreshadow the horrors to come. Indeed, the victims of the epidemic are not to expect any medical treatment should they fall ill, or any intervention by the police if violence breaks out among the patients. The state thereby declares the withdrawal of its mechanisms of protection and security from the internment facility, applying its lethal force only against those who attempt to leave the hospital without permission. The authorities, stricken by fear of being exposed to the contagion, adopt by default a policy of neglect, so that conditions in the hospital quickly deteriorate into squalor and filth. The rapid spread of the epidemic results in the overcrowding of the hospital, as over 240 patients, both the blind and those infected by the ailment, are forced to inhabit a space intended to hold half that number. Moreover, the quantity of food supplied to the inmates turns out to be inadequate, and the famished inmates waiting avidly for the containers are cut down by machine gun fire when they surprise and throw into a panic the guards dropping off the food.

The toilets quickly begin to overflow in the overcrowded building, but the authorities fear contamination too much to send anyone to fix the pipes. The patients thus frequently step into piles of excrement in the hallways, left behind by those who could not hold back until they have reached the yard. Unable to wash, they sleep and have sex in beds in which they have defecated:

> It is not just the state to which the lavatories were soon reduced, fetid caverns such as the gutters in hell full of condemned souls must be, but also the lack of respect shown by some of the inmates or the sudden urgency of others that turned the corridors and other passageways into

latrines, at first only occasionally but now as a matter of habit. . . . It was
not just the fetid smell that came from the lavatories in gusts that made
you want to throw up, it was also the accumulated body odour of two
hundred and fifty people, whose bodies were steeped in their own
sweat, who were neither able nor knew how to wash themselves, who
wore clothes that got filthier by the day.[29]

The overflowing toilets cause the patients to wait until nightfall to void their
bowels in the yard, often over the thin layer of dirt covering the bodies of the
internees killed by the guards. The situation, already hellish and dehuman-
izing, grows markedly worse when a gang of thugs that has established itself
in one of the wards seizes control over the food supply. They force the other
internees to hand over their valuables in exchange for their share of the food.
Once their victims have given up all their jewelry, watches, and other precious items, the gangsters demand that the other wards send them women to
satisfy their sexual urges. After the women are forced to endure sexual violation at the hands of the thugs, which results in the death of a woman who
had been suffering insomnia, the protagonist, known only as the doctor's
wife, resolves to take action. When, after four days, the thugs again summon
the women in her ward for another night of mass rape, she stabs their leader
in the throat with a pair of scissors. As a result, the inmates in her ward
decide to fight back against their tormentors. A fellow female patient succeeds in setting fire to the room inhabited by the brutes, and though she per-
ishes in the blaze alongside her tormentors, the fire allows the others to
escape their confinement.

The protagonists in *Blindness* and *Children of Men* are thrown out of their
normal conditions of life into dangerous and life-threatening situations, in
which their actions come to have a determining effect on the fate and well-
being of others. In *Children of Men*, the disillusioned office worker and former
activist Theo Faron is roped into the underground activities of a militant
immigrant-rights organization by the pleas of his ex-wife. After she is
betrayed and murdered by her fellow militants, Theo becomes the protector
of Kee, an African teenager who has somehow become pregnant and thus
represents the hope for humanity's future. In *Blindness*, the wife of the oph-
thalmologist feigns infection in order to remain at her husband's side after
he has succumbed to the epidemic. The fact that she still possesses her sight
enables her to kill the leader of the thugs and lead those in her group to shelter and safety after they venture out into the city, where they discover that

everyone has gone blind. Both Theo and the doctor's wife are forced to take action in a transformed reality, but first must come to grips with and accept the truth that they cannot go back to the certainties and habits of their previous ways of life. They must accept the fact of being exposed to constant danger and, in the case of the doctor's wife, the indignities of sexual violation. To defend the lives of those whose care and safety have been entrusted to them, they must also ready themselves to take the terrible step of committing actions that would be unimaginable under normal conditions, such as taking the life of another human being.

The dilemmas and predicaments that confront Theo and the doctor's wife arise out of the grim conditions created by a state that simultaneously resorts to brutal force while abdicating the basic function of protecting the well-being of the citizens. In addition to shooting down the internees who, crazed by hunger, move too quickly toward the food containers, the soldiers guarding the hospital in *Blindness* turn aside the pleas of the patients when they complain that the thugs are unfairly withholding their share of the food. The attitude of the guards is that it would be better for the inmates to kill each other, because "there will be fewer of them" to cause trouble.[30] A state policy characterized by a combination of disproportionate force and malign neglect is found in *Children of Men* as well. As in *Blindness*, the security forces prefer to shoot noncombatants than to expose themselves to increased levels of danger: a group of frightened men and women, waving white handkerchiefs in an attempt to get out of the crossfire between the troops and militants, is cut down by the former as they try to leave their building. In the film, government forces routinely terrorize and abuse the suspected migrants caught in round-ups and transported to the internment facilities. The film recreates in the background of the scenes in which Theo and Kee enter the camp at Bexhill the iconic images of torture and prisoner abuse that were committed by U.S. troops against Iraqis at the Abu Ghraib prison, such as the now iconic figure of the hooded man standing on a box with electrical wires taped to his body and the half-naked man terrified by a German shepherd snarling at him. Yet, though the British government in the film deals harshly with the refugees, it also encourages its own citizens to end their own lives by promoting a euthanasia kit called Quietus, the advertisements for which ("you decide when") are ubiquitous. Thus, when Theo tells Jasper that even if a solution to the problem of infertility were found, it would do no good, because the world had already gone to "shit," his words also underscore the awful impasse whereby the state has committed too many atrocities to back away from its brutal and inhuman policies.

The kind of state that emerges in both narratives is the neoliberal state in a more advanced stages of decomposition, in which actions and policies it once confined to a periphery or to foreign territories, such as the practice of torture or the doctrine of force protection in which the danger of terrorism makes a target of any civilian, become routine for the security forces charged with defending the First World homeland itself. The situation that prevails calls to mind the argument of Alain Joxe that the United States is building a neoliberal empire that triggers the "multiplication of savage contemporary wars."[31] For Joxe, the problem with the American empire is that it is one-sidedly economic in its orientation. This neoliberal empire cannot but exacerbate strife on a global scale because it balks at assuming the traditional function of historical empires, which is to "take responsibility for protecting the subjugated societies" and "enrich the conquered peoples as much as the conquerors."[32] Ceaseless strife becomes for the British government in *Children of Men* the status quo it defends with force, as the perpetual threat of violence grants the state justification for its brutal security policies and relieves it of the obligation to provide minimal services for the refugees it apprehends. Under neoliberalism, the nightmare is no longer that of an overbearing, totalitarian government that seeks to control every aspect of an individual's existence, as in George Orwell's *1984*, but rather the decaying and disintegrating state that selectively withdraws its powers of jurisdiction and abandons various categories of people to their fate, subjecting them to the will and appetites of the least scrupulous among the abandoned.

Thus, in the novel *Blindness* the doctor's wife muses that the mass outbreak of sightlessness not only dooms most of the newly blind to a terrifying and isolating death, but also makes manifest the condition of helplessness that has prevailed among human beings before they lost their sight. After the interned make their way into the city where everyone has finally gone blind, the doctor remarks that many of the houses must contain rotting bodies and that what the blind need most is organization. His wife replies:

> A government. . . . An organisation, the human body is also an organised system, it lives as long as it keeps organised, and death is only the effect of disorganisation. And how can a society of blind people organise itself in order to survive. By organising itself, to organise oneself is, in a way, to have eyes.[33]

The wife thus accounts for her unimpaired eyesight as indicative of her capacity to organize the group as well as her obligation to bear witness to the horrors that they have experienced but cannot see. Her sight enables her to perform the act that eventually brings about the liberation of the group from the hospital. It is her vision, understood in both the physical and spiritual senses, that is crucial in preventing the others in her group from being reduced to the brutish condition of the elderly woman in whose building they take refuge. This woman, driven mad by her solitary, troglodytic existence, has regressed to an animalistic condition, living off the raw flesh of the rabbits and chickens whose carcasses litter her apartment. More shockingly, she compels these creatures into violating their natural patterns of behavior by making them eat meat. The reversion to a bare, animal-like existence centered on catching and devouring one's prey leads not to a return to nature but rather to the further manipulation and corruption of nonhuman forms of life. As the old woman reasons, to the horror of her listeners: "animals are like people, they get used to everything in the end."[34]

In *Blindness*, it is the wife's miraculous retention of her sight in the midst of an inexplicable epidemic that proves to be the salvation of the other characters. Similarly, the resolution of *Children of Men* also rests on a miraculous event: the birth of a human child after eighteen years of worldwide infertility. As in *Blindness*, the intervention of an inexplicable event serves as an occasion to unveil the elementary workings of social relations, in this case the care and awe, but also the hubris and rapacity, shown by those who find themselves in the presence of the infant. The aging hippie political cartoonist Jasper makes arrangements for Kee and her companions to travel to the coast, where she is to be met by scientists based in the Azores, but proves to be a poor judge of character when he entrusts them to the care of the sociopathic soldier Syd. Upon discovering Kee's newborn infant, Syd, who sells marijuana grown by Jasper in the internment camp, tries to turn her and Theo over to the state to collect the bounty placed on their heads as wanted fugitives. On the other hand, Marichka, a woman who works with Syd and is described by him as an "Arab, gypsy, whatever," right away devotes herself to safeguarding Kee and her daughter. Marichka initially appears to be a shady figure, with eyes dulled and wearied by an everyday reality pervaded by fraud, deceit, and brutality, who ekes out a living by trafficking drugs and possibly human beings. But it is through her courage, resourcefulness, and steadfast dedication that Kee, Theo, and her baby are able to sail out to meet the ship manned by the scientists working to develop a cure for infertility. Though Marichka can barely communicate with Kee and Theo, her actions nevertheless prove to be indispensable in enabling them to achieve their quest.

The devotion and grace shown by a stranger to Kee and Theo casts a harsh verdict against the government that has decided to deal brutally with the waves of migrants seeking refuge. Indeed, the refusal of the state to give shelter and protection to the refugees in effect cuts the state off from the source of its salvation. But as indicated by Theo's observation that it is "too late," the numerous scenes of violence through which he passes (angry and dispossessed youth throwing rocks at a bus; a high-rise on fire, evacuated by security forces; the bombing of a café; cells containing refugees about to be interned, lamenting their fate) reveals a grim and absurd quandary in which the state exerts excessive force for the sake of shoring up an essentially hopeless situation. It is, to be sure, difficult to imagine the state bending to the will of the militant refugee-rights organization called the Fishes without triggering another, perhaps even more formidable, crisis, yet the spectacle of pomp and opulence that greets Theo on the way to visit his cousin Nigel, a minister in the government, discloses that the imperative to preserve the privileges of the political and financial elite has taken precedence over the need to confront the challenge of a drastically altered reality.

Although the film does not dwell on the luxurious escapism enjoyed by the wealthy and powerful at the twilight of the human species, it nevertheless provides a sharp counterpoint to the preoccupations of the ruling class. Nigel, proudly showing off Michelangelo's *David* when Theo enters his apartment, speaks half-jokingly of his regret that his office failed to rescue the *Piéta*, which had been smashed by vandals. Later on in the film, at the Bexhill internment facility, Theo, Kee, and their guides hurry past a mother wailing at the heavens while the body of her dead son lies across her lap. While the Fishes resort to armed struggle against the state, they are no less under the sway of the desperation that has afflicted the whole of society—their leader Luke, for example, has no compunctions about endangering Kee's infant in his determination to keep the baby girl from falling into the clutches of the government he hates. The Fishes set out to trigger an uprising which they hope will somehow spread into British society, but prove incapable of adjusting their plans to safeguard the child that may be the last hope of humankind.

*Children of Men* and *Blindness* emerge as allegories of the present socio-political impasse, in which neoliberal capitalism still reels from the shock of the global financial crisis while confronting a bleak future of environmental catastrophe and resource scarcity. Yet, the weakness of global capitalism, or the prospect of its collapse, has not benefited its ideological adversary. Rather, as John Gray points out in a recent article, "Neoliberalism and social democracy may be dialectically related, but only in the sense that when the neoliberal state collapses it takes down much of what remains of social democracy as well."[35] The crisis of infertility and the epidemic of blindness thus correspond to a present that cannot be grasped according to social and political doctrines premised on progress and abundance. They underscore the fact that we have not yet awakened from the afterlife of dead ideas, in which an "irrational faith" in progress serves to sustain social bonds and enables individuals in capitalist society to continue making sacrifices and compromises to preserve the existing order.[36] But such a medicinal lie has reached the end of its effectiveness, even for the terminally disenchanted. Instead, scarcity imposes a new reality that can only be mapped by those instincts and intuitions that have been left to languish in the era of easy abundance. As acts of worldmaking, speculative narratives such as *Children of Men* and *Blindness* evoke the disruptive and wrenching character of the experience of historical change as it would befall the citizens of affluent societies, who have grown accustomed to the belief that they have surpassed the condition of scarcity and the conflicts provoked by it.

Whereas *Children of Men* and *Blindness* depict a fantastic situation of lack and absence in order to signal the dissolution of the certainties and expectations of the posthistorical, late capitalist world, the comic *Fables* concentrates its speculative energies in its striking portrayals of familiar imaginary characters engaging in realistic intrigues and confronting dire contingencies. In an interview, Bill Willingham describes the protagonists of his series as "immortal, traditional people" who not only have "been alive for thousands of years," but also "tend as a community to cling to old ways."[37] Maintaining this premise has aroused controversy among the comic's readers—for example, after an abortive revolution carried out by some of the talking animals, Snow White, as deputy mayor, rejects the "modern social philosophy" of mundane society that exonerates the violence inflicted by the rebels.[38] Yet, Snow White and her colleagues prove themselves adept at learning from their reversals and crises. After punishing their ringleaders, they adopt crucial elements of the program devised by the revolutionaries, including an assault on the fairy-tale homelands using modern weapons and advanced technology to overcome the sorcery and vastly superior numbers of the Adversary's forces. But what is perhaps most noteworthy with respect to the question of historical consciousness is the readiness with which the protagonists of *Fables* refer to duty and obligation in carrying out their actions. This sense of duty and obligation, however, is not based on any feudal code. Rather, it is rooted in a covenant that the Fables have made with each other, agreeing to forgive the crimes and misdeeds they committed against each other in the homelands, in recognition of the precarious interdependence that is necessary to confront and deal with the forces that threaten their existence. The covenant of course serves only to mitigate conflict, as many of the storylines dramatize the clash between individual ambition and group responsibility. Willingham thereby creates a vivid depiction of a community struggling to defend itself against the forces that seek its destruction while undergoing changes of leadership and contending with internal divisions.

An age in which competition for limited resources and environmental catastrophe serve as the major sources of global conflict is in significant ways a return to the historical past to which we have become oblivious. As John Gray observes, scarcity and the attendant evils it brings, such as wars fought over access to rivers and fertile land, are in fact the norm in history. What is exceptional and an aberration, in historical terms, is the incomprehension with which we greet such developments, not least their recurrence in our own time: "if we find the emergent pattern of conflict unfamiliar, it is because we are still haunted by nineteenth-century utopian visions in which the spread of industry throughout the world ushers in an age of perpetual peace."[39] Fanciful as the vision of a prosperous, economically interdependent globe might come to appear since the attacks of September 11 and the subsequent wars in the Middle East, our predominant political models remain wedded to the promise of abundance and the expectation of never-ending growth. Even the primary adversary of liberal democratic capitalism, state socialism, fought and lost the ideological battle on the terrain of economic prosperity, as it failed to match the rising standard of living delivered by the capitalist economies. What this means of course is that, intellectually and psychologically, we are largely unprepared to take the measure of a reality in which scarcity becomes increasingly the dominant factor of social life. But to confront this reality we must first relinquish the world that has shaped our expectations as well as our apprehensions—the sociopolitical order that is at present rapidly deteriorating into a utopian fantasy that licenses self-destructive passion while calling upon murderous force for its defense. The speculative, properly worldmaking imagination at work in *Blindness* and *Children of Men* exposes the lack of vision and the extinction of the future such a fantasy necessarily entails, while the fairy-tale protagonists of *Fables* struggle to maintain their community without succumbing to the therapeutic illusions that encourage the denial of harsh exigencies. In these narratives, the act of worldmaking awakens us to the necessities we have ceased to imagine while bringing us face to face with the field of actions and possibilities imposed on us by a world that is returning, in arduous and unexpected ways, to the narratives we thought were beyond or behind us.

# 4

# THESE GREAT URBANIST GAMES

## NEW BABYLON AND SECOND LIFE

### THOMAS M. MALABY

Michel de Certeau, the French social theorist perhaps most attuned to the fraught nature of the relationship between designed spaces and everyday practices, took a moment in his landmark *L'invention du quotidien. Vol. 1, Arts de faire* (1980, translated by Steven Randall in 1984 as *The Practice of Everyday Life*) to muse about the rise of technology and its possible saturation of everyday experience, and what that would mean for the future of the city. He imagined that the proliferation of technology in an unbounded sense would dissolve what had been a distinction between "proper" institutional spaces and the unbounded spaces of the quotidian. He continued:

> The system in which [people] move about is too vast to be able to fix them in one place, but too constraining for them ever to be able to escape from it and go into exile elsewhere. There is no longer an elsewhere. Because of this, the "strategic" model is also transformed, as if defeated by its own success; it was by definition based on the definition of a "proper" distinct from everything else; but now that "proper" has become the whole. It could be that, little by little, it will exhaust its capacity to transform itself and constitute only the space . . . in which a cybernetic society will arise, the scene of the Brownian movements of invisible and innumerable tactics. One would thus have a proliferation of aleatory and indeterminable manipulations within an immense framework of socioeconomic constraints and securities: myriads of almost invisible movements, playing on the more and more refined texture of a place that is even, continuous, and constitutes a proper place for all people. Is this already the present or the future of the great city?[1]

This question of how technology may make imaginable a new kind of environment, characterized by a kind of totality that contains infinite improvisation, finds striking and concrete expression in two "urbanist" projects, one never realized and one host to hundreds of thousands of people today. New Babylon, the postwar unitary urbanist project of the Dutch painter Constant Nieuwenhuys (known as "Constant"), and Second Life, the virtual world made by Linden Lab of San Francisco, each lie almost exactly twenty-three years to either side of de Certeau's writing. His description of the totalizing containment of the new city, and how it would provide a context for the "Brownian movements of invisible and innumerable tactics" (in reference to the assumably random motion of particles in a fluid, named after the botanist Robert Brown), serves equally well for both projects, at least in their utopian aims. Both of them sought to make use of design and technology to accomplish a seeming contradiction: to contrive and control a space for utterly free and self-governing action. In doing so, they each—though seemingly entirely unrelated in their histories (and apparently unknown to de Certeau)—drew upon related notions of play and creativity—productive play—and prompted strikingly similar conundra of governance and authority.

Constant, who was a founding member of the Situationist International with Guy Debord, worked on New Babylon from 1958 until 1973. This proposed city (which would, theoretically, cover the globe) was intended to prompt all people to express their creativity through their constant reconfiguration of its open and malleable living space. Explicitly designed for *homo ludens*, in this "great urbanist game,"[2] social life was to be constituted by architectural play. But, as Mark Wigley has noted, "play was the whole point of New Babylon but not its mode of production."[3] As designer of this universalizing and revolutionary playspace, Constant's role necessitated the contrivance of open-endedness, and thus implicitly relied upon the very artistic authority that the Situationists had rejected (Constant left the Situationists in 1960). In Second Life, an online architected social space that also claims to be an infinitely malleable forum for creative expression, the same tension is in place. Linden Lab, its creator, has made a product that is supposed to make itself, based upon ideals of universal access and unconstrained creativity and concrete techniques of game design, but Linden Lab also confronted the designer's contradiction of occupying a position of deeper access to Second Life's code, to what is "under the hood."

In what follows I briefly draw some of these connections in order to spark thinking about the nature of making worlds under postbureaucratic imaginings, and how these cases illuminate the different influences of play in that effort on both sides of the Atlantic. I hasten to note that in doing this I am delving into an area not originally my own—not being, to take just one more fitting possibility, an architectural historian. As a cultural anthropologist that studied the making of *Second Life* by the small group of people at Linden Lab in San Francisco, I grew interested in connecting such efforts to the broader arc of thinking about design as worldmaking and certain strands of architectural thought. In encountering Constant's New Babylon, I was struck by the depth of parallels in the cases and intrigued to find out what might be learned from considering how their differences reflect their culturo-historical situations, so I offer the following connections in the hope that it may be helpful for beginning to think about how notions of play as a productive force influence worldmaking, but in ways that reflect culturo-historic specificities. Such a conversation about architecture, design, play, and technology may further help us to understand the histories and ideals behind the digital architectures that increasingly mediate our everyday actions.

## Constant and New Babylon

The scholarship on Constant is distinguished, but far from extensive. In 1999, his drawings from the project were the centerpiece of an exhibit about New Babylon at The Drawing Center in New York, and the center also hosted a symposium that brought a number of scholars on Constant together, as well as Constant himself, who was in attendance (he died in 2005). In what follows, I rely heavily on the volume published thereafter, which includes many images from the exhibit along with participants' essays and an interview with Constant.[4] There are other works that more directly trace the influence of Constant and the Situationists on architecture and urban planning,[5] but my interest here is shaped more by the specific parallels between New Babylon and Second Life.

What was New Babylon? The design for the city called for two planes, one above the other, with living space in between. Both planes would be suspended above the ground (via cables from large columns that dot the New Babylon landscape), allowing for traffic underneath, along the ground, and with the top of the upper plane available for aircraft use. The city was to expand not as one ever-larger shape, but via multiple, networked corridors of this interconnected space.

The planes are never broken off from the network, which is marked by a center-less, branching arrangement of "sectors." It was in the vertical spaces

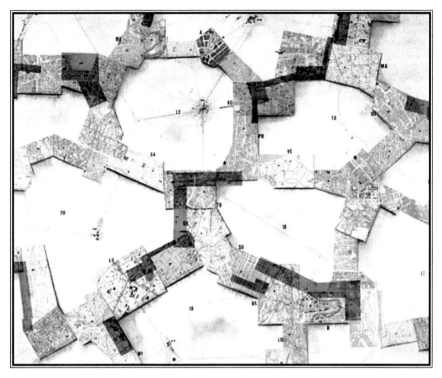

———————————————— Constant Nieuwenhuys. ————————————————
Symbolische voorstelling van New Babylon, 1969.

sandwiched between the planes where everything was to happen, and where
design would practically vanish, along with the distinction between artist
and non-artist. This was the living space, and it was meant to be infinitely
configurable by its users. As de Zegher puts it:[6]

> The inhabitants drift by foot though the huge labyrinthine interiors,
> perpetually reconstructing every aspect of the environment by changing
> the lighting and reconfiguring the mobile and temporary walls. For this
> *homo ludens*, social life becomes architectural play and the multiply
> interpretable architecture becomes a shimmering display of interacting
> desires—a collective form of creativity, as it were, displacing the tradi-
> tional arts altogether.

The project was never realized, but was extensively modeled by Constant
in elaborate small-scale constructions that still give architects pause. In
them, intricate cabling, often fanning out from tall pillars, suspends carefully
fitted plexiglass, enclosing the living space, above mostly featureless white

paper that denotes the ground. But as Wigley has noted, what actually happens in this living space is always blurry and undefined, the indeterminacy of its representation in Constant's models and drawings set against the exacting and specific demonstrations of how the space is made possible. "Inside, things are always blurry. . . . Constant continually blurs both the play of desire, which cannot be specified without blocking it, and the support of that play, which cannot be represented without it being mistaken for frozen play."[7]

It is not a surprise that such an ambitious and utopian project relies on no longer fashionable assumptions about technology and production. Constant imagined—as have many going back to Karl Marx (and forward to *Star Trek*)—a fully automated system of production, one that would free individuals from having to act for any other reason than to fulfill their creative impulses. In New Babylon, all of this automated production took place underground, the only evidence of the machinery being the small points (perhaps for ventilation) that would protrude very slightly aboveground (often at the center of the open spaces in the branching network of sectors). As Wigley puts it, "New Babylon is a seemingly infinite playground. Its occupants continually rearrange their sensory environment, redefining every microspace within the sectors according to their latest desires. In a society of endless leisure, workers have become players and architecture is the only game in town, a game that knows few limits."[8]

Thus is Karl Marx reconciled with Johan Huizinga; to play is to be creative is to be human, with creativity standing in for Marx's picture of the human as the maker. In New Babylon, *homo faber* and *homo ludens* are one under the rubric of creativity. In the symposium interview of 1999, Constant outlines his ideas in this area specifically:

> Huizinga, and his *homo ludens*, was thinking about a state of mind, not about a new kind of humanity; of human being, but in a certain sense a state of mind, of certain temporary conditions of human beings. For instance, when you are at a carnival, a feast, a wedding party. Temporarily you become the *homo ludens*, but then the next day you can be the *homo faber* again. He has to earn his pay. Marx . . . says creativity is a state of mind. A man cannot always be a painter. He is only a painter when he paints. . . . That is close. I have always tried to reconcile those two points of view, those visions of Marx . . . and Huizinga.[9]

New Babylon, in a sense, was about designing for play, because play was for Constant the essence of creative human activity. This brings us to the role of the child in this conception of play. The child represented creation in several important ways for Constant, and for several movements of which he was a part, including the Dutch Experimental Group (founded in 1948), COBRA, and the Situationist International. For these movements, the social order itself was the target for radical reconfiguration. Artists, as a category, were complicit in an exploitative social order, and thus the distinction between artists and non-artists had to be broken down. One way this was done was by the exhibiting of children's drawings alongside those of members of the movement, something COBRA did in the early 1950s.[10] This concept of the value of children's playful work was tied to an idea about the primitive, in the sense of the original or primal, in which children's creativity was taken as an instance of purely human creativity before the twisting and confining influence of social institutions.

But this conceptualization of the child and creation had moral overtones as well in postwar Europe. The first question asked of Constant at the symposium interview was about this connection to the art of the child in the work of him and his cohort, and Constant's reply begins with an articulation of the above point about the primitive, with this elaboration:

> Not exactly the child. Not only the child, but going back to the origins
> of creation—of artistic creativity. We cannot think of COBRA without
> thinking of the situations we were in after the war, the situation of com-
> plete emptiness. . . . Especially in Holland it was nearly nothing for these
> young artists, so that we turned to what was the only thing that looked
> at least like creation, like spontaneous expression of humanity.[11]

The vast destruction of the war, and its moral horrors, left European thinkers like Constant reaching for a source for (re)creation that would be outside the received social order, exemplify the essentially human, and thereby recoup moral ground. Huizinga's legacy for Europe, at least for these movements generally and New Babylon specifically, was a particular conception of play, one that elevated the child and focused on the unschooled, noninstitutional play that distinguished childhood.

For Constant it was not enough to valorize this form of creativity. He sought to actively bring about a new urban landscape that would foster it. And herein lay a contradiction, for to do that Constant had to seize some degree of artistic, in this case architectural, authority. His plans for New Babylon began at almost the same time that he cofounded the Situationist International, in 1958, but he left that same organization in 1959, frustrated by what he saw as a resistance to applying the ideas of the movement on the part of Guy Debord and others, who for their part saw the rejection of any special artistic authority as the very point. The problem, as Constant saw it, was the need to take an active role in prompting the kind of society they wanted; a question of the authority that makes, in a way, social policy possible. As Constant put it, "It's not enough to say that everybody is an artist. I have said this long before Beuys, other people have even before me—the surrealist movement, for instance. What is important is to figure out how this creativity, this sleeping creativity . . . can be woken up."[12]

By 1959 Constant already had experience in attempting to architect play. After COBRA disbanded, Constant joined Aldo van Eyck in designing playgrounds in Amsterdam. In New Babylon, Constant continued in the effort of designing for play. "Children's creativity remained Constant's model, but its products were no longer to be simply imitated. As with the playgrounds, it was a matter of making spaces for play rather than reproducing its patterns. Like van Eyck, Constant used a highly controlled abstract geometry to facilitate an uncontrolled play."[13] This was "designed confusion"[14] or, as I would put it, contrived indeterminacy.

In this way Constant embarked in his distinctive way on a program to find a means of governance that we might call postbureaucratic. In rejecting the existing modern bureaucratic institutions that had defined the social order (and were implicated in the horrific war), he and his contemporaries found an alternative in childlike play. But Constant took a further step and sought to work through how to contrive such play, how to employ controlled design that would prompt uncontrolled play within the spaces of New Babylon. Such play would embody a contradiction. It would be self-governing, to the extent that the use of New Babylon's spaces was completely under the control of its residents. But this of course elides the role of the designer, or anyone with access to control over the conditions of the domain as a whole. Just as only the tips of the automated machinery can be glimpsed aboveground everywhere, if one were to look, so the social position of the maker, *homo faber* of a different order, is everywhere and nowhere.

Play for Constant in his war-ravaged Europe stood as a productive and morally innocent, childlike force, one that could nonetheless through design be prompted and contained in order to remake the urban (in fact, all) landscape.

Constant and New Babylon.
Photograph by Bram Wisman, 1968.

## Linden Lab and Second Life

Catherine de Zegher, director of The Drawing Center during the 1999 symposium, drew out some of the implications of New Babylon in an era of networked technologies. While the Web had already arrived, Second Life was still
four years away (in fact, its founder Philip Rosedale had at that point just quit
his job as the Chief Technology Officer of Real Networks in order to found Linden Lab). But de Zegher's comments seem prophetic, if at times they seem to
overstate the parallels between New Babylon's theoretical lack of constraints
and the seemingly unconstrained web:

> Prefiguring the current debate about architecture in the often placeless
> age of electronics, Constant seems to have conceived of an urban model
> that literally envisaged the World Wide Web. In the network of sectors
> in New Babylon, one configures his or her own space and can wander in
> an unobstructed way from site to site, without limits. In this respect,
> Constant's project represents the spatialization of a virtual world, where
> people can move, meet, and interact anytime, anywhere. As an un-
> limited communication system, the work is as radical as ever.[15]

This could almost serve as a mission statement for Second Life, which, like New Babylon, sought to bring everyone (indeed, in aspiration, everyone on the planet Earth) together in a space where they would have freedom to play in an unconstrained fashion and access to the tools for creation. In a way, Second Life *is* New Babylon, or an attempt as close as we may ever see.

What is Second Life? It is a virtual world, just as de Zegher put it, but now that term has come to denote a category of persistent online spaces for social interaction. While the first ones were text-based, the largest now have three-dimensional graphics, and users participate in them through their avatars, representations of their bodies in this virtual space. Many of them are games in a foundational sense, that is, they have shared and established game objectives (such as World of Warcraft, Ultima Online, Lineage II, or War-hammer Online). World of Warcraft is the largest, claiming more than twelve million active subscribers. Others are sometimes called "social virtual worlds," and do not have shared and established game objectives. Second Life is one of these and has, by some accounts, upwards of 500,000 active users. Second Life's distinctive feature is that all users have access to 3-D modeling, scripting (programming), and texture-mapping "tools," ones that allow them to make interactive objects in the world. Just as important, users own the intellectual property rights to their creations (which cost next to nothing to reproduce), and can control how they are distributed to other users, including the possibility of market transactions in the in-world currency, Linden dollars. When I began doing research at Linden Lab in December 2004, approximately 13,000 users had created accounts in Second Life—small by the standards of the virtual world industry (at the time the original Lineage, a game primarily popular in East Asia, boasted over two million users worldwide), but this number was beginning to rise at an increasing rate, and by the end of 2005 they had over 120,000 registered users.

Governance of Second Life is supposed to be minimal as well. While Linden Lab provides that world's landscape, creating continents and countless small islands, what is built on this virtual land is left almost entirely up to the users. This style of governance shares with Constant's efforts the distinction between those acting freely within a domain and those with the authority or access to architect that domain in its entirety, but when we explore the ideological and practical roots of Linden Lab's approach, the path could not be more different from Constant's Marxian views. Recent work has charted how some of the most important developments in computing and networking technology in the United States were inextricably linked to political and more broadly ideological interests. Works by journalists[16] and, more recently, academics[17] are helpful in filling out the culturo-historical landscape from which computers emerged, particularly in the San Francisco Bay area. Specifically, these works reveal how the development of these technologies and their makers' aspirations for them were inextricably linked to general attitudes about authority that characterized the postwar period.

In these works there is a common theme: among this emerging culture one finds a remarkable and mutually confirming combination of a deeply held skepticism toward "top-down" decision-making—with a corresponding resistance to (and even resentment of) the institutional control of technology—and a deep faith in the ability of technology, when made widely available, to provide solutions. The contrast here is with computing as it existed in institutions through the 1960s: mainframe computing demanded specialized and controlled access to the most powerful tool in an institution, and its enduring image is that of the mainframe in the glass room, accessible only by a priesthood of those empowered to tend it. The attitude that arose in reaction against this image, these books suggest, reflects the anti-establishment politics of the period and found purchase in the distinctive disposition of engineers toward new technologies, new corporate organizations, and a particular version of libertarianism. As Coleman put it:

> Programmers over decades of intense interaction come to viscerally experience the computer as a general purpose machine that can be infinitely programmed to achieve any task through the medium of software written by humans with a computer language. The technological potential for unlimited programmable capabilities melds with what is seen as the expansive ability for programmers to create. For programmers, computing in a dual sense, as a technology and as an activity, becomes a total realm for the freedom of creation and expression.[18]

The issue of creation and engineering is central to Linden Lab's project in particular, as the making *of* the world of Second Life stands in a strange and mutually constructive relationship to the making *in* the world on the part of its users.

But there is another strand of this thought that has a direct bearing on Linden Lab, and it brings us back to the issue of play and games: emergent properties and how legitimate they are as a basis for self-governance. A new style of work practice came out of World War II and the cold war that followed, with that era's constant demands on the United States to innovate in a number of areas (the atomic bomb being the most famous example). In places like MIT's Radiation Lab, members of the military, industry, and academy had to find a way to work together despite the fact that no single vertical institution governed them all.[19] The successes produced by such collaborations resonated with ideas put forth by some of their members. Norbert Wiener and Julian Bigelow, through war-related research on systematizing anti-aircraft weaponry, had begun to apply the metaphor of computing on a grand scale to humans and their society. As Turner writes, "Wiener and Bigelow offered up a picture of humans and machines as dynamic, collaborating elements in a single, highly fluid, socio-technical system. Within that system, control emerged not from the mind of a commanding officer, but from the complex, probabilistic interactions of humans, machines, and events around them."[20]

We see already a contrast with the European scene, as many historians have noted. Whereas Europe was left ravaged and broken by World War II, the United States emerged confident and masterful, the new superpower on the world stage. It should not surprise us, then, that a tracing of ideas about play as they influenced Second Life has a very different tenor. For an understanding of Linden Lab, one effect of the rise of this thinking about socio-technical systems and controls was the implicit legitimacy that such emergent effects seemed to have. The suggestion (and it is one that can be traced all the way back to Adam Smith's "invisible hand") is that the emergent properties of complex interactions enjoy a certain degree of rightness just by virtue of being emergent. The emergent effects that complex spaces like virtual worlds generate depend upon this open-endedness, the lack of determinacy in the environment and participants' actions in it, and this open-endedness is to a certain extent contrived.

In thinking about how these ideas connect to the American conversation about urbanism specifically, it becomes worthwhile to note the link to the ideas of Jane Jacobs, who lodged her own strong critique of modernist urban planning in her landmark *The Death and Life of Great American Cities* (1961). Jacobs argued that great cities, like New York, were great because of how the contingent and at times inefficient led to a social vitality. The jumble of inherited practices, architectural styles, and larger projects (subway lines) threw people together in a mix of circumstances. Here, too, is a faith in the emergent, in this case the aggregate and historical processes that generate governance organically. The targets of Jacobs's critique were in some ways the same as Constant's and the Situationists': those presuming that a top-down form of rationalized control was the best hope for achieving social goods. Jacobs' book and its ideas circulated around Linden Lab, and were the touchstone for a number of initiatives that sought to promote Second Life's self-governance[21] (for an extended discussion of the influence of Jacobs's ideas on Linden Lab, see Malaby 2009). But the contradiction is not hard to see. Jacobs celebrated the uncontrived, and showed up the folly of the modernist project in aspiring to a kind of total planning. Linden Lab, however, was engaged in the attempt to contrive this vital open-endedness, just as Constant was; this was not top-down rationalist planning, but it bespoke the same will to govern the conditions for action. And just as Constant departed from the Situationists over the issue of the imperative to act from an authoritative position, even in a post-bureaucratic fashion, so do we find a similar tension in Linden Lab's embrace of Jacobs' ideals in the midst of its own deep authority.

But we can go further, and recognize a different kind of play in this formulation of socio-technical systems. Ken Kesey and the Merry Pranksters, staples of the 1960s counterculture and close to Stewart Brand of the *Whole Earth Catalog*, made use of games in their efforts to overcome vertical authority. As Turner describes:

> [Ken] Kesey and the Pranksters turned to various devices to distribute and, ostensibly, level . . . power. One of the devices was a simple spinner. The Pranksters regularly played a game in which a number of them would sit in a circle. Someone would spin the spinner, and whoever it pointed to would then have full power over the group for the next thirty minutes.[22]

Another example is a game they played with the *I Ching*; a person would toss a set of coins and then consult the book for a correlating bit of text, which would then be taken as guiding action. Thus, the Merry Pranksters sought to invest power in game-like *processes*, aided by technology. It was *game design* that they engaged in—the combining of constraining rules and sources of indeterminacy (the coins, the spinner). Kesey and the Pranksters had only familiar, "analog" sources of stochastic contingency ready to hand, the accessible computers that followed soon after allowed for a vast multiplication of both controls and contingencies and eventually contributed to the ability to produce the online simulated worlds of today.

The implication, I suggest, is that play for both projects was central to the conception of a postbureaucratic form of governance. But whereas play in Europe for projects like Constant's was imbued with the child and the primal, in the United States, for an important strand of thinking and practice about technology, play was imbued with notions of individual mastery over a complex system. A core idea exemplified in Brand's *Whole Earth Catalog* was of an individual, amid a complex system of affordances, pursuing enlightened self-interest, and contributing to collective and emergent effects that were thereby legitimate. On this view, authority is collectively generated out of many individuated acts of agency within a system. With the spinner and *I Ching* games, the Pranksters sought to architect that circumstance. That is, they sought not only to provide "tools" to people amidst the unbounded world of the everyday, but to set up a circumstance of constraints and possibilities *within which* that individual pursuit of enlightened self-interest would take place. But something very important changes when it is no longer simply the provision of tools that is the aim, but rather the broader project of contriving (and providing) the conditions—the system, in a sense—in which those affordances are encountered and used.

This line of thinking about play as a kind of individual mastery can be traced to an important thinker about play who developed Huizinga's ideas on the American side of the Atlantic, Mihalyi Csikszentmihalyi (1990). For Csikszentmihalyi, play can be found wherever people face an ongoing mixture of pattern and unpredictability that demands a practiced mastery of performance (what he calls "flow"), such as for the factory worker who happens to confront the properly engaging mixture of constraint and (perhaps dangerous) possibility in manipulating multiple machines and objects. Practiced makers of cedar shingles, for example, deftly handle the slight variations in every piece of wood that comes their way as they coordinate their bodily movements in extremely close proximity to two open and spinning saws. Csikszentmihalyi's focus on a state of mastery aligns well with the ideas of Wiener and others who saw individuals as active and performative participants in complex systems. To a certain extent, then, when many Lindens imagined their users, they imagined game-players in this way. They were gamers in a highly individualistic sense. For many Lindens, a game constituted, at root, a challenge to an *individual* to act within an open-ended system, whether that game involved other players or not.

Both of these projects, appearing in such different times and places, reveal themselves as not so different in their final aspirations, nor so different in the hopes they invested in productive play. But the productive play for each were so different, coming to these designers through such vastly different paths, that we are left reconsidering how universal and transhistorical the idea of play could possibly be. Instead we may find it more useful to consider play in a way similar to how William James saw religious experience, never found in some universal form but rather appearing in great variety, reflecting the myriad times and places for human life.[23] Here, the turn to a primal and innocent child's play in Europe seems a completely different move than the appeal to a masterful, individual gamer in the United States, yet both were held to be productive, and embodied the hopes of designers for generative action in postbureaucratic eras.

# 5

# FORMAT TELEVISION AND ISRAELI TELEDIPLOMACY

TASHA G. OREN

The formally dressed Ethiopian man stands at an outdoor podium. His audience, a large group of journalists and commentators from over ten countries across the African continent, has gathered at this Ugandan resort. Now they wait, fanning themselves against the hot midday sun. The young man can surely sense their skeptical glances as he stands, head down, anxiously rearranging his notes and patting at his damp neck. Behind him, seven women and six men in their twenties sit facing the audience; among them is a Russian-born software engineer, a Swedish-émigré finance student, a German-born businesswoman, a political science student of Iranian heritage, and a Belgian-born marketing major. They, too, are visibly nervous as they wait. Finally, the speaker clears his throat. "My name is Elias" he begins tentatively, "and I am a Zionist."

Elias and his team are on a mission. By the end of the day, after presentations and a question-and-answer period, this audience will cast ballots, and the group on the stage will have a winner and a loser. This is one of many such challenges for Elias and his teammates, all game show contestants on the Israeli reality program *Ha'shagrir*.

Based on a format illicitly borrowed from producer Mark Burnett's *The Apprentice, Ha'shagrir* (The Ambassador) employs all the familiar (and formulaic) tropes of the popular U.S. and British television format: a group of young and ambitious contestants, divided into teams by gender, compete in a series of challenges issued by an imposing expert judge. In each episode, the two teams scramble to complete the challenge while negotiating personal rivalries, clashing perspectives, and unforeseen complications. At the end of each installment, they gather for evaluation and judgment by a panel of experts. A winning team is rewarded, a losing team bickers to pin blame, a single loser is identified by the judge and dispatched off the show with a dismissive but ceremoniously intoned catch phrase.

Other formal conventions further signal the show's kinship with the globally dominant reality show format: the thematic, game-like introductory opening sequence, where each contestant strikes a bravado-infused pose while their first name flashes on the screen; the overly dramatic musical leitmotifs that accompany each segment; the fragmented, conflict-seeking editing technique; the personal "testimonial" audio and on-camera interviews by contestants reflecting on their experience; the solemnity of the dimly lit boardroom where judgment takes place; the delayed, tension-building pacing of the judgment segment; and finally, the "exit" interview voiceover, as the booted contestant, suitcase in tow, leaves for home.

Indeed, these television conventions have become ubiquitous and instantly recognizable as programmatic staples for many viewers all over the globe. *Ha'shagrir* resembles many other such programs in all but one detail: on this popular show, the contestants compete to be named "The Ambassador," charged with representing an Israeli foreign policy perspective to an all but hostile world.

In what some critics have likened to a viral contagion, format television (and particularly the reality show competition format) is everywhere, as contestants dance, cook, sing, redecorate, lose weight, start businesses, fall in love, or merely survive in close quarters. Astounded by the consistent, near-global popularity of formats like *Survivor*, the *Idol* franchise, and *Big Brother*, as well as the proliferation of other lower-rent (but still reliably successful) reality programming, most television scholars have focused on specific programs' representational strategies, embedded social values, generic and narrative strategies, or on the overall cultural impact of nonscripted television. Yet few have attempted to address the format exchange and global duplication process as both a cultural and industrial phenomenon, or consider its implications for theories of media and globalization.[1]

Moreover, the focus on "reality" as a generic component has estranged many scholars from the real story: not all reality programs are formats, and the broad category of format television extends beyond reality TV. And while formal influence, exchange, "cloning," and adaptation have long been staples of international television, the current rate of circulation, flow, trade, and "pirate" adaptation of global television formats is transforming the international mediascape.

In what follows, I consider the Israeli program *Ha'shagrir* as an exercise in political and cultural worldmaking. In reading the show as both exemplary of the global format phenomena and curiously, tellingly, and essentially Israeli, I will suggest that global formats (and their specific, local adaptations and reiterations) offer a new understanding of media globalization and the unique role television still plays in a public envisioning of an interconnected globe. The format's particular role in worldmaking, as I argue in this chapter, occurs on two, linked but distinct, levels: first, at the local level (represented here by the Israeli *Ha'shagrir*) the program's content endeavors to both represent an Israeli view of the world (doubly so, as the program is about both media and political representation) as well as offer the possibility of intervention, a remaking, of the world it finds. Second, on a global scale, the format convention itself partakes in a televisual worldmaking, as it articulates a unique relationship between the viewer's national identity and a media-centric articulation of global culture.

The notion of a global culture (and indeed, of a global consciousness) is itself worldmaking in the sense that it is always fabricated and intimately tied to a shared imaginary; a willful, constructed sense of the world that attempts to capture a global collective from a particular (local) vantage point. In this way, I argue that some media texts not only offer an image, a feel, and a sense of the global but also function to impart a level of local presence, participation, regard, and even (if seldom) influence, in the collective global reality they construct. This opening for change may be illusory in terms of demonstrative institutional or legislative power, but it is culturally invaluable. And, as daily headlines remind us, we cleave the cultural from the political at our peril. To this, the analysis below hopes to make the case for why television—that old, nearly discarded technology—still matters.

Within the loose disciplinary confines of global media studies, nationalism and television are historical co-conspirators. As scores of scholars have argued (myself included), the history of television is replete with the medium's specific, explicit (and often aggressive) articulation as, first and mainly, a national medium. In fact, institutional histories of television are told primarily and necessarily as narratives of location, national ideology, and—if only perceived—expressions of collective culture and identity. To this extent, early histories of television are by definition histories of national aspiration and distinction. However, contemporary television development, along with a broadening of the media field to include satellite, Web-based media, and other global content flows, presents challenging new opportunities to reconceive television's place in the global media field. This "field" is not only a content exchange and commercial marketplace but also a larger cultural frame of reference that shapes our collective sense of the global.

According to media scholar Graeme Turner, many researchers working within media studies have adopted a stance of "techno-political hierarchy" toward emerging interactive and Web-based media when regarding traditional television.[2] A rhetorical marriage between border-crossing technology and postnationalist aspirations, this perspective regards television as a dying technology, wedded to the outmoded nationalist perspective of top-down distribution of power and ideological closure. By contrast, digital media is celebrated as democratizing, user-oriented, progressive, and global: "The closer to the global consumer we come . . . the further we are from the nation state . . . the technology liberates the consumer from political and regulatory containment."[3] Here, Turner further notes an exuberant enthusiasm to endorse and embrace a model of postnational, globally felt television consumption (mostly via the internet) as both progressive and widespread. Indeed, satellite television, Web-based programming, mobile media, convergence technology, and the growing popularity and accessibility of regional and transborder television—in addition to the robust trade in "finished programs"—pose questions for traditional television scholarship to take account of a growing transnational media presence. As television scholar Jean Chalaby observes, "International TV channels are not simply deterritorializing but deterritorialized cultural artifacts themselves. Many of their features, including coverage, schedule and patterns of production, tear apart the relation between place and television."[4]

However, both the dilution of television as a site- (and technology-) specific medium and the emergence of a postnational media world appear overstated or at least only partial truths when one considers the average nightly offering in television marketplaces all over the world. The current shape of television, and the popularity of formats in particular, challenge much of the received common thinking about global/local distinctions in television production and what they mean within a broader cultural and political context. They do so primarily through categorical interference on the one hand, and critical disdain on the other: formats do not sit neatly under either "import" or "local production" classification—eluding received dichotomies of global sprawl vs. local cultural distinction. Further, since they are, for the most part, critical forehead-slappers but ratings bonanzas, they are often condemned as both the worst manifestation of global homogeneity and local articulations of parochial and nationalist prejudice.

As texts, formats are difficult to classify. Since formats exist primarily as economic commodities and a production term (as opposed to textual "genres" or "program-types," for example), it is best to start there in defining them: formats are popular serial programming formulae that are adapted, franchised, bought, mimicked, or even "stolen," to be produced in multiple localities worldwide. Unlike imported "finished" programs, formats are an odd economic unit, as what is bought, sold, and exchanged is a set of rules and, often, a backlog of knowledge. A format "package" is first a set of rules and conditions that make up the specific format program—this, in the industry, is known as the "format engine," a term that recalls the video-game industry's name for the basic set of common software protocols each game-type shares.

As one format producer put it: "a format is all about the rules you put on an idea."[5] This definition is simple, elegant, and right on the money. A format is seemingly content-free; format is a protocol. Format devisors create and "tweak" a set of visual, formal, and structural elements into an engine and a format pitch. In one classic example, Mike Briggs, the UK talk show host who is credited as the devisor of *Who Wants To Be A Millionaire*—and later went on to co-form the UK format production giant Celador International—pitched the *Millionaire* engine as: a major prize, "giving contestants a set of possible answers, offering a series of 'lifelines', using a host with a supercilious manner, and soundtrack and lighting to dramatic effect."[6] "If you cannot say it in a paragraph," a format producer once explained about the basic engine pitch, "you cannot say it at all."[7]

As television scholar Albert Moran defined format, it is "a set of invariable elements in a serial program out of which the variable elements of individual episodes are produced."[8] In terms of its economic and industrial use value, the format is generally defined in opposition to the transnational model of program import/export trade. The format, as opposed to the finished or "canned" television program, is an easily replicated and adaptable framework licensed through the international television market for local adaptation.

In addition to the rules themselves, the format package and license agreement includes a wealth of documentation (known in the trade as the "Bible"):

a collection of careful and minute detailing of all production knowledge and history, design specification, visual, graphic, and audio materials, character and staging notation, and any marketing and rating information from past iterations of the show (if any existed before its current franchising).[9]

As an economic unit, then, the format can be thought of as recipe or blueprint, yet, as Moran further insists, format is not a tangible product. Rather, it is a technology of economic and cultural exchange and a service that facilitates certain televisual possibilities.[10] In short, it is a globally distributed container for locally produced content.

Such a definition finds the format a site of contention between scholars who argue to maintain focus on national articulations of identity through television texts, and those who look beyond the nation as a formative analytical category. Both positions draw strength from media's symbolic work in shaping a sense of the world for its audience. Here, the inherent power (and import) of media's role is not so much their concrete representational quality, but rather a more amorphous fostering of globally scaled understandings of allegiances, divisions, belongings, interests, and difference. Just as the nation-centered stance insists and affirms the resiliency of national identity in the face of globalizing media, a counter position calls attention to media's role in an ongoing cultural realignment of identities along with developments in media mobility, media forms, taste-formations, and access within contemporary globality.

Sociologist Ulrich Beck has influentially charged the former with methodological nationalism, dismissing as outmoded the view that nation-state is the primary organizing principle of analysis, and famously dubbing it a "Zombie category." Within television studies, Beck's work has informed media scholars like Kevin Robins and Asu Aksoy, who not only critique the national approach as lacking in nuance and imagination but also as being a stake-holding cheerleader for top-down nationalist ideology.[11] As they argue, television scholars who have recently articulated the centrality of nation in their discussions of global television and media culture "mobilize the rhetoric of political pragmatism and realism, intending to convey the idea that the old national model still 'works'—and aiming to rule out possibilities that there could be any meaningful potential in new transnational or global media developments."[12]

Arguments like these are valuable in their insistence on alternative identity formations through media, and their caution against academic

automation. And while in Robins and Aksoy's hands "The Nation" looms as
a stifling and homogenizing soul-prison, their argument also resonates with
a kind of fatigue for the standardized essay that keeps restaging, ad infini-
tum, a celebrated nation-local's triumph over global-western groupthink.
Yet, at its weakest, the argument falls into the same dialectic system it aims
to reject when it casts the national as a thin, singular, ideologically pungent
broth, to the rich, fragrant stew of multilocational, multicultural, postnational complexity.

For one, the possibilities of alternative, transnational models of media do
not preclude, nor describe, the current experience of intimate, domestic,
and, more often than not, nationally based programming. The proliferation
of format television, in particular, provides scholars with ample examples of
programs that anchor a sense of collective recognition to mundane details of
social interaction, habits, routines, shared practical knowledge and familiar
internal divisions, differences, and conflicts. As Finnish television scholars
Minna Aslama and Mervi Pantti observe in their study of reality television
formats, the sense of national belonging is not by any means bound to an
authoritative, official version of culture or identity, and as another television
scholar, Sharon Sharp, has recently argued in a study that compared various
national productions of the "wifeswap" formula, format reality programs
often invoke the nation precisely through the staging of and emphasis on
internal conflicts over region, gender, race, or class.[13] Moreover, as I will
show in returning to the Israeli example, formats can also employ globally
developed televisual conventions to articulate frustrations and acknowledged tensions within these nationally organized structures of experience.

### Ha'shagrir's Global Journey: One Guilt Trip At a Time

As a television show, Ha'shagrir is a striking example of Israeli self-
consciousness and global media anxiety. At its thematic core is the long-held
belief within Israel that much of the animosity felt toward it throughout the
world is the result of the country's failure in the arena of public relations—of
"hasbara" (literally, "explanation"). The show's engine has contestants sent
on missions that seek confrontational situations in international settings (on
university campuses, encounters with a skeptical foreign press, sales-pitches
to international businesses, meetings with foreign leaders, etc.) and every
such encounter enacts the same tension: contestants face negative attitudes
about Israel, attempt to address questions of politics and policy, and try

mightily to change hearts and minds. The show's twin central preoccupations are, of course, self-representation and global media scrutiny. The
original show promo (which ran on Israeli TV and online before the first
season aired in late 2004) began, tellingly, with a CNN logo. As images of
various violent bombing sites, gun battles, and other footage of international
conflict flash on the screen to ominous music, a breathless male voiceover
proclaims, "in a world where television and newspapers are the battlefield,
Israel sometimes finds itself with its back against the wall." An abrupt shift
in music ushers a new low-angle shot as young men and women, clad in
sober business suits and clutching rolling suitcases behind them, stride
through the frame.

With a new touch of warmth and enthusiasm, the voiceover now continues, "only the best will be able to represent Israel in a world of media." The
next sequence introduces the participants and the panel of three judges (a
prominent PR specialist and former IDF spokesperson, a former director of
the Israeli secret service, and the senior political correspondent for Israeli
television). As contestants and judges assemble around a gleaming boardroom table at the historic King David Hotel in Jerusalem, site of many state-
sponsored diplomatic encounters, the head judge, Nachman Shai, explains,
"the struggle over Israeli hasbara in the world is perhaps the greatest challenge that stands for us as Israelis in the current period. One of you will fulfill this difficult and demanding role." A quick montage of various locations
follows with a shot of the competitors boarding an El Al plane and the
voiceover, "their journey begins now: real missions in the real world."
Another montage, in a familiar format style, follows: competitors arguing, a
close-up of an emotional contestant who appears devastated ("you need to
think fast," cautions the voiceover), an empty stage (voiceover: "make deci-
sions under pressure"), a meeting hall, and a close-up on a gavel as the
voiceover warns sternly, "every mistake can be critical!" The camera now
settles for a group shot, and the voiceover concludes with the show's challenge: "Who has what it takes? Who will stand up to the pressure, far away
from home? In front of a hostile crowd and tough questions? Who will be
(dramatic pause) . . . the Ambassador?"

In the first season (2004–2005), the show proved to be one of the highest
rated of the season, despite lukewarm critical reception. Notably, the program's use of U.S. and European capitals as both visual icons and challenge
settings in the first season located Israeli anxieties about representation and

public opinion in what the show's own lingo described as "the nerve centers of global media." The second season appeared to expand the show's scope and correct its limited, Western focus by aiming for a global vision.

Titled "The Ambassador: Five Continents," the second season (2005–2006) represented a more ambitious and expansive vision: an improved global, civilian Israeli hasbara and, as the show's producer, the Keshet Network, touted in promotional materials, the "new and prestigious international production." This time, the program's theme stressed mobility: from the international scope of the missions, to the change in the ambassador position itself—scrapping its headquarters in New York for a traveling, worldwide agenda—and even to the addition of a new judge, a former pilot and noted Israeli war hero. Even the opening promo insisted on an outward-looking, global program of diverse contestants (and Israeli self-representation) on the move. Most strikingly, as the show's overall emphasis turned more self-consciously global, its televisual style became even more tightly associated with the specific expressive pallet of format television. The first episode, for example, opens on a nighttime caravan of gleaming cars as they wind around a grounded airplane, their headlights repeatedly striking the lens as they move to park in a neat row in front of an enormous hanger. Dramatic music punctuates the highly choreographed moment when all car doors open in unison and fourteen suited young men and women step out and walk in a neat row toward a large conference table, located, inexplicably, in the middle of the hanger. Music and camera style strive for a sense of bombastic drama and significance as the three silhouetted judges enter the hanger, their footsteps amplified above the imperious score. The overall effect stresses the "no-place" location of the hanger—emphasizing the show's focus on world travel and agile readiness—as it playfully invokes generic echoes of the format's own standard tongue-in-cheek histrionics and thrillers in which such clandestine meetings are common preludes to intrigue.

The second season's premise reflects a shift toward a de-centered view of global media, with the United States (represented in the show as exclusively New York City and Washington) demoted from its first season status as the "nerve center of the world." This shift may have had something to do with the plunging rate of world public opinion toward the United States in the Bush era (declining steadily to an all-time low in 2005),[14] but also a developing "nodal" view of global politics and opinion-making. This reconfiguration of the global map further reflects a contemporary, de-centered, and de-hierarchialized notion of globalization that, as sociologist and cultural critic Zygmunt Bauman described, is characterized by a new indeterminacy of "self- propelled" world affairs and "the absence of a centre, (or) a controlling desk."[15]

However, beyond the political and cultural implications of the new season's spin on global media, televisual considerations of more exotic locations, new types of challenges, and overall novelty was surely a factor. By 2005, Israeli viewers had become accustomed to seeing their entertainment shot in New York, Paris, or London (common location shoots for Israeli TV programs). However, a group of Israelis dancing with African tribesmen in a traditional welcome ceremony, exploring the bar scene on a frigid night in Stockholm, or having an audience with Uganda's president, Yoweri Kaguta Museveni, or former Soviet Union President Mikhail Gorbachev (all segments in the second season of the show), were impressive novelties and notable accomplishments for Keshet, the show's production company and one of the two largest Israeli commercial TV producers and exhibitors.

Aside from the diversity in contestants and locations, however, the show's basic engine remained unaltered. In each episode, the groups were dispatched to a different location and competed to complete and best their rivals in a mission that invariably included a challenge to Israeli PR and a confrontation with a skeptical (and sometimes explicitly anti-Israeli) interlocutor. True to its generic allegiances to format television, each episode emphasized emotional conflicts, political machinations, and strategic sniping among contestants; featured rapid editing and an indication-heavy score; and was structured according to the formulaic repetition of segments, assignments, ceremonial judgment, and the invariable, final send-off. "Turn in your portfolio and go home."

Despite the rigid formula that made the show's look, sound, structure, and narrative-making strategies a classic and instantly familiar format, *The Ambassador* also fits perfectly into Israel's particular media past and the preoccupation of "self to the world." As I've written elsewhere, Israel's television origins are sourced in the image of broadcasting as a kind of border-crossing electronic visiting card. The notion that broadcasting could help Israel's self-representation and "speak to" Israel's enemies (and Palestinian residents) was widely regarded as even more important for television's founding than what programs could say to Israeli citizens. The idea of harnessing television in the service of *hasbara* was a primary motivator for the establishment of state television in 1968, the year that followed Israel's occupation of East Jerusalem, Gaza, the West Bank, the Sinai, and Golan Heights in the Six-Day War. It is then significant that *Ha'shagrir*'s first season, in the fall of 2004, was less than a year after then–Prime Minister Ariel Sharon's historic reference to Israeli conduct in the territories as "occupation" and his reported—and, to many, astonishing—change of heart over Israel's policy of withdrawal. The show's airing corresponded with a fierce internal debate over dismantling settlements in Gaza and the media spectacle of violent clashes between Israeli soldiers and evacuated settlers in the summer of 2005, just weeks after the first season's finale.

Despite *Ha'shagrir*'s ultranationalist concept, the political priorities of articulating the nation are repeatedly and studiously challenged in practically every episode of this hugely popular program. In various settings around the world, the contestants are addressed with challenging, often hostile, questions about Israel's basic moral position, the abuse and humiliation of Palestinians, or Israel's refusal to consider the right of return or cease its settlement building activity. In these confrontations, contestants are rarely in control and are often caught at a loss for words, or worse, as they misspeak. In a famous incident in the first season, a contestant was unceremoniously dumped from the show after she defensively asserted, during a visit to Oxford's campus, that "Israel has never taken anything from anyone." This, the august panel concluded, was simply the wrong answer. Far from smoothing out ideological inconsistencies, the show seems to relish moments in which the contestants falter in the face of such challenges. Their awkward equivocations are highlighted and mercilessly repeated within the show, on its Web site, and in previews for future programs. And, in telling repetition, the winning contestants are those who prevail through charm, personality, and an affable skill to circumvent specific policy discussions in favor of communicating Israelis' love of peace and hopeful vision for a better future. While it unquestionably supports and celebrates national identity and the underlying myth of Israel's poor PR, the show rarely regards such identity and nationalist pride as unproblematic, and instead gives voice and moral credence to a range of political realities and non-Israeli perspectives, undermining the show's premise as easy explanation for Israel's status. It is this very tension that animates the space between the format's global game-like protocol and its local content and meaning.

In *The Ambassador*, this tension is elevated to thematic heights by positioning a local iteration of a global format within the context of national soul-searching and global performance. Said differently, the program enacts a nation's acute anxiety over global scrutiny through a globally ubiquitous media product.

As offered here, the case of *The Ambassador* is (instructively) extreme in its explicitness, and fits the Israeli fixation and hyper-awareness of national identity under a critical, global gaze. True to format programs all over the world, *Ha'shagrir* appropriates the global format code to articulate specific and explicit national identities for their audiences. Yet, how and why does this happen? In other words, having defined the format, discussed its controversial standing on both sides of the nation-centered global media debate, and suggested the Israeli example as just such a text for national negotiation, this essay has not yet addressed the format's *global* popularity, and how it too participates in the "worldmaking" vision I've alluded to earlier. So, how do formats make a world as they address a nation? How does this media world differ from other television programs (and, indeed, other media content at large?) and, of course, why should all this matter?

## Contemporary Televisuality: Global Participation and the Pleasures of Difference

As Moran and Keane recently suggested, the format phenomenon now itself constitutes an alternative model of media globalization.[16] While the phenomenon of formats is easily dismissed as mere industry clamoring to repeat a proven money-maker, Silvio Waisbord argues that they are better understood as revealing important developments in the globally interconnected television industries and institutions on the one hand, and the efforts of transnational producers to deal with the resilience of national cultures on the other.[17] The simple economic advantages of formats over original productions and "canned" imports is surely an important factor, as are the local development of commercial television and the internationalization of the television marketplace.[18] Another important factor, however, as Timothy Havens points out, is the rapidly changing and standardizing television profession itself.[19] As a generation of professionals worldwide begins to think about TV in similar ways, they likewise define the imaginary connections that bind together different segments of the public both within and beyond the nation-state. These forms of standardization are, Havens argues, far more powerful (and, for Havens, pernicious) than the representational strategies of television texts, the meanings that viewers make from television or global patterns of media ownership. Waisbord makes a similar point while posing a counterargument: "structural regulations and institutional expectations limited programming choices, for programming trends to become truly globalized, television systems needed to be patterned along the same principle."[20]

In light of such stylistic and economic centralization, the future, as Graeme Turner suggests, is in indigenizing: "The way to examine the local within the global is through mapping processes of appropriation and adaptation rather than proposition of any thoroughgoing specificity or uniqueness."[21]

Global standardization of the institutional shape of television here actually facilitates (indeed, demands) a shift in the logic of programming. In this global logic, systemic conventions of the apparatus are both deterritorialized and naturalized, and production is at once localized and standardized. Yet, this is a process that television has seen before: the news show, the interview program, the sitcom, the soap, and the variety show are all base-formats that have specific, recognizable, and classifiable codes. These soft protocols of content organization emerged—through particular processes of exchange—within various television systems, and quickly solidified with the naturalization of a televisual space in each context. The current codification of format protocols around the world is, then, a turn deeper into the very essence of television itself (repetition, modularity, variation of content within formulaic form, etc). In its current shape, this process cannot be separated, as Havens, Waisbord, and others observe, from the growth of a cosmopolitan industry elite whose shared business sensibilities and homogenizing tastes make up a large part of the explanation for format growth.[22]

At the same time, a central tenet of this homogenized understanding of the format's appeal—along with its globally shared formal conventions—is its essential, ever-present, particularity. Moreover, one fundamental difference characterizes the current shape of format when compared to earlier television texts: contemporary formats invoke local specificity *through* their global feel. While format adaptation existed throughout television history, the practice has largely gone unacknowledged outside the television industry itself.[23] For example, two hit U.S. shows of the late 80s and early 90s,

*America's Funniest Videos* and *America's Most Wanted*, appeared as distinct and original texts without any revelation of their origins as a popular Japanese program or German and British formats. By contrast, *Big Brother, Survivor, Idol,* and *So you Think You Can Dance,* as well as *Ugly Betty*—all massive international hits that ushered in the format era—are read, and often promoted, in terms of their proliferation, popularity, and global presence. Thus, the format's recent large-scale standardization has also produced a meaningful shift in its mode of self-representation as a text—a newly found reflexive self-consciousness in light of its acquired visibility.

Reading the Japanese iterations of *Who Wants to Be a Millionaire* and *Survivor,* Koichi Iwabuchi notes that the shows make wide reference to their constitution as local versions of global formats that are popular all over the world. Iwabuchi concludes:

> The format business has given audiences a pleasure in sharing the common frameworks and the irreducibly different appearances that manifest in local consumption. Put differently, what is being promoted is not simply global localization that aims to adopt the common to the difference but also local globalization that makes audiences feel glocal, that is, a sense of participation in a global society through the reciprocated enjoyable recognition of local (in most cases synonymous with national) specificities articulated through the shared formats. The western gaze of modernity thus melts into a global modernity.[24]

As Iwabuchi suggests, the sense of (and pleasure in) "global modernity" is fundamentally dependent on the presence of a recognizable, irreducible difference that comfortably and assertively sits within the shared format engine. The complex web of global and domestic linkages that television systems (and audiences) find within the format exchange were similarly—if less buoyantly—described by one Australian format producer as "parochial internationalism."[25]

I would further suggest that formats, in their very existence and acknowledged structure of local repetition within a multinational framework, can do more than just express national identity in content: they often *cement* the national quality of television.

The Israeli iteration of the dance competition format *So You Think You Can Dance* (*Nolad Lirkod*), for example, was heavily promoted as an international format sensation and compared (even within the text of the show itself) to the *Idol* format—also a hit in Israel. However, its first episode (the obligatory pre-season audition segment with its ritualized, heavily edited clips of triumph and ridicule) began with historic 1948 footage following the declaration of Israel's formation as a state, when hundreds of Israelis broke into spontaneous celebratory dancing in the city streets. The segment continued with contemporary footage from various locations in Israel, where groups gather to dance in styles ranging from folk to the cha-cha, krumping and ballet. Layered over clips of spinning toddlers, hip-hopping youth, and swinging elderly couples, the host's voiceover confirmed Israel's special affinity to the show's subject (with more than a hint of comic flare): "Israelis were born to dance . . . we're a nation of dancers. The English celebrate with a drink in the pub, the French luxuri-ate with a nice fois gras . . . and Israelis, we dance!" This effort to locate the dance format in such over-the-top nationalist context is amusing precisely in light of the show's formal allegiance to the globally popular *So You Think You Can Dance* format—whose American version is familiar to the Israeli audience. The format's essential playfulness and global reproducibility thus anchors its audience in watching, reading, and experiencing this and other format texts as having deep local resonance, nested within a larger format logic that is fundamentally televisual and globally connected. As the example above illustrates, an important aspect of the format as a modular unit of television programming is that it often travels, and announces itself, *as* an iteration. As such, it offers a supple model for media globalization that does not perceive local production as a response or opposition to a global push. Rather, it understands the specificity of the local as necessar-ily dependent on its participation within—and unique take on—the shared global.

I do not argue that such negotiations of local formats in a globalizing tele-vision environment function in this way in every case. Certainly my interest in the Israeli examples is due to their excessive and self-conscious employ-ment of nationalist tropes, as well as the remarkable resonance and fit of these contemporary themes with Israel's national and television history. However, I do want to stress that *when* such national expressions or invoca-tions appear within format television, they do so in the context of inter-national presence and participation. Such global acknowledgement is not just about references to one national identity in comparison to others, but in full textual acknowledgment of the format qua format, as a local version of a globally traveling form.

## Conclusion: Location and Peripatetic Televisuality

As a self-contained text, *Ha'shagrir* can easily be read as a typical cultural symptom of the long and drawn-out "post Zionist" crisis in the Israeli ideological mainstream. As such, the text fits snugly into a model of repairwork, a way to rescue and reinvigorate a globally embattled and internally tarnished "visionary nationalism."[26] And, despite the show's relentless focus on the failures of its own strategic logic of charm-offensive, and the awkward acknowledgement of a final, nonnegotiable, equivalence of morality and policy responsibility, the show does maintain and even celebrate the hope of a neo-Zionism that is both transformative and globally amiable. In this, it defies— in spectacular fashion—any argument about nationalism's media demise. And, as I've argued, while the case of Israeli telenationalism is certainly extreme, it is far from unique or anachronistic. As various scholars have suggested in recent work on national iterations of global formats, the assertion of nationalist identity is often a central thematic link within the program.

However, in thinking about this program and its linkages to both an existing global media culture and an imagined sense of global interconnectedness within national particularity, it is important to consider that such deeply felt, unique, and contextual national impulses are so "naturally" packaged in the most formulaic, ubiquitous, and globally available televisual convention.

Since global formats emphasize a playful, standardized televisuality, this quality is also essential to how meaning is made (and solutions are posed) in *The Ambassador*. It is here that the naturalized televisual logic of format and its specific set of expressive tools meet and profoundly shape local expressions of particularity, as Israel's self-conscious preoccupation is processed *through* the circumscribed protocol of a globally legible televisual style. The strict and limited set of expressive outlets (available only as time-limited game-like challenges of private strategizing and public performance) provide an odd but ideal staging ground for a national perspective-shift. Stripped of all complexities, subtleties, and "special conditions" that have always accompanied Israel's grappling with its political and military realities, national conduct is here subjected to an entirely different reality: the simultaneously intimate and othering logic of reality television. The format, then, not only allows for a deconstruction of sorts in Israeli political rhetoric, but its popular legibility *as* a global format reinforces and amplifies the same global scrutiny that is *Ha'shagrir*'s thematic core.

That television's relationship to space can no longer be taken for granted is indisputable. However, the current explosion of format television challenges our understanding of how this relationship has reconfigured itself. No doubt the current success of global formats is intimately tied to a particular logic of globalization—both capital and popular. It is also an especially good example of how contemporary global cultural exchange differs from older models of influence and imperialism, while simultaneously unseating revered characterizations of local culture as resistance to the crushing span and ubiquity of global/Western media products or cosmopolitan aspirations for a postnational mediascape. Arguments that insist on a break or opposition between national experience and global or transnational consciousness conflate the former with state-powered nationalism from above, and sweepingly ascribe chauvinistic and insular disposition to various articulations of national linkages that may operate quite differently, ignoring currently occurring multiplicities that *necessarily* make up the national experience of viewing. More important, they cut off the possibility of national address as *part* of the meaning viewers make of transnational media texts. Here I suggest the international format as one such textual category where the national frame comes into view precisely *because and within* the understanding of such programming as multinational reiterations.

The *feel* of the global is dynamic, fluid, and highly subjective—the living product of a constantly shifting matrix of political, cultural, institutional, ideological, symbolic, and personal clusters of association. It also replicates and multiplies across various registers from individuals to identity- or location-based communities and societies, nations and regions among them. Through televisual codes, representational strategies, viewer address, and cultural currency, *Ha'shagrir* engages in a very specific kind of worldmaking: fashioning an image of the world—and Israel's place in it—that at once confirms and destabilizes cherished excuses for political failures. Undergirded by the logic of global format, the show projects the myth of hasbara as both true and impossible, seen from here and there, within and outside. The anxiety of media scrutiny is here inseparable from the therapeutic powers of global perspective.

This Janus-faced function ceases to appear as a paradox when one considers that the contemporary television format itself evokes a parallel logic: the local is felt in the whole of the global, the global embraced at the site of the particular. How else is the world made real?

# 6
# MEDIATING "NEUTRALITY"
## LATINO DIASPORIC FILMS

YEIDY M. RIVERO

In a series of articles about recent *telenovela* production and thematic trends, Colombian media scholar Omar Rincón indicates that there is a new type of product on the market: the "neutral" telenovela.[1] Produced in Mexico (via Televisa), and Miami and Colombia (via Telemundo) for the U.S. Spanish-language and global television markets, this telenovela subgenre is characterized by five principal tropes of "neutrality"—neutral accents, neutral territoriality, neutral culture, neutral expressions, and neutral morality. Similar to most programming produced in Miami, the neutral accent in Spanish is equivalent to a Mexican accent and it is utilized in the narrative to appeal to the Mexican majority that comprises the U.S. Hispanic audience. The territorial neutrality, on the other hand, places the narrative in a geographical space without history and culture. The cultural neutrality, similar to the territorial neutrality, functions through the avoidance of cultural practices, signifiers, and political references that might connect the narrative to a specific country. The expressive neutrality is also closely tied to the previous neutrality tropes but, in this case, the neutrality refers to the evasion of jargon or phrases associated with a country or region. Lastly, moral neutrality operates by including less risqué subjects, conservative themes, and Catholicism as a way to avoid "offending" the audience.[2]

The neutral telenovela with its cultural sanitation, its moral conservatism, its verbal performances of *Mexicanness*, and, while not mentioned by Rincón, its whiteness coded through the *mestizaje* [racial mixing] discourse, is the latest media element wrought by globalizing forces. The neutral telenovela is also an additional phase in the eradication of the local that has affected some Latin American and Spanish Caribbean television systems and

the U.S. Spanish-language television scene. Since the late 1980s, small television markets in Latin America and the Spanish Caribbean have been saturated with Mexican imports. Today, Mexico and Miami are the centers of
television exportation for the region, positioning the neutral telenovelas as
the main products for industries that rely on imports to fill up their prime-
time schedules.[3] As expected, this programming selection is also part of the
major U.S. Spanish-language television networks Univision, Telefutura, Telemundo, and Azteca America. Whereas these networks might include telenovelas from Brazil, Colombia, and Venezuela, the bulk of programming
comes from Mexico. In terms of locally produced shows, these networks'
"pan-ethnic" programming, similar to the neutral telenovelas, includes
people from various ethnic backgrounds yet, in appealing to its largest audience constituency—Mexicans—they frequently eliminate ethnic distinctions
by purposely accommodating verbal and visual performances that are associated primarily with Mexican modes of cultural representation.[4] Directly
and indirectly, these industrial processes have begun to silence certain cultures, peoples, and experiences from today's geo-linguistic mediascape.

Given these television trends, I see a need to recuperate a series of Spanish Caribbean and Latin American films produced in the post-1980s era that
narrate the migratory movements, interactions, cultural practices, and
struggles of particular U.S. Latino groups. I am thus proposing that we look
beyond the region's television homogenizing tendencies and explore "the
plurality of 'worldmaking'" present in films that, in terms of their themes
and intended audiences, might be categorized as Latino diasporic films.[5]
Films such as *La guagua aérea* (Puerto Rican), *Nueba Yol*, and *Nueba Yol 3: Bajo
la nueva ley* (Dominican), and *El espíritu de mi mamá* (Garifuna) create
counternarratives by mediating the invisibility of certain immigrant stories
and Caribbean-Afro diasporic subject positions in today's de-centered and
clearly Eurocentric regional mediascape.[6] Generally speaking, these films
might be disregarded for lacking character and plot development, for inef-
fectively imitating Hollywood cinematic conventions, or, in one particular
case, for dreadful acting. However, I contend that the importance of these
texts does not reside in what scholars might deem their "artistic value" but
instead comes from their re-articulation of histories and their incorporation
of people, stories, languages, accents, cities, and cultures that are gradually
disappearing from commercial media outlets "at home" and "abroad." By representing historically situated migratory patterns, social conditions, places,

and *very specific* verbal and bodily performances, these films are archives that re-create and thus document elements of cultural repertoires that have been displaced by globalizing media forces.[7]

In this piece I examine *La guagua aérea* and *Nueba Yol* and consider how these films recreate migratory movements, construct and in some cases transform ethnic groups' interactivity, and reproduce culturally explicit verbal and bodily enactments. My analysis is informed by the work of cultural geographer Doreen Massey and folklorist Richard Bauman. Although these scholars' academic writings do not address the topic of cinema, they nonetheless provide useful analytical tools for examining films in relation to textual representations of "places," social-spatial relations, and vernacular cultures.

In her recent work, Doreen Massey theorizes the impact of globalization with respect to space, society, groups, mobility, and individuals' access or lack of access to resources and goods.[8] Criticizing scholars who exclusively center on transnational economic processes, free trade, and who, as a result, create a universal narrative from "one geographical speaking position," Massey proposes a spatial approach for understanding globalization.[9] For Massey, space is "a product of interactions," a "sphere of possibilities and multiplicity," and it is "always in a process of becoming."[10] Consequently, by understanding space in terms of power relations, social constructions, exchanges, and encounters of diverse yet juxtaposed "narratives and histories," a *place* can be viewed as *a meeting place.*[11] A "place" might therefore be conceived as "the particular articulation of social relations, including local relations 'within' the place and those many connections which stretch way beyond it."[12] According to Massey, "places" are then entwined to locality but also to a host of interactions and influences that, as a result, destabilize a "mythical" conceptualization of the local as a site of historical seclusion.[13] At the same time, "places" are experienced through a variety of positionings, which consequently challenge a one-dimensional, essentialist, and hegemonic notion of identity and belonging.[14]

Coming from a discipline that researches the local, microlevel aspects of cultures, Richard Bauman's work focuses on performance and, in particular, verbal performance. While Bauman has extensively theorized the relationships between ethnographer, performer, performance, and audiences, I am interested in his conceptualization of "verbal act" as performance and his meaning of "communicative competence." For Bauman a verbal act "may comprehend both myth narration and the speech expected of certain members of society whenever they open their mouths; and it is performance that brings them together in culture-specific and variable ways."[15] As performance, a verbal act goes beyond "an artful text," the recognition of "standard language," and the comprehension of a language's literal meaning. Verbal acts refer to "ways of speaking" and they are beholden to the performer's skills and on the audience's competence to uncover the culturally specific meanings that inform a performance. As Bauman writes, "performance rests on an assumption of responsibility to an audience for a display of communicative virtuosity, highlighting the way in which the act of discursive production is accomplished, above and beyond the additional multiple functions the communicative act may serve."[16] To be sure, "competence" does not come from an imposed and static meaning of culture but instead it relates to the relationship between performer and audience and their knowledge about a variety of definite cultural practices.

At first glance, the theories of Massey and Bauman may seem to be in conflict. After all, in her work, Massey has been highly critical of fixed constructions of "place and home" in which identity is based solely on discourses of national or local belonging. In contrast, Bauman addresses the local-performative aspects of cultures that are recognized and employed by people from particular communities. Then again, as Massey clearly states, "I absolutely [do] not want to give up on the ability to appreciate local difference (it is one of the reasons I became, and remain, a geographer)."[17] More to the point, in Massey's theorization of globalization, she problematizes people's movements from the periphery to the center, their ongoing exclusion at the center, and also, as David Morley explains, their access to resources, goods, and information.[18] Accordingly, in drawing on Massey's and Bauman's work, I am calling attention to filmic representations of migrations, "places," and cultures, to contemporary media travels and their displacements of specific bodily and verbal enactments through the tropes of "neutrality," and to the audiences' mediations of their local or immigrant experiences through their consumption of these texts.

I begin with *La guagua aérea*, concentrating on how this film utilizes an airplane as an "activity space" for familial-ethnic interactions.[19] Even though the film has a simplistic nationalistic agenda, the multiple vernacular references included in the narrative nonetheless generate spaces for diversion from the narrow political discourse that informs the text. I then move to

*Nueba Yol* and focus on this film's reassessment of New York City's *Latiniza-tion*. I explore the ways in which the film appropriates yet also transforms the Spanish-language media's pan-ethnic construct by representing New York City as a Latino/a but ethnically specific "place." Taken together these films are meaningful media artifacts that comment on and re-create internal/ external power relations and multiple cultural practices while the characters are "at home," "en route," or already "away" in the United States.

## *La guagua aérea:* The Airplane as an "Activity Space" for Familial Encounters

Loosely based on Luis Rafael Sánchez's collection of short stories, poems, and interviews entitled *La guagua aérea*, Luis Molina's 1993 comedy of the same title depicts a December 20, 1960, midnight flight from Puerto Rico to New York City. A voiceover narration and images of the Isla Verde International Airport initiate the film's explorations of Puerto Rican migrations to the United States. The narrator's opening line—"I will never forget that Decem-ber 20, 1960"—immediately establishes a temporal distance between an unspecified present and an individualized and nostalgic past. Still, even though this past is uttered as the narrator's personal experience, the tempo-ral specificity of December 1960 intentionally maps broad economic and political significations that would resonate with a Puerto Rican audience.

Approximately fifteen years have passed since the first massive post-WWII Puerto Rican migration to New York City, twelve from the year in which the islanders elected their first governor and witnessed the launching of the Operation Bootstrap industrial economic model, and eight years from the island's transition to commonwealth status. In 1960, Puerto Rico was beginning to experience its rapid, albeit short-lived, economic growth. The middle and upper classes were indeed benefiting from the political and eco-nomic transformations even as the poor and working-class remained at the margins of modernization. Consequently, in *La guagua aérea*, temporality, place (the airplane), and people unfold into a cartograph depicting Puerto Ricans' complex relationship with the U.S. and their ambivalent relationship with their own local, diasporic, and diverse ethnic selves.

Through an array of characters, the airplane becomes the location for representing fragmented experiences within Puerto Rico's local and dias-poric communities. En route are those enjoying the financial opportunities brought by the island's industrialization, sharing an aisle with those on the working-class periphery; there are those who are in favor of Puerto Rico's commonwealth status mingling with those who are against it; there are also those who are escaping from a shady past and are attempting to start a new future; and there are those who are already part of the circular back-and-forth movements that characterize Puerto Ricans' post-1950s migratory patterns. On an individual level, the plane manifest is an ideological and social cross-section of the island, including, among others, the *jíbaro* [Puerto Rican male white peasant] narrator, a prostitute with a heart of gold, a successful pro-U.S. businessman, a married and unfaithful womanizer, a man who pretends to be blind, the head of Puerto Rico's Department of Education English-language program, a "modern" and allegedly sexually liberated woman, and two Newyoricans.[20] The airplane, like the translocal nation it reflects, also has an American presence in the form of two American flight attendants.[21] As expected, the American women are utilized in the narrative to both reemphasize the United States as the colonial oppressor and to ridicule what is understood in Puerto Rico as U.S. intolerance for ethnic, racial, and cultural differences.[22] With this population on board, the airplane becomes an "activity space" for familial encounters wherein, due to the spatial confinement, these diverse Puerto Ricans and Americans are forced to interact with each other. As a result of these exchanges the airplane also becomes a *place as a meeting place* for the articulation of social, political, and cultural experiences and differences.

Most of the passengers' motivations for traveling to New York are revealed through their conversations with each other.[23] It is precisely through these dialogues that the process of economic modernization, the push and pull factors leading to migration, and the difficulties endured by those in the diaspora, are explored and criticized. The characters that most clearly illustrate the diverse impact of Puerto Rico's 1940s and 1950s political and economic transformations are the successful businessman Orlando Colón, the poor *jíbaro* narrator Faustino Román, and two nameless working-class Newyoricans.

Orlando Colón embodies the pro-commonwealth ideology and the Puerto Rican middle-upper class who profited from the new economic environment. He is traveling to New York on business, is educated and fluent in English, and he highly admires what he constantly refers to as "the wonders of the American civilization." For Orlando, the misery of the immigrant community in New York is a product of their own laziness, something that he sees as an innate characteristic of the Puerto Rican people. Faustino Román on the other hand, symbolizes the pro-independence/nationalistic ideology. He is traveling to New York to look for his oldest son, who migrated to the United States to earn money in order to pay for the family house. For Faustino, the real Puerto Rican is the one who holds onto the land and who rejects the process of economic modernization that is ruining the land/homeland. Finally, the two nameless Newyoricans personify the struggles, financial difficulties, and racism endured by members of the Puerto Rican diaspora. They dream of a future return to the island because, as one of them states, New York has "a sky without stars."

Whereas through Orlando Colón, Faustino Román, and the two Newyoricans, the narrative tries to problematize the distinct ways in which the social and economic transformations of the 1950s affected various sectors of the Puerto Rican translocal communities, the one-dimensionality of these characters creates a binary construction that simplistically defines what a real Puerto Rican is and is not. In *La guagua aérea* a Puerto Rican's "worthiness" and "unworthiness" is exclusively based on an individual's support for or rejection of U.S. involvement in Puerto Rico. Even though in the film it is evident that Puerto Ricans experience their sense of belonging in different ways and that the "local" has been influenced by the U.S. presence, those who do not conform to hegemonic "mythical" notions of identity are ostracized. Therefore, Orlando Colón, the "Americanized" and successful businessman, is constructed as the most despicable and traitorous Puerto Rican on the plane, and, by extension, throughout the local and diasporic nation.

Besides the fact that *Puerto Ricanness* is defined through a nationalistic political position, the selection of a *jíbaro* as the film's hero generates a patriarchal, racial-Eurocentric, heteronormal, and gendered hierarchical structure that symbolically annihilates past and present members of the translocal ethnic family.[24] Additionally, and interrelated to these exclusions, in *La guagua aérea* women are silenced, especially regarding Puerto Rican politics. Although a Newyorican woman addresses the issue of prejudices against Puerto Ricans in the United States, men are primarily the ones who debate Puerto Rican politics and economic processes. In sum, *La guagua aérea* is a political pamphlet that limits issues of ethnic authenticity based on a narrow, male-centric, and heterosexist nationalistic discourse.

Despite all the aforementioned problems, the film includes a variety of characters and cultural references that, to a certain extent, expand the political-nationalistic definition of *Puerto Ricanness*. In *La guagua aérea*, the "ways of speaking"—the jokes, the insinuations, and the gossip, as well as the gestures, music, dancing, and "disorder"—create spaces of what Richard Bauman refers to as "the culture-specific constellations of communicative means" that can be fully understood only by those who have "communicative competence."[25]

The first and immediate frame of Puerto Rican "ways of speaking" is the film's title. Whereas, as I previously mentioned, the title is borrowed from Luis Rafael Sánchez's book, the use of the word *guagua* [bus] binds the film to locality and, to a certain extent, Spanish Caribbeanness, given that in Latin America the only groups who use the term *guagua* for "bus" are Puerto Ricans, Cubans, and Dominicans. This seemingly minor detail can be decontextualized in different ways. For instance, in Mexican vernacular language, *guagua* means baby. Thus, based on the title, some people might think that the movie is about a "baby who travels or flies," when in reality the film's title tries to convey the ongoing, back-and-forth working-class movements that have characterized Puerto Rican migrations to the United States from the late 1940s to the 1980s.

In *La guagua aérea*'s diegesis, verbal acts are utilized as indexes of characters' social class, education, and levels of assimilation or knowledge of U.S. culture (through the use and misuse of the English language).[26] For example, the Newyorican woman uses a sporadic "you know" in English, which indicates that she has been living in the United States for some time and has thus appropriated and incorporated general English phrases into her speech. At the same time, her "way of speaking" also has elements of what is considered in Puerto Rico as *jíbaro/a* speech to convey her working-class background. On the other hand, the teacher and head of Puerto Rico's Department of Education English-language program speaks *very proper* Spanish, pronouncing all the syllables in each word, a verbal act in total opposition to the *jíbaro/a*-working-class speech, which is characterized by the omission or substitution of letters in words. In addition the English instructor has mastered the English language and corrects other people's inaccurate use of terms. Her verbal performances reflect her formal education, a factor that situates her as a highly respected individual regardless of her economic status. Hence, in *La guagua aérea*, the *jíbaro* speech, the sporadic inclusion of English words, and the *correct* use of Spanish and English communicate very specific cultural nuances regarding the location of these individuals in the diegesis.

While the verbal acts generally reflect the characters' class, education, and/or assimilation, another variety of cultural behaviors transcend and at the same time complement the culturally specific "ways of speaking." These performances relate to vernacular-familial practices at both the individual and communal level. Contrary to the verbal acts that still resonate in contemporary Puerto Rico, some of these cultural references recreate performances that were more common in the past (for instance, passengers clapping when an airplane has landed safely), while others surpass the specificity of the diegesis' temporal location. The fact that the narrative takes place in December provides an opportunity to depict cultural elements that are associated with the Christmas season, such as playing instruments (guiros, maracas, and guitar), singing, dancing, and eating seasonal dishes.

There are other, more subtle cultural references that would only be perceived by those versed in the realm of the vernacular. Some of these practices include bringing the nuclear and extended family to the airport, crowding around the gate instead of forming a single line when boarding, sharing food with strangers, or talking to someone on the airplane who is sitting ten rows away. By representing what an outsider might see as exaggerated, chaotic, and disorderly, but which a cultural insider would recognize as familiar, *La guagua aérea* satirizes the ethnic self and invites those with "communicative competence" to engage with the film, recognize themselves and others, and laugh about it. This satirizing of the "self" is not the "masochistic humor" that Freud theorizes in relation to what he as well as others define as self-hatred ethnic humor but instead should be viewed as a filmic reconstruction of the carnivalesque, of multiple corporeal and verbal practices and beliefs that inform Puerto Rico's vernacular cultures.[27] And it is precisely through this satirizing of the ethnic self that the narrative suggests that, for instance, not every Puerto Rican woman wants to get married or is sexually repressed, that some members of the ethnic family financially trick others, or that, despite the semi-official Catholic religion, Afro-diasporic religious practices might be considered the underground quasi-official belief. Thus, while in the last shot there is a static image of the *jíbaro* and a voiceover narration that reasserts a singularized "sense of place," the parade of Puerto Ricans illustrates that, whether at "home," "en route," or "abroad," there are fissures to an all-encompassing identity exclusively based on a nationalistic political discourse of belonging.

If, in *La guagua aérea*, the flight from Puerto Rico to New York City is an "activity space" for familial encounters, in the comedy *Nueba Yol*, New York City, and specifically Washington Heights, is a *place as a meeting place* where various Latinos/as interact. By accommodating Dominican, Puerto Rican, Cuban, and Mexican immigrants, *Nueba Yol* re-constructs New York City as a Latino "place" of "social interactions and co-presence," an ethnic inter-activity that relates to "a geography of social relations" within Washington Heights, across Central Park (in Spanish Harlem–El Barrio), throughout the city, and beyond it (in the Dominican Republic and in Puerto Rico).[28] In *Nueba Yol*, Washington Heights, an Upper West Side New York City area historically inhabited by racialized groups (Irish, Eastern European Jews, and African Americans) is ethnically rebuilt as Latino and primarily as Dominican.

## *Nueba Yol:* The Diasporic Place Where the Spanish Caribbean and Mexico Intersect

Angel Muñiz's commercially successful 1996 film *Nueba Yol* addresses the post-1980 working-class migrations of Dominicans to New York City as well as the Latinization of the city.[29] Through the experiences of Balbuena, a poor, black, humble, honest, hard-working, naïve, illegal, and very pleasant Dominican man, the filmic depiction of New York's Latinization and, as a result, of *Latinidad* departs from a pan-ethnic and singularized Hispanic-Latino identity. As Agustín Laó-Montes argues, Latinidad does not signify a "single identity formation but rather a multiplicity of intersecting discourses enabling different types of subjects and identities and deploying specific kinds of knowledge and power relations."[30] From the selection of the movie title (a Dominican and also Puerto Rican vernacular pronunciation of New York), to the racial and class markers of the characters' bodies, to the use of culturally specific jargon, *Nueba Yol* generates a discourse of Latinidad that includes Latino diversity but that is framed through the Dominican working-class immigrant experience.

While *Nueba Yol*'s construction of Latinidad is influenced by market imperatives, it nonetheless allows for a distinct cultural-ethnic presence in which Spanish Caribbean and Mexican immigrants verbalize their shared experiences—everyday financial problems, issues of assimilation, and/or homeland nostalgia—while utilizing their respective accents, jargon, and performative-bodily cultural practices. Equally important, *Nueba Yol*'s New York City is not only Latino-ethnically plural and working-class but is primarily black and mulatto. Consequently, *Nueba Yol*'s New York is a *place* where bodies, accents, and jokes produce multiple spaces of differentiation, which symbolically articulate the movements from the third world periphery to the first world periphery and the "ethnic/racial hierarchies" of the pre- and the not so post- "colonial/racial domination."[31]

*Nueba Yol*'s narrative begins in Santo Domingo. Balbuena, the film's protagonist, has lost his beloved wife and, with her death, he has lost his hopes and dreams for the future. Living in a poor barrio and with sporadic jobs, Balbuena has tried to obtain a visa to the United States without any luck. As he says, "only those with money and connections and who do not have any financial need get the visas." It is not until Fellito, Balbuena's Puerto Rican friend, makes an illegal deal with a raging queen who happens to be the American consul in the Dominican Republic that Balbuena is able to migrate to New York City.

Whereas, in *La guagua aérea*, *Americanness* is embodied through two bigoted women, in *Nueba Yol* the United States is portrayed through a hedonistic and materialistic gay man. Besides stripping the United States of its masculine-power position in a clearly homophobic way, what is interesting about Fellito, the American consul, and Balbuena's interactions, is the ways in which the United States–Puerto Rican dilemma is represented from a Dominican point of view. It is evident that Fellito has had a long business relationship with the consul that might have involved some sexual favors. Obviously, in this heterosexist inversion of United States–Puerto Rican colonial-colonized roles, the Puerto Rican macho is on top of the negotiations. Still, according to *Nueba Yol*, Puerto Rico has already "sold"—prostituted—itself. Thus, as long as Puerto Ricans use their associations to help their Dominican brothers and sisters, they can do whatever they please with the unscrupulous, exploitative, and imperialistic United States.

Eager to work hard and begin a new life, Balbuena together with Fellito arrives in New York. Fairly soon, Balbuena discovers that life there is not as easy as Fellito had promised. Two weeks after his arrival he has not found a job and Fellito has vanished. Furthermore, Balbuena's cousin, who has provided shelter since his arrival, could not continue to accommodate seven people in a two-bedroom apartment. Balbuena needed to find another place to live. Feeling nostalgic for his homeland, he wants to return to the Dominican Republic as soon as possible. The only avenue of happiness is with Nancy, a Dominican woman who, after residing in New York for several years, has decided to go back to the Dominican Republic.

Thanks to the help of a Mexican restaurant owner, Balbuena finds a steady job cleaning the restaurant. The dream of a future return home and the possibility of reuniting with Nancy provide Balbuena with the drive to work two jobs and rent an inexpensive and unappealing room in a house/former bordello owned by an alcoholic Cuban woman. *Nueba Yol*'s last images show Balbuena in the Dominican Republic, getting married to Nancy, happy and financially stable because he was able to pay off the loan he received to buy the visa.[32]

In *Nueba Yol*'s New York City, the contemporary conflicts and racial/ethnic hierarchies among Dominicans, Puerto Ricans, and Mexicans are not explored. As Arlene Dávila notes:

> In New York City's hierarchy of Latinidad, for instance, to distance oneself from the lowest ranked racial/ethnic groups in the city is to estrange oneself from Puerto Ricans, and increasingly, Dominicans. These groups are considered to be lazy, uneducated, loud and less "cultured" as compared to the more cultured, hard working, and ethical Mexicans, a discourse positioning them as the premier "good immigrant" and prospective model citizens.[33]

These ethnic and racial hierarchies, as Dávila argues, are intertwined with and "shaped by" Latin American and Spanish Caribbean racial ideologies and U.S. "racialist processes."[34] Contrary to New York City's Latino relations, *Nueba Yol* generally recreates an amicable environment among Dominican, Puerto Rican, Mexican, and Cuban immigrants, who are all trying to survive financially and culturally in this working-class and unwelcoming city. Still, the film contains some underlying criticism regarding particular ethnic groups. Whereas the narrative certainly condemns Dominicans in terms of taking financial advantage of family-ethnic members, and for participating in illegal-drug trafficking activities, the harsher Latino depiction is reserved for Puerto Ricans.

The most pathetic and morally dubious character in *Nueba Yol* is Fellito, a man who, as one discovers toward the end of the film, is a crack addict who assaulted his good friend Balbuena. Even the alcoholic Cuban woman is more sympathetic given that, based on the narrative, her alcoholism is a product of raising her children on her own in an inhospitable New York City. In other words, despite their immigrant privileges, 1960s Cuban exiles have also suffered in a futile attempt to achieve the so-called American dream (a theme explored, to some extent, in the 1980 Cuban American film *El super*).[35] On the other hand, Puerto Ricans, who have not had to worry about visas or *la migra*, have squandered the advantage of American citizenship. But not only are Puerto Ricans depicted as socially apathetic, they are also seen as highly untrustworthy people who would do anything to protect themselves.

This problematic depiction of Puerto Ricans can be viewed as a response to the anti-Dominican sentiment that informs Puerto Rico's society and not necessarily to the relationship between these ethnic groups in New York City. Although there is friction between Dominicans and Puerto Ricans in the city, their shared experiences as racialized immigrant-minorities have been influential in fostering political, social, and cultural coalitions.[36] Conversely, in Puerto Rico, as Jorge Duany argues, Dominicans have been blamed for the country's social ills, such as drug-trafficking, unemployment, and criminality.[37] Furthermore, in the island's vernacular culture, Dominican immigrants—most of whom are primarily black and mulatto—have been constructed as lazy, illiterate, and lacking intellectual skills. This racialization, as Jorge Duany has extensively analyzed, is rooted in Puerto Rico's Eurocentric nationalistic discourse and its exclusion of blackness from the national imaginary.[38] Therefore, Fellito's character could be seen as a product of the Dominican and Puerto Rican ethnic, racial, and cultural tensions beyond New York City.

At the opposite end of the New York City–Latino spectrum, Mexicans are constructed as the most diligent, financially solvent, and supportive group within the community. In an attempt to attract the Mexican majority that comprises the U.S. Spanish-language media market, *Nueba Yol* reproduces the discourse of Mexicans as the "premier good immigrants" and "model citizens." Therefore, even though in New York City Mexicans are the smallest Latino subgroup among Puerto Ricans, Dominicans, and Mexicans, and the least powerful of the three groups in terms of New York City politics, they nonetheless have a prominent role in *Nueba Yol*.[39]

Besides this market-driven representation, there are drastic distinctions between *Nueba Yol*'s Latinidad and the U.S. Spanish-language media's contrivance of *Mexicanness* as "the embodiment of generic Latinidad."[40] These differences relate to the diegesis's specific geographic locations, the bodies/people that populate these locations, and the performative acts included in the narrative. These elements describe an immigrant experience that has points of commonalities with past and contemporary Spanish Caribbean and Latin American migratory movements to the United States, but that concomitantly articulate the particularities of the post-1980 Dominican migrations.

First, the place where Dominican, Puerto Rican, Mexican, and Cuban characters interact is Washington Heights. The A train, the street signs, the George Washington Bridge, and the Cloisters re-locate Latino exchanges to what is known by Latino New Yorkers and Dominicans "at home" and "abroad" as Quisqueya Heights. In other words, the narrative translates-moves the Mexicans and Puerto Ricans who reside in Spanish Harlem–El Barrio, and the Cuban majority who live in Union City, New Jersey, to this Dominican-populated area. This translation then transforms Nueba Yol (New York City) into an exclusive area: Washington Heights. Therefore, although as a verbal act, *Nueba Yol* (the title) resonates with a Puerto Rican vernacular "way of speaking" and, at first glance (and based on the title) it could be re-contextualized as a film about the Puerto Rican Nueba Yol (i.e., El Barrio), the diegesis's geographical and cultural specificity, and the multiple nonverbal signs, frame the city as a Dominican–Washington Heights "place."[41]

Second, and interrelated to this geographical and ethnic-cultural rebuilding of New York, besides the two Mexican men and the Cuban woman, Balbuena, Fellito, his extended family, Nancy, and the people on the streets of Washington Heights, are primarily blacks and mulattos. This coloring of Washington Heights portrays, interconnects, and expands the Afro-diasporic presence that comprises New York City's Latinidad. That is, the Dominican characters' race not only maps—racially speaking—the Dominican exodus but it also creates a symbolic cartograph of previous Spanish Caribbean and Latin American Afro-diasporic movements to and settlements in New York City. This ethnic and racial cartograph also alludes to New York City's "residential apartheid," wherein since the early twentieth century, many Spanish Caribbean and Latin American immigrants (as well as other racialized ethnic groups) have been pushed to impoverished areas.[42]

Hence, Balbuena's black and mulatto Dominicans in Washington Heights are allegorically linked to the early-twentieth-century Puerto Ricans in Harlem, the 1930s-1950s Cubans who were dispersed throughout Harlem and the Upper West Side, the 1940s-1950s Puerto Ricans who moved to East Harlem, Hell's Kitchen, and the South Bronx, and the 1970s-1980s Garinagu (plural for Garifuna) from Honduras and Nicaragua who settled in Harlem and the South Bronx. As a result, the blackness and *mulataje* of *Nueba Yol*'s characters articulate the "colonial/racial domination" in the Spanish Caribbean and Latin American periphery and in the United States—New York City center.[43] At home and abroad, nonwhites have experienced the legacy of colonialism, or what Aníbal Quijano calls "the coloniality of power," that is, "the continuity of colonial domination over indigenous and black populations" by white elites.[44]

The issue of marginality along the periphery brings to light a third point— *Nueba Yol*'s blackness transcends Washington Heights. Balbuena's Santo Domingo barrio is exclusively populated by black and mulatto individuals. This indexical grounding is utilized in the narrative to portray Balbuena and his friends' positionings in terms of race and class and also regarding the community's Afro-diasporic cultural practices.[45] In other words, blackness signifies class and social locations on the margins of the periphery, as well as a realm of cultural enactments that are part of the Spanish-Caribbean Afro-diasporic vernacular cultures.[46] This Afro-diasporic cultural component is clearly seen in Balbuena's Santo Domingo farewell party. In this scene, Fellito, Balbuena, and approximately fifteen friends from the community are singing a song entitled *Me voy pa' Nueba Yol* [I am going to New York], playing drums, and dancing. Through the rhythmic performance of the drums and bodies, this filmic representation creates a trans-Spanish Caribbean space that is interconnected through black music and bodily movements. Accordingly, the *Me voy pa' Nueba Yol* musical and communal enactment can be viewed as a foreshadowing element that moves Balbuena from a black vernacular cultural "place" (his Santo Domingo barrio) to another black cultural "place" (Washington Heights). In this way, this act is also part of the symbolic cartograph that maps some of the Afro-diasporic elements of New York City's Latinidad.

The song *Me voy pa' Nueba Yol* underscores another point of departure between *Nueba Yol*'s Latinidad and the U.S. Spanish-language media's Latinidad—verbal acts. The aforementioned song utilizes Spanish Caribbean slang and verbal-vernacular pronunciations. For instance, the communal chorus sings *"yo me voy pa' Nueba Yol,"* in which the word *para* [to] is pronounced *pa*. In grammatical terms, this is an incomplete and thus incorrect pronunciation of the preposition, yet, it clearly reflects the vernacular way of speaking in the Dominican Republic in particular, and in the Spanish Caribbean in general. The song also includes words such as *pana*, which means buddy in Puerto Rican slang, and *Boricua*, a term for Puerto Ricans commonly used on the island, in the Spanish Caribbean, and in New York City (as JLo clearly tells us in "Jenny from the Block").

The speech patterns on display in *Me voy pa' Nueba Yol* are used throughout the film. In *Nueba Yol* there is no attempt to construct what Mexican and Spanish-language television have conceptualized as "neutral" Spanish (i.e., upper-class Mexican Spanish). Quite the opposite. The language and accents utilized by each of the characters relates to the ways of speaking commonly associated within the Latino ethnic group in question. For example, the Cuban woman has (as culturally expected) a Cuban accent and the Mexican characters employ words such as *chamba* [work] or *manito* [friend-man], a type of speech that is mostly associated with the Mexican working-class culture. To be sure, these Mexican verbal enactments have been extensively represented in U.S. Spanish-language television networks through cultural artifacts such as Mexican Golden Era movies, telenovelas, and other types of programming imported from Mexico. Therefore, the Mexican working-class "way of speaking" is also part of the "neutral" Spanish-language media Latinidad construct. Nonetheless, in *Nueba Yol* this Mexican speech is only one of many ways of speaking existing alongside Dominican, Puerto Rican, and Cuban accents and words. These diverse verbal acts represent a variety of sounds, tones, and culturally specific terms that resist the verbal and cultural homogeneity projects of U.S. Spanish-language television. Hence, for those familiar with New York City's Latino cultures, these verbal performances are not a cacophony but instead they might be seen (or heard) as a more realistic manifestation of the languages, voices, and jargon of some of the Spanish Caribbean and Latin American immigrants who live in the city.

*Nueba Yol*'s narrative geographical locations, black and mulatto characters, Afro-diasporic elements, and ethnic-specific cultural performances directly challenge the U.S. Spanish-language media discourse of a single, Eurocentric Hispanic identity. Instead of silencing differences and imposing one image of Latinidad, *Nueba Yol* embraces some of the ethnic, racial, and cultural aspects that comprise New York City, and more broadly, the U.S. Latino/a population. Both *Nueba Yol* and *La guagua aérea* are part of what Agustín Laó-Montes calls *latinization from below*, "the processes of Latino self-fashioning that arise from resistance against marginality and discrimination and as expressions of a desire for a definition of self and an affirmative search for collective memory and community."[47] These two films recreate distinct ethnic, racial, migratory, and communal encounters and cultures, a variety of representations that, while influenced by market imperatives, also respond to the movements of people and the progressive displacements of experiences, languages, and voices in today's mediascape.

### Rereading Latino Diasporic Films: Toward a Reassessment of Places, People, and Cultures

The issue of understanding recent Latino diasporic films' constructions of places, migrations, ethnic relations, cultural performances, and verbal acts is extremely relevant given that these films are, for the most part, designed for the entertainment and pleasure of particular communities at home and abroad. I am not saying that the only significant aspects of these films are ethnic-social interactivity and culture, but rather that by considering the aforementioned elements one can recuperate a variety of films that may not be masterpieces but that are highly important cultural artifacts for particular communities. Lastly and interrelated to what is mentioned above, while in this chapter I performed a textual analysis, I want to make clear that a key aspect in reconsidering *La guagua aérea*, *Nueba Yol*, and other Latino diasporic films derives not only from an examination of the texts but also from the audiences' interpretation of these texts. For example, do Latino diasporic films' intended audiences mediate television's displacements of their cultures through their consumption of these texts? Do these films expand the audiences' conceptualization of migration, space, and cultural performances? Is it possible for Latino diasporic films to alter or to cement particular immigrants' perceptions of other ethnic groups? These are some of the questions that might shed light on how audiences at home or abroad negotiate contemporary media travels and their displacements of locally specific enactments.

The advent of the "neutral" telenovela, the push for verbal and cultural homogeneity, and the progressive elimination of locally produced programs in some Latin American and Spanish Caribbean television markets present a disturbing picture regarding the medium's capacity to function as a cultural, political, and social forum. As I indicated elsewhere, when the local ceases to exist and the performances of cultures have no resemblance to the struggles that comprise the national, multifarious quandaries arise.[48] It is for this reason that in places where television only broadcasts "neutral" telenovelas and imported shows, it might be time to turn off the sets and look for other media outlets that depict a locally inspired socio-political, cultural, and ethnic landscape. Latino diasporic films, films in general, and other artifacts such as theatre, music, and performance art might become the primary spaces that re-articulate the "plurality of worldmaking" in Latin American, Spanish Caribbean, and U.S. Latino communities. In an era of globalization, these fictional narrations offer us new perspectives on how people understand themselves, their cultures, their worlds, and the worlds of others.

# 7

# KILLING ME SOFTLY

## BRAZILIAN FILM AND BARE LIFE

AMY VILLAREJO

Media flows between the two largest countries in the Americas, Brazil and the United States, intensified in the years following the First World War and continue today. From initial treatments of Brazilian culture as "exotic" or as a "third world" surface for aestheticization, North American filmmakers, video artists, and mass culture producers now mine Brazilian culture largely for images of megacities and urban poverty, drug lords and violence in the *favelas*, or poor neighborhoods. In turn, Brazilian cinema and television industries increasingly see the United States as a distribution venue and profit generator for Brazilian media, including these images of cities under siege. This chapter explores the traffic in images across the Americas as a model for interrogating other sites of global media exchange, seeking to account for uneven power relations, racial dynamics, and processes of transculturation that distinguish intermediality and worldmaking from previous modes of understanding cultural production.

In brief terms, I seek to revisit a set of questions that were framed from the late 1950s through the 1980s through the discourse of "Third Cinema." This category—always one that betrayed internal tension and threatened to collapse—enfolded a number of different cinematic projects that suggest a need to move beyond "Third Cinema."

Third Cinema originally described a cinema of anti-colonial struggle, from Gillo Pontecorvo's *Battle of Algiers* (1966), chronicling the Algerian revolution, to Ousmane Sembène's films tracing the liberation of Senegal, to Argentinians Octavio Getino and Fernando Solanas's *Hour of the Furnaces* (1968), to Tomás Gutiérrez Alea's *Memories of Underdevelopment* (1968), reflecting upon the early moments of Castro's Cuba. Fueled by a concatenation that included, as Roy Armes has noted, "opposition to the Vietnam war, student revolt, a new consciousness on the part of American blacks, the emergence of armed guerilla groups in Latin America, developments within the communist world opposing China to USSR in terms of revolutionary strategy," filmmakers in the 1960s believed in the political function of cinema within what Armes calls the "euphoria of revolution."[1]

Further, it described an anti-commercial cinema, rooted in national-popular struggle. In the case of Brazil, *"cinema novo"* ["the new cinema"] opposed itself to the incursion of Hollywood-style spectacle as well as allegedly indigenous popular genres such as the *chanchada* films (films set in Rio de Janeiro that showcase the modernity and urban splendor of the city, incorporating music and popular traditions associated with *carnival*, and featuring irreverent humor from a populist perspective). The *cinenovistas* (proponents of *cinema novo*) proposed a persistent distinction between the commercial mainstream and the political avant garde. In the key theoretical elaborations of Third Cinema in its moment—for example in the now-canonical "For an Imperfect Cinema" by Julio García Espinosa and "Towards a Third Cinema" by Solanas and Getino—we witness an attack upon Western formal perfection in works of art, whether demanding, in the former essay, the destruction of the artist's elite isolation (and a film practice that "finds its audience in those who struggle") or, in the latter, a subversive mode of filmmaking dependent upon the destruction of both commercial cinema ("first") and the author's cinema ("second cinema").

Finally, it described innovation and experimentation at the level of form as much as content. In many African instances, for example, "Third Cinema" drew upon folklore, traditional myths, and legends to tell stories about the emergent nation and the complexities of postcolonial modernity; in the Brazilian context, as Robert Stam shows, the theme of "first contact" and historical relations between Afro Brazilians and Indians suffuse the increasingly politicized representations.[2] Frequently dependent upon allegory, though not all reducible to allegorical structure, the films tend to establish complicated relations to national history. In the manifestos for Latin American cinema, calls for the deformation of capitalist images and the cinematic rupture with traditionalism (which is in turn coded as complacency) dominated a passionate rhetoric that sought breaks with the past and the invention of a promising future.

Even the most prominent discussions of "Third Cinema" undertaken more than twenty years ago suspended the designation as a question precisely to "re-pose the question of the relations between the cultural and the political."[3] Indicting the left's sentimentalism regarding third worldist politics, the 1986 Edinburgh International Film Festival conference yielded the book *Questions of Third Cinema*, which sought to "draw attention to different, non-English approaches to cultural politics."[4] The conference organizers marked the ostensible passing of a moment and of a conceptual frame (both "third world" and "Third Cinema") that seemed adequate to that moment, which was characterized by the dominance of the national frame, the declaration of a break with the colonial order, and the promise of a national-popular culture articulating the vision and needs of a people newly empowered to shape its image. "Third Cinema," born of cold war politics, furthermore traveled on a utopian impulse to establish political categories rather than describe them.

The moment clearly has changed. But how, exactly? The "third world" is no longer a coherent descriptor, but a host of questions remain about how to "world" the world, that is, how to designate sociopolitical realities and possibilities in the wake of neoliberal reorganization and globalization. I will not attempt to chart even those strains of postcolonial thought that have had the greatest impact on my own understanding of the conceptual tools that can reframe the Third Cinema question. Such an undertaking exceeds the scope of this essay, to be sure, but it also presumes that one can pause in the midst of uneven practices (varied sounds and images, feelings and thoughts) in order to render a diagnosis. Here I would wish to ally myself with Franz Fanon's text, more than fifty years old today: his address to the second Congress of Black Writers and Artists in Rome in 1959 (printed as the chapter "On National Culture" in *Wretched of the Earth*). In two justifiably famous passages, he calls for the "native poet" (organic intellectual, postcolonial feminist, queer social activist) to immerse, to be taken, to be open:

> It is not enough to try to get back to the people in that past out of which they have already emerged; rather we must join them in that fluctuating movement which they are just giving a shape to, and which, as soon as it has started, will be the signal for everything to be called into question. Let there be no mistake about it; it is to this zone of occult instability where the people dwell that we must come; and it is there that our souls are crystallized and that our perception and our lives are transfused with light.[5]

Even if the enlightenment metaphors today seem strained, we may dwell within this "zone of occult instability" in thinking still about cultural production, what Fanon characterized as "the whole body of efforts made by a people in the sphere of thought to describe, justify, and praise the action through which that people has created itself and keeps itself in existence."[6] "Postnationalism" and urban post-state globality talk, as well as neologisms like "glocal" that cover the very problems they seek to address, forget the task of describing the effects of weakened states under globalization, the struggles for survival within them, and the production of discourse from positions significantly different than those anti-colonial articulations Fanon chronicles. Here I take inspiration from Gayatri Spivak's deconstructive use of the idea of "inter-diction" to put these historically dense formations into play, "repetition in rupture," "a practice that does not take sides, but uses what is strategically important."[7] These questions remain, too, in the domain of cinema. What I focus on here is the latter task: how to describe the transformations in cinema from "Third Cinema" to a more commercial, narrative form that nonetheless embodies a political voice in Brazil today and circulates both intermedially and transnationally.

The flows of Brazilian cinema to North America and vice versa, then, have a long history, one traced by Stam and other major scholars of Brazilian cinema. In the chanchada, the genre I mention earlier, Brazil exported an image of the country that has persisted: the musical celebrations of carnival, the popular and comedic traditions of the music hall and the circus, and the wily assertion of *malandragem*. The latter stresses the nobility of the poor and the vanity and futility of the elite classes exemplified through the figure of the lazy but flippantly clever Bohemian. If that genre persisted as the face of Brazil's national cinema, it did so alongside other state-subsidized or state-financed film initiatives through the periods of World War II, Brazil's neofascist government, and its more recent authoritarian regime, the dictatorship that lasted from 1964 to 1984. Already by the mid-1950s, the "godfather" of cinema novo, Nelson Pereira dos Santos, had criticized the popular genre and its aping of the Hollywood studio system (as well as the North American dominance of film exhibition, itself a partial product of the so-called Good Neighbor Policy), producing one of the first breaks with the commercial cinema in his film *Vidas Secas* (*Barren Lives*, 1963). That film adapts communist author Graciliano Ramos' novel from 1938 about a family living a hardscrabble life in Brazil's North-East region and delivers a strong indictment of social injustice.

Displaying some of the same stylistic innovations that characterize Italian neo-realism (i.e., the use of nonprofessional actors, location shooting, hand-held camerawork, and a limited script), the major formal contribution of *Vidas Secas* is its "overexposed" look, achieved by rejecting the use of camera filters. The surface of the image thus comes to signify the oppressive conditions of the *sertão* (the Brazilian backcountry or bush). Other cinema novo films, such as those by the influential director Glauber Rocha, adopted different thematic and aesthetic strategies (more Brechtian, lyrical, and baroque) but helped to popularize cinema novo especially in the first world sites of Europe and the United States. As Brazilian film critic Paulo Emilio Salles Gomes put it, even as he celebrated the movement, "[cinema novo] remained an accurate barometer of young people aspiring to interpret the will of the colonized."[8] This is not a very positive assessment!

In other words and emphatically, there has never been a straightforward relationship between the state, the national, and the popular. Strands of both commercial genre cinema (such as the chanchada) and the political energy of films associated with cinema novo continue, however, to define the aesthetic, political, and thematic projects of much Brazilian cinema, even if both are deformed in the intermedial climate of the present. The legacy of the chanchada continues in a fascination with postmodernity and its surfaces, with music and carnival, and with the pulse of the city, mostly the dramatic cityscape of Rio de Janeiro. If cinema novo mostly pursued a fantasy of Brazilian subaltern life, it nonetheless offered a cinematic vocabulary (much but not all of which was indebted to realisms of various sorts) for expanding the role and look of popular culture in Brazil and for keeping questions of political consciousness on the table.

Between the years of cinema novo and today, Brazil, like much of the world, has witnessed unprecedented social change and urbanization, leading particularly in Brazil's largest cities of São Paulo and Rio to dramatic contrasts between rich and poor inhabitants, white and black, who live side by side. Documenting the lives of city residents, especially the *cariocas* of Rio, has become an urgent national task in ostensibly holding up a "mirror" to Brazil's large underclass and thereby attempting to render a more inclusive world picture. It is important to note here that very few Brazilians can attend the cinema: only about 6 percent of the population buys movie tickets each year, and the country has the second highest ratio of inhabitants to theatres in the world.[9] The idea, then, that cinema alone can represent the underrepresented to themselves is seriously flawed, and it has become increasingly the case that television and television/cinema hybrids have taken the lead as the popular form capable of continuing a discussion about national culture, about the impact of globalization on the subaltern city population, about the city as a social space, and about the relationship between culture and political change. Brazil, in other words, helps us think intermedially about worldmaking. Without delving into significant detail about corporate organization, it is perhaps important also to remark that cinema and television converge in the massive entity called Rede Globo.

## Cities and Brazilian Cinema

The genre that has emerged as the new voice of Brazilian moving image culture is the favela film, first popularized with the massively popular film *City of God* (Fernando Meirelles, 2002), which takes place in a neighborhood that is not exactly a favela but has some of the same elements. Realist films concentrating upon life in the city's poor neighborhoods/shantytowns depict some of the features that make such areas unique, drawing from a discourse of cinematic cities under siege. I will rehearse a bit of that literature before specifying the ways in which the film that becomes my focus zooms in upon architecture, control, and music.

Questions regarding media and urban publics have proliferated in cinema and media studies. European city films of the 1920s and 1930s, Weimar "street films," postmodernist virtual cities produced in films like *Blade Runner* or *The Matrix*, sociohistorical contexts for urban sites of production, film noir: all of these have been useful sites for exploring, to borrow Edward Dimendberg's title, "spaces of modernity." (The literature here includes Dimendberg's *Film Noir and the Spaces of Modernity*, the works of James Donald and Sabine Hake, and the essays in Linda Krause and Patrice Petro's *Global Cities*, among others).[10] I share with John David Rhodes, author of a wonderful book about a particular filmmaker (Pasolini) and a particular city (Rome), the sense, however, that often these discussions about cities and cinema, in Rhodes's words, "assume a rather abstract, diffuse character; often the 'city' might even be only an imagined city—a fabrication of set design and cinematography."[11] In *Expediency of Culture*, George Yúdice reminds us in stark terms that we must address specific and localized cities, for they speak their own facticities:

[i]n Rio, as in other major Latin American urban centers, poor black and mulatto youth have no citizenship rights to speak of. They are not protected by the police; on the contrary, the police, often in cahoots with *justiçeiros* or vigilantes, harass them in the best of cases, and in the worst, murder them and leave their corpses on the street to serve as a warning to others. Human rights organizations' records show that in 1991 in São Paulo alone, the military police killed 876 "street youth." That number was expected to increase to 1,350 in 1992. In comparison, 23 youth were killed in similar circumstances in New York, a city about the same size as São Paulo. The point is not so much that in São Paulo the police kill thirty-eight times as many youth as in New York (although that itself is a telling statistic), but that the method of dealing with unemployment, lack of educational opportunity, hunger, and racism is "social cleansing" of the poor.[12]

Yudicé and other writers on Latin American geography, such as Teresa Caldeira in her powerful book *City of Walls*, confront an urban landscape in which processes of social differentiation, as Yudicé puts it in a haunting phrase, "render commonality difficult if not impossible" (Yudicé, 123). Purposeful and not so purposeful acts of occupying space in these cities (that is, being seen and being heard) might performatively assert a mode of belonging to a fractured and dissolute polity, but, as with any performative, there is no guarantee of success in those acts. Similarly, media responses can easily be folded into complicit spectacle. Even those forms of critical media that seem to promise to crack through that complicity can themselves become commodified cultural objects.

These kinds of analyses and alternative genealogies—not of "the city" as undifferentiated urban space but of cities under siege, cities to which we are umbilically linked in global networks—powerfully chart the fraying of normative ideals of modern city life, which include a sense of openness, fluidity, and coexisting unassimilated differences. Caldeira provides a snapshot of the contours of the normative ideal:

Although there are various and sometimes contradictory accounts of modernity in Western cities, the modern experience of public life is widely held to include the primacy and openness of streets; free circulation; the impersonal and anonymous encounters of pedestrians; spontaneous public enjoyment and congregation in streets and squares; and the presence of people from different social backgrounds strolling and gazing at others, looking at store windows, shopping, sitting in cafes, joining political demonstrations, appropriating the streets for their festivals and celebrations, and using spaces especially designed for the entertainment of the masses (promenades, parks, stadiums, exhibition spaces).[13]

In contrast to this modern ideal, Latin American cities like Rio, megacities like São Paulo, and smaller cities throughout the world display an *aesthetic of security*, in which fortresses, barriers, walls, surveillance cameras, dogs, barbed wire, coded keypads, armored cars, and machine guns enforce social differentiation and grant prestige. This aesthetic recognizes the possibility of permeability (let's call that an index of the modern city), and armors itself precisely against it. The wall creates a zone of relative safety that peremptorily denies social integration. Public spaces harbor threat. To walk is to challenge the hegemony of the elite. Spaces calibrate effect in new rhythms; the wall cannot extend everywhere, and so anxiety and fear become dispersed. According to Jabor with respect to Rio, "Dark strollers in sandals and shorts fill the streets of the Zona Sul. They intuit the fear of the 'middle classes' and promenade with pride. White cariocas become indignant, as if only they were the true native city dwellers."[14] These, and I wish to emphasize this point, are not cities that legislate inclusion on the model of distributive justice; by the 1990s, the normative ideal of city life proposed, for example, by Iris Marion Young (in her important essay "City Life and Difference") of a "being together with strangers" seemed out of reach for many of the world's largest cities.[15] Violence and poverty create new cartographies of (at least) the global city, traced in films of the past decades that stress the movements of and constraints upon *young people*: workers, hustlers, prisoners, addicts, street dwellers, lovers, artists, musicians. And they have moved to television and back to film. Whether redemptive, despairing, or critical, these visual mappings foreground the violence of social differentiation and explore obstacles to meaningful forms of social life, if not to life, i.e., adulthood itself.

In these favela films, three structuring features dominate:

1 **Architecture as *mise-en-scène*.** These films plot the architecture peculiar to the favelas, which were built to house displaced populations. Rising from the edges of much more prosperous neighborhoods, the favelas are informal networks of self-construction, homes cobbled together irregularly and with poor-quality materials. Many lack streets and are instead laced together by steps and alleys. They involve steep inclines and difficult-to-access zones of living. The favela films frequently inter-

est themselves in the movements of outsiders through these unfamiliar or alienating geographies or, conversely, demonstrate how the residents/communities are adept at navigating these territories. Cultural anthropologist Caldeira identifies new patterns of segregation associated with these "cities of walls" and understands the architectures emerging in cities like São Paulo as producing new forms of citizenship within these divided cartographies.[16] Tense with drama, the architecture invites an investigating and mobile camera, keen to reveal its interior logic and its social geographies.

2 **Control.** Due to the impotency of Brazilian state power in relation to forces of privatization and enclosure, many of the favelas are under the control of drug lords or traffickers, immune from the police, who cannot penetrate their complicated geography. Heavily armed young men exert force and regulate social relations, establishing a culture of violence that is seemingly inescapable. Many of the films thematize the encounter between uncontrolled petty violence and the incompetency or inefficacy of the police, tracing cycles of violence and retribution that suggest no alternatives to vigilantism and arbitrary forms of control. In recent films such as *Elite Squad* (Jose Padilha, 2007), the violence is extremely graphic in the style of video-game "first-person shooter" assaults on human targets who move through the favelas as though through a computer-generated maze. Even when less graphic, the films focus on violence as a momentary eruption of force, an everyday occurrence, and a fact of life more than an interruption of a noncoercive and peaceful polity.

3 **Music.** Finally, in the favela films, music serves as a means for expression of the will for change and as a vehicle for social mobility, a way out. In Jeff Zimbalist's film, *Favela Rising* (2005), nongovernmental organizations (NGOs) provide instruction in the music of Afro-Reggae to the young inhabitants of the Vigário Geral favela, where a notorious massacre of young people by the police took place in 1993, creating an alternative to the life of the drug traffickers and, most important perhaps, creating for Brazil's underclass a community that functions and persists in the face of tremendous odds against survival. Not surprisingly, many of the lyrics of the rap and hip hop songs emerging from this combination of culture and music dwell on issues of life and death, survival and struggle. While *Favela Rising* is shown primarily to audiences outside of Brazil, several projects,

such as those led by anthropologist Esther Hamburger, invite favela residents, mostly young people, to cast a critical eye on images of them circulated through the media, and they are making media themselves to speak back to these exported images.[17]

## Antônia

Fernando Meirelles, director of *City of God*, has spawned a veritable franchise. With a number of colleagues, he adapted *City of God* for the small screen: the television series, *City of Men*, loosely followed the narratives of two boys from the movie as they grew into young men tempted by the lives of the drug lords. That television series, in turn, was made into a feature film of the same title, a demonstration of how the synergy between television and film production by the entity Rede Globo functions as intermedia, here as brands that cut across NGOs, media markets, CDs, and internet activity. A product also of Globo Filmes, *Antônia* benefited from production funds of the International Film Festival in Rotterdam and traveled the festival circuit in Europe before being released on DVD. I bought my copy at the North American drugstore chain called Rite Aid.

Let me begin with a quick synopsis, then analyze a song (to which I'll only gesture, due to copyright laws about citation). The film follows four young women from the Brasilandia neighborhood of São Paulo, a low-income neighborhood with many features in common with the favelas of Rio de Janeiro. Together, they call their singing group Antônia, their name for their band but also a way of naming "one woman's story" through four exemplary women named Preta, Barbarah, Lena, and Mayah. Members of the underclass, each woman faces obstacles to survival and well-being beyond those of poverty and race, whether in the form of abusive boyfriends, children to care for where resources may be lacking, patterns of familial failure, or local instances of violence. The film ultimately focuses on Barbarah, whose brother Duda and brother's boyfriend Jose are attacked, badly injuring Duda and killing Jose. While Barbarah, Lena, and Mayah eventually leave the group, they all for some period of time persist with Antônia, finding a manager, Marcelo, and eventually gaining some exposure outside of their neighborhood performing for increasingly white and wealthy audiences.

Appearing in the title sequence over a steep street's ascent that permits a glimpse into the densely packed neighborhood that surrounds them, the women move quickly from a neighborhood performance (about which more in a moment) to a gig for white, wealthy partiers at which they perform the song "Killing Me Softly." This performance is a key scene that signifies their unity and their possibility: they figure, in that unity, a sense of national possibility. Because the song is begun by the white host of the party and dedicated to his sweetie, the sound editing bridges his strained and warbling version of the song with the members of the group improvising their English-language feigning of the lyrics. What they do well is harmony; it is never clear, however, how they understand the English-language lyrics, begging a question about the role of pure sound or, better, harmonious sound as itself an image of sociality.

This performance is a complicated and uneasy scene, complicated as much for the layers of what it stages as for the affect it solicits. Let me unpack the layers. First, it distinguishes in social position between the members of Antônia and the audience for whom they perform: the white "playboy" (a generalized and pejorative term for the privileged class to which the bridegroom belongs) is singled out and ridiculed for his poor voice, but we see others partying and circulating in the background of the image. While we know from the relentless visual and narrative work the film does to locate the women in their neighborhood that stresses that they belong to a different world, the film also stages the risks of their consumption as spectacle and as exotic by their privileged counterparts, a risk obviously also taken by the film we are watching. They might be heard simply as background, a bland and depoliticized harmony that contrasts sharply with the image and sound they presented earlier in their signature song for the neighborhood (Brasilandia) performance.

Second, as we see at the end of the performance when he joins Antônia on stage, the manager Marcelo has clearly taken charge of the group, promoting them to the audience and steering their course based upon his perception of their talents and potential directions. This is not an indictment of the narrative as sexist—in that a male manager controls the group's fortunes and profits himself from their talent, although we could certainly raise our suspicions about how frequently this is the case for female performers. Neither is it to allege that there is some unmediated and free zone of exchange where women control their bodies and talents and sell them more "appropriately" or autonomously to the elite. What is most important about Marcelo's presence in controlling this performance is that it subtly points our attention to the situation described by the *lyrics* of the song, in which a doubling of intent and effect make it impossible to discern female and male agency. Another way to put it is that the lyrics raise questions about effect and property/propriety that this scene wishes to stage, again doubling the reflexive work of the film as a whole.

"Killing Me Softly"—which is very well known in the United States through a recording by Roberta Flack and has been covered by many performers in the United States, Europe, and abroad—was apparently inspired by the feelings of a young woman upon hearing a performance by folk-rock singer Don McLean, best known for a long verse song called "American Pie." Registering the way in which another's performance can seem to reveal the very truth of one's self, in which the listener and performer seem to merge, the lyrics traverse a number of emotions such an experience can provoke. Beginning with the anticipation of a promising performance ("I heard he sang a good song, I heard he had a style"), the chorus moves quickly to the depths he accesses in the woman's/narrator's experience, where he strums her pain and kills her softly.

The complexity, if not hyperbole, of this phrase—killing me softly—gets suspended in the next verse in favor of shame. Becoming flush ("I felt all flush with fever") is a hallmark of shame, which moves through contagion, from one person to another without regard for bodily or psychical boundaries. Even though the singer is the object of the crowd's attention, the listener/narrator now feels embarrassed and somehow discovered in the depth of her emotions and in the secrets contained in the letters she feels as though he is exposing. In the penultimate verse (one not performed in this version by Antônia), the listener/narrator wills the singer actually to stop and feels she has lost the capacity for that intersubjective recognition she has fantasized from the beginning. Finally, in what functions as the last verse, the singer and/or narrator fuse voices into nonlinguistic expression, through oohs and las that belong to neither or to both and follow the melody of the verse into the chorus. In the folds of these sounds, neither Portugese nor English reigns: the performance offers the multilingual and nonlingual compromise of global culture, in which we respond to something like distilled harmony, while it also raises questions about whether it's ever possible to fuse in this way beyond one's own locatedness. In short, it's a *very* careful reminder that we, and I mean we white North American folks, are watching.

I probably don't need to point out the sexuality of this unfolding scene, nor how the phrase "killing me softly" references those little deaths that are at the heart of the sexual act. Without discarding or discounting the coding of all of this intersubjective and fantasmatic exchange as sexual and fore-closing thereby a reading through them, it is also possible to read it as an allegory of audio-visual expression offered by this film in a context in which it is the state which is "killing us softly."

In this film, the formal device of the "girl group" that is Antônia already makes a unity of a plurality of women's experiences. In the press surrounding the film and in the documentation of the film's making, the director, Tata Amaral, emphasizes how her process was that of a "semi-documentarian." She recruited actual singers from the favelas or low-income neighborhoods of São Paulo such as Brasilandia, and she asked *them* to invent and name their characters. Some of these names signify in Brazilian Portugese: for example, Preta is also the name for a racial category slightly darker than a mulatta.[18] Mayah in turn invokes the pre-Columbian civilization and hence the presence of indigenous peoples in Brazil. In these senses, even the names invoke social categories. Amaral's script was an open one, in which the actors improvised the vast majority of the dialogue, and the women wrote and developed their own original musical numbers for the film, with the notable exception of "Killing Me Softly."

Others on the production team emphasize the documentary aspects of the process of filmmaking. In shooting on location in Brasilandia, connecting with the neighborhood in which the fictional narrative unfolds, the sound recordists and designers faced extremely noisy conditions and used a great deal of ambient sound as a result, giving the film the acoustic texture of the streets. Likewise, the camera was always handheld, allowing the camera operator to locate his actors within social frames and allowing him to use cinema verite style framing, especially in scenes involving dialogue, where the cameraman, much as noted *verité* documentarian Albert Maysles did, re-frames responses to reveal their emotional truth. Sometimes the makers capitalized on surprises: in the title shot, a train unexpectedly rolled into the subway station in which they were filming and stopped exactly midframe, providing the perfect geometric surface for the film's title; unobtrusive and careful lighting allowed filmmakers to capture these surprises, as well as to create fluid interior-to-exterior movements using mostly natural light.

All of these elements of the production process lend force to the argument that the film's realist aesthetic is driven by the desire to communicate collectivity, or the experiences of many; that is, the experiences of many women like the women we see on the screen, the experiences of many of the residents of poor neighborhoods such as those we see on the screen, and the experiences of many urban Brazilians such as we see on the screen. It also seeks to communicate the sounds of many musical traditions and movements. Preta's family in the film is an evangelical Christian one, and we witness her mother leading a gospel session in the living room of their home. Preta's father, we learn, has been a failed samba performer, referencing a key musical movement that maintains a powerful presence in Brazilian cities. In opening with DJs and hip hop performance, the film gestures to the African American musical and stylistic influence on Afro-Brazilian music and Afro-Reggae more recently. And the group Antônia covers a range of styles in its own performance, from "rap" (an acronym, we should remember, for "rhythm and poetry") to hip hop to folk.

Antônia is thus a film as a collective product and the name of one woman simultaneously functioning as the name for four women who in turn signify many women. How does the film imagine the connections between its audiovisual textures, surfaces, and its audience, between its vision of individual transformation and social change? Through the very same mechanisms the song references and stages in its performance in Antônia: that is, through structures of anticipation, through the rubric of shame, through the contagion of affect (including the affect of music), through the translation of specificity into pure sound, and through the fusion of voices (genders, social positions, races) into harmonious unity.

As I suggested, anticipation is key to an image of social mobility. In the scene that precedes the first appearance of the group, all of the women are giddy with the prospect finally of taking center stage, having served in the capacity of backup singers for the male DJs in the opening performance (and, the narrative tells us, for three long years). An overdetermined interface between popular culture—a shared sense of female hip hop, a "common sense" of what that image and sound entails—and the particularities of these women's lives appears. Manifested in clothing (taken from the actors' own wardrobes), vocal performance, and self-stylization, a set of possibilities unfolds for what these women might become as artists and as commodities on an urban market. "Style," in the lyrics of "Killing Me Softly," should, in other words, not be underestimated as an enunciation of becoming; as the women develop a style, one that is marketable by Marcelo, they travel a vector of social mobility that remains potential even if it is narratively unfulfilled for the bulk of the film's duration. (I will give away the last scene: a moving reunion of the group in its flashiest and catchiest performance.)

This vision of potentiality is tainted, however, by shared experiences of violence, victimhood, and social stigmatization. In *Antônia*, the narrative figure for such stigmatization is the revelation that Duda, Barbarah's brother, is gay. The revelation comes after he and his boyfriend are brutally, fatally, attacked. Unusual for the favela film is any focus whatsoever on women's complex lives; almost unheard of is any positive and almost unremarked instance of a character's homosexuality. (A fuller account would here chart the nuances of a history of sexuality in that country that involves codes of display and spectacle that exceed rigid and reductive Western binaries of straight and gay.)[19] A previously helpful neighbor, for example, refuses to help Duda mount the forbidding concrete steps to his home, afraid that he will be stigmatized for associating with a gay man who did not actively reveal his sexuality. But this specific stigmatization spills beyond the bounds of identity into a more generalized sense that these people live imperiled lives: that the omnipresence of violence that threatens to render them mute, impotent, and scared becomes a facet of everyday social life that, like shame, spreads like a contagion throughout poor neighborhoods in Brazil's cities and beyond, into the abject lifeworlds of the North-East and the interior. By no means a new trope, that the poor are flooded with feelings of shame and inadequacy, here these feelings are met with a defiant assertion of survival, voice, and longing for change that comes in the music itself. I want to be clear that I am not suggesting that queerness overwhelms and overcodes persistent survival, but I am noticing how rarely and, yes, how arrestingly queerness overlaps figures of such vocal emergence.

Thus the thesis, posed in the lyrics to "Killing Me Softly" but really staged in both the song's performance and in the film *Antônia* as a whole, that sounds and images, rhythms and poetry, harmony and glances, have an affective force and can produce change. In a story Preta tells to her daughter Emilia at the end of the film, she condenses the point neatly: "Once upon a time, a beautiful girl walked along the street. Her name was . . . Antônia. Antônia loved to sing. Her singing transformed things. She sang and everything changed. The bad things turned to good things." We could, as Emilia does, enumerate the good and bad, wishing that the rains didn't destroy peoples' houses, for example. And it's true that *Antônia* the film is, as the characters say when they reunite at the prison (where Barbarah is incarcerated for killing the boy who attacked her brother and his lover), "a song about the things we want to change," some of which seem out of reach, naïve, utopian, or resistant to the usual political glosses. But "a song that tells our story" is also a song that can feed the local into something broader, just as the final verse of "Killing Me Softly" makes "ooh" and "la" into just as helpful a nonnational grammar of intersubjective exchange as its previous verses.

It is finally this sense of collective voice as *potentia* that leads me to introduce that which it sings against: a state pushed to the point of dissolution, itself impotent in the face of crime and violence and unable to corral its institutions into effective instruments of survival. Within the civil society, a generalized disregard that easily translates into a wish for genocide permeates the social fabric. I quote at some length from an ethnography of street children:

> *Avoidance* is better understood if we don't think of it as a quality exclusive to beasts, typecast criminals, or potbellied soldiers with a thirst for blood and destruction. "Killing those dirty little things" might be suggested by the upright doctor who offers free, humanitarian care, a man flanked by his children and grandchildren. Just as easily, it might be suggested by the university anthropologist who, after a brief period in the field with the kids, is pontificating, searching for a way to translate into sanitary, intellectual argot the mentality that he, as a resident of Rio, shares with the vigilante, exterminators, soldiers, members of organized crime syndicates, and frivolous housewives. "They don't want citizenship; they want to take over the city."[20]

"Avoidance" might be another name for "killing softly" in a literal sense, that is, another name for what Giorgio Agamben would call naked or bare life: a product of the biopolitical fracture between "naked life" and "a People" upon which he has written so eloquently. "[T]he capitalist-democratic plan to eliminate the poor," he observes, "not only reproduces inside itself the people of the excluded but also turns all the populations of the Third World into naked life."[21] "Naked life" is here a figure for that "people" that capitalist modernity has created within itself but that it can no longer tolerate. Figured as threat, as contagion, as extrapolitical, and as an "intolerable shadow," "naked life" is not only produced through paranoia and psychosis but through the everyday narratives of those who appear to be the very scaffold of civilized modernity. This productive process is a form of "killing softly," to which cinema responds with a cry that is at times inchoate, but it can be seen to be straining the vocal registers and image repertoires, directed toward survival. Here I would make my final point that this film *harmonizes*: it does not reduce difference into equivalence or make sameness a requirement for simultaneous expression or exaltation. Harmony is not a product but a process: it is not a bland synthesis but a constant movement of the creation and destruction of tension. Without seizing too quickly on a trope for the politics of Brazilian cinema today, this one will do. For now.

# 8

# THE MAN, THE CORPSE, AND THE ICON IN *MOTORCYCLE DIARIES*

## UTOPIA, PLEASURE, AND A NEW REVOLUTIONARY IMAGINATION

CRISTINA VENEGAS

*And if there is any hope for America, it lies in a Revolution, and if there is any hope for a Revolution in America, it lies in getting Elvis Presley to become Che Guevara.*

—Phil Ochs

An eyewitness reported that upon facing his executioner in the little schoolhouse in the Bolivian highlands, 39-year-old Ernesto "Che" Guevara said, "Shoot, coward. You're only going to kill a man."[1] After he and his comrades were executed, Guevara's body was flown to the nearby town of Vallegrande, laid out Christ-like on a deathbed in an austere laundry-room with half-opened eyes. The eerie image of his death was captured in photographs and on film. Newspapers reported that communist Revolutionary pursuits in Bolivia had come to an end. The date was October 9, 1967.

If his contribution to the Cuban Revolution had not already immortalized him, the events following Che Guevara's death secured his mythical status in the pantheon of revolutionary heroes. A symbol of ideological resolve, tenacity, and moral conviction, the revolutionary's body, now a corpse, became invested with immense political meaning both by those who venerated him and those who scorned him. His hands were severed in order to make a definitive identification, his face disfigured in a crude attempt to make a death mask, and the corpse, arms tied behind the back, was tossed into an unmarked grave by the Bolivian military. For Vallegrande, where these events took place, the dead Che literally became a Christ symbol and a lay saint. Buried in anonymity, his enduring presence became legendary in the Bolivian mountains. Popular culture referred to *la maldición del Che*, the Che curse, a narrative that reiterated mythic post mortem events, telling of mysterious tragedies suffered by many of the people associated with his capture and execution. It is a fact that most of those involved died within the next decade.

The novelistic account of the deaths is woven into the mythology of Che, confirming the great loss of the Argentine guerrilla hero to Latin America, and to the ideology of the Left. It is a formidable narrative of revolution, inflated with heroism and idealism. The real story adds ridiculous irony to the sublime fiction. The severed hands and death mask were hidden away by a Bolivian general who admired Guevara's ideals. The CIA pursued the general until he left Bolivia to live in Cuba. Before leaving, he gave the hands—in a jar filled with formaldehyde—to a Bolivian journalist who in turn kept them hidden under his house until he was able to return them to Che's family. Thirty years later, in 1997, Guevara's remains were found buried near an airstrip in Vallegrande, and returned to his family in Cuba, where he received a state funeral in the province of Santa Clara, site of a then newly built museum and mausoleum.[2] Amid celebrations to commemorate his memory, Fidel Castro symbolically declared that Che was, "fighting and winning more battles than ever."[3] Whether brought to life by mourning, filmmaking, or commerce, the complexity of Che Guevara's "resurrection" is worthy of examination as a factor in postmodern consumerism, in which politics have become a matter of style in search of substance.

### Traveling Revolutionary Texts

The chronicle of Guevara's death and his iconic status are no secret. These topics have filled the pages of at least eight books, and fueled several feature films and documentaries. Yet an evolving significance of the life and legend lies outside these media, in various strands woven around the representation of Guevara. This is seen particularly in the renewed circulation of his image and ideas surrounding the worldwide release of Walter Salles's film *Diarios de motocicleta* (*Motorcycle Diaries*, 2004). In the film, the character of Ernesto Guevara evolves in the adventure of travel.

His nascent consciousness discovers the "other" Latin America, and the gulf between disadvantaged people and the ruling system of power. Observing

Gael García Bernal in *Motorcycle Diaries* (2004).
Universal Pictures.

first the plenitude of the land and its people, Ernesto focuses on commonalities woven together, and on geography, forging new ideas about political identity. The people he encounters are marked by the violence of colonialism, authoritarian political projects, and imperialist economic adventures. There is a moral bias to his political cause that illuminates and ignites political movement. Ernesto finds power in the experience of being on the road, in knowing Latin American society and culture more deeply.

Continuously appropriated in postmodern culture, the visual representations and concepts of Che "travel" (in the fashion described by Edward Said), as new revolutionary texts conflate with previous ones. The film serves as an example of the resultant merging of the represented—Guevara—with the on-screen representative—Gael García Bernal. Both become "revolutionary" icons used by marketing and publicity machines, and by Bernal himself. The conflation conjures up a new set of political connotations for Latin American film, politics, and the historical relationship between the two. The body of Che Guevara, already invested with politics, creates a media body politic. Precedents for this process lie for example in the figures of Ghandi, the Indian bandit-turned politician Phoolan Devi, and Christ. *Diarios* brings forward the internationalist impulse of Che Guevara's time. At work here is a process of re-articulation through iconicity combined with stardom. This occurs in the realm of new global, rather than ideological, identities, and is sustained by more basic utopian impulses founded on the pleasure produced by the contradiction of Guevara's image used as pop icon.

The journey of the revolutionary texts of Ernesto "Che" Guevara and the narrative of the Cuban revolution find substance in *Diarios*—and later in Steven Soderbergh's *Che: The Argentine* (2009)—beginning with political rhetoric in the mountains of Cuba and moving through time and space to find expression today as a Che street performer donning pink silk military fatigues in Barcelona.

They form part of a constellation of political projects in Latin America that are linked intertextually and historically. Together with Latin America's other revolutionary struggles, from Mexico to Patagonia, they have become a set of powerful symbolic references, constantly deployed to define the region.

Writing about Central America, Román de la Campa argues persuasively that personal and war diaries, *testimonios* and novels, themselves beget revolutionary and insurrectional events linked in an endless self-referential revolutionary narrative.[4] His postmodernist summary proposes an intricate web of personalities and texts that brings together Che Guevara and, among others: Emiliano Zapata, hero of the Mexican revolution; Alberto Bayo Giroud, a veteran of the Spanish Civil War; Augusto César Sandino, Nicaragua's anti-U.S. revolutionary leader in the early twentieth century; Fidel Castro, Cuba's revolutionary leader; Farabundo Martí, a revolutionary leader in El Salvador; and the members of the Ejército Zapatista de Liberación Nacional (EZLN) in Chiapas, Mexico. For de la Campa, both the act of revolution and the description, in different genres, have a political outcome. In this way, action and its narrative come together as the temporalities of writing and being, both containing expressive possibilities of the future. The texts reference social projects still unfinished, a just society of new individuals, in a particular form of utopian thinking. The writing continually points toward a future, giving force to the idea of potential and becoming.

Che Guevara (and the others mentioned above) left not only diaries, but also letters, producing an archival and material presence, which has become the subject of multiple new expressions. Most enduring is the commercial appropriation as markets redefine the icon's ideological weight by its reproduction. This was seen, for instance, when in 1968 publishers and politicians haggled over the international rights to Guevara's Bolivian diary, which

———————————————— Street performer in Barcelona. ————————————————
Photo courtesy of Roman Baratiak.

documents the experiences of his final insurrectional campaign (and which was confiscated by the military when he was captured). However, the book's ideological weight trumped any financial deal. At issue was establishing (and maintaining) the authenticity of the manuscript, which "in the wrong hands" (those of the CIA, for example) could become a tool to undermine Cuba's

Revolution further. Publishing the Bolivian Diary first in Cuba and immediately thereafter in Chile, France, Spain, Mexico and Italy, and distributing thousands of free copies before its officially sanctioned publication by Bolivia, Fidel Castro's government showed its historical and political importance alongside its market value.[5] Sidestepping trade norms in this way, Cuba controlled the diary's content and preempted what it saw as crass commercialization that characterizes the conversion of revolutionary texts into marketable commodities.

The endless linking of revolutionary texts that de la Campa investigates leads to another way of thinking about the path ideas take as they travel from one historical moment to the next. For Said, dissonance is created by the distance and manner taken by an idea as it travels from its moment of conception where, with revolutionary narratives, the insurrectional force is located, to its many iterations and appropriations.[6] Cuba's consistent counter-role illustrates an alternative path taken by revolutionary texts across eras: in the case of Cuba and Che Guevara, the texts retain much of their original political character, the signifier still points to the signified. It has traveled some distance from its inception, but far less than Guevara's image on an Absolut vodka billboard or a bright pink "Che" cell phone sleeve. The distance covered by the time of the evolution of Che Guevara into Salles' Ernesto in *Diarios* falls somewhere between the result of the appropriation by Cuba and the product of adoption by the market. The film and its texts serve then as an example of a new type of audio-visual landscape that overlay political and commercial territories. Such appropriation by media compared to commercial and political appropriation of revolutionary texts invites exploration of the mechanisms and consequences in play in order to discover their potential and their impact.

The mass circulation of the images produced by *Diarios* and the stardom of García Bernal reveals in particular the place of utopia in today's revolutionary imagination. Again, the deployment here needs to be considered in contrast to that of the Cuban state, which reflects a more ideological and social manipulation toward ideals where politics tries to evade markets even as commercial issues wield obvious influence. The Cuban government used Guevara's burial in 1997 to revive the ideals of the failing Cuban Revolution. Reeling from catastrophic economic chaos after the end of the Soviet socialist bloc, the state promulgated the notion of a resolute and invincible revolutionary project, encapsulated in the slogan "*socialismo o muerte*," even if it was harder to deny the incongruity of the utopian project with the chaotic reality and the exhaustion of the masculine image of the revolution. During the state funeral, Cubans bid farewell to Che Guevara, replenishing the political and cultural value of his image while they did so. But the Cuba of 1997, when Guevara's remains arrived in Santa Clara, would have, as the saying goes, made the revolutionary turn in his grave.

The economic downfall of the 1990s tested the extent to which the people of Cuba could endure personal sacrifice as tourism defined the new economy. The symbolic return to Cuba of the *heroic guerrilla's* "body" coincided with the increasing value of other Cuban bodies—those sold in prostitution, as the body was the only thing left to sell for profit. It was Che *cum* Lazarus helping to resurrect the Cuban cause, even if temporarily. Alive or dead, these revolutionary bodies gained in political and market value. Guevara's persona, which had never waned in the Cuban cultural sphere, and the historical convergence of his burial in Cuba in the midst of Cuba's greater integration into a world economy, figured as a powerful cultural icon calling back from oblivion ideas of resistance. His appeal was not only emotional but also moral, and defiant even beyond a presumed grave.

As in Vallegrande, Bolivia, Guevara's myth in Cuba was again associated with Christ but this time through an official Cuban government lens rather than motivated by popular imagination. During Pope John Paul II's visit to the island in 1998, the first papal visit to Cuba in more than forty years, the Che/Christ parallel was in full graphic display: a gigantic image of Jesus Christ was placed next to Enrique Avila's 1993 monumental sculpture of Che in Havana's Plaza of the Revolution, where a million people gathered to hear the Supreme Pontiff. Religious faith and faith in revolution were linked through enduring yet seemingly incongruous icons. The concurrence of these two images at a time of political uncertainty had a twofold value: it allowed the Cuban state to take advantage of the event's ubiquitous media coverage to present a mediated image of tolerance and socialism, and to realign the symbolism of Che with resilience. The return of Che's "body" in 1997, the Pontiff's visit in 1998, and the state's consistent reliance on revolutionary rhetoric— and its reverberation throughout the hemisphere by Venezuelan president Hugo Chavez and Bolivian president Evo Morales—show a persistence in Latin America of well-traveled revolutionary ideas.

The conflation between Christ and Guevara in the juxtaposition of their images by the Cuban state has a far greater parallel in the commercial realm.

The transformation of revolutionary texts and therefore political force by media into instruments of capital also produces conflation. In *Diarios*, the dead body of Guevara joins with the live body of Gael García Bernal. The fusion of the *guerrillero* and the star brings together insurrection and historical reconstruction as a weak form of politics in global film culture. Guevara propagated the grand, if now questionable, idea of Latin America as a force for pan-American unity as hailed by earlier liberators such as Simón Bolivar or José Martí. This idea now circulates globally alongside a grandiose revolutionary imagination associated with the geopolitical "South" of heroes and revolutions, uprisings and victories. Rather than politics rooted in the socialist ideals of solidarity and equality, this conflation promotes a consumerist utopia and associated pleasures. The commercialization and media content set in motion by *Diarios* demonstrates, then, a combination of original events, their mythic evolution, and the cultures of celebrity and consumerism. The result has the appearance of a political force, since real revolutionary power has derived from the ingredients both of historical reality and of its legends. The additional layer of consumerism, however, may drive those it captures only to the utopia it invents, a palliative distraction from the usual darker political forces that wield real power in Latin America and internationally. The overlaying of the real revolutionary character and events with the actor and filmic narrative appears to create a global cultural force with a power borrowed from the revolutionary concepts that it adopts, but a power that diverts from its real revolutionary origins. The surface representation of and around *Diarios* substitutes for the substance it represents.

### Celluloid Che and Consumer Culture

If Che's death in 1967 had signaled the end of a postulation of utopian projects worldwide, the return of his remains to Cuba meant the guerrillero was really dead, and utopias in the waning twentieth century therefore seemingly even more impossible to conceive. In La Higuera, the hamlet where Che was captured, authorities were determined to erase the material traces of his existence. In subsequent years, every attempt by the town's people to erect a commemorative bust of the revolutionary met with repression. For the town, the material tribute to past ideals embodied the significance of being linked to the broader project of Latin American resistance. Eventually, the military stopped destroying the memorial, and the bust of Che was allowed to stand. Did this moment of death, return, and rebirth also constitute the hero as a

consumable icon rather than a revolutionary threat? Probably so, since
Ernesto Guevara's political consciousness and solidarity were influenced by
crucial events and thinkers of his time, including: the Bolivian revolution of
1952, which granted suffrage to indigenous people; the CIA-backed overthrow
of Guatemalan president Jacobo Arbenz in 1954; the Algerian War of Indepen-
dence (1954–62); and the extremes of the cold war represented in the nuclear
stand-off of the October Missile Crisis in Cuba (1962). The final burial took
place in a decidedly different, post–cold war world where Guevara's ideas, his
presence, and above all the consumption of his image no longer signified a
threat to imperial or capitalist projects.

It is precisely the concern that the power of the sign has diminished, that
Guevara's image has been tamed, which led veteran Argentine filmmaker
Fernando Birri to take up the topic in his documentary *Che: muerte de la
utopia? (Che: Death of Utopia?* 1997). In the film, Birri weaves together his own
poetry and political views while questioning the possible continuing existence of utopia as a social and philosophical construct as well as a possible
site of resistance and hope of liberation. Using the "man on the street" interview strategy, Birri talks to a variety of people in disparate locations: young
tourists entering a Michael Jackson concert in Germany, and at the Berlin
Wall; visitors to the EuroDisney park outside Paris; dancers at the Tropicana
Club in Cuba; Bolivian peasants; university students in Havana; citizens of
Buenos Aires; Latin American and European intellectuals. Of them, Birri asks
two questions: "Who was Che Guevara? What is utopia?" The responses vary,
revealing a range of emotions and cultural knowledge, some surprisingly
penetrating. In the eyes of one, Guevara "was a normal person who modeled
the idea that in Cuba is known as the New Man"; for another, "an idol, a star
in Latin America"; "a trouble-maker, so he [was] never appealing"; "a great
idealist and romantic hero." To a young Argentine student, utopia "is defined
by its own failure; failures that didn't consider human costs." To a tourist at
the Berlin Wall, utopia was "Money, happiness, tolerance, better distribution
of material wealth; only thinking about today."

*Che: muerte de la utopia* thus attempts to disengage Guevara's moribund
political project from the temporal dislocation that diminishes its impact.
Birri's highly nostalgic salvage operation is not to answer, but to retrieve, the
traces of ideas that might once again flourish in the circularity of time. The
film grapples with the reality of radical politics that haven't fared well over
time while still proposing the necessity for utopian thinking in the context of

a world still in need. In doing so, Birri sets loose the idea of Che from the constraints stemming from his relationship to an earlier era, reinvigorating a broader and more important space for considering the future, for asserting the force that lies behind the face on the t-shirts.

*Diarios de motocicleta* portrays Guevara's ideas as influenced by Marxism, the Peruvian political philosopher José Carlos Mariátegui, and the Chilean writer Pablo Neruda; these influences are clear from Che's diaries and speeches. Yet, the actual leftist perspective developed by Guevara would go on to gain credibility and force by being rooted in Latin American political thought, and the consideration of the foreign ideological project of the Soviet Union as a strategic counterbalance to North American power. The film dwells on a simpler, less intellectual phase of political development, meeting audiences largely unengaged with politics, and presenting an individualistic, pre-political agent of hope and change.

The historical contours of the landscape lose some of their harshness as Salles frames and softens Ernesto's political formation with the lushness and beauty of the extreme topography. International mining interests drive people from their lands in the Chilean Atacama Desert, arid and unforgiving, but nevertheless captivating; the presentation of the architectural complexity of Machu Pichu matches the original diarist's appreciation of the site as a product of sophisticated ancient indigenous knowledge and culture; however, it also becomes an invented grand setting for the Guevara of *Diarios* to first articulate the possibility of armed struggle. The pan-American worldview emphasized by the Latin American Left after the Cuban revolution proposes hemispheric and cultural unity as a political strategy against the imperialism of the North and Europe. The film invokes this encompassing view with Ernesto's journey across countries but imbues its latent political influence with the romanticism of almost any dramatized road trip. And, again, where *Diarios* captures the life-changing impact on Guevara of the leper colony in San Pablo, it also travels far from the politicization seen in the original diaries. The real Guevara's political awakening and understanding of the inequities between North and South America find workable narrative symbolization in the colony, where the worst leprosy cases are marginalized on the south bank of the river, while the hospital is found on the north bank. As articulated by Leftist intellectuals, isolation and solitude, notable attributes of the two leper communities, are hallmarks of colonizing projects; the colony also exhibits a kind of cultural awareness that is marked as a quality of strength in the revolutionary ideas that galvanized an entire hemisphere throughout most of the twentieth century. The symbolization, though, reaches beyond sympathetic emphasis and summary when it has Ernesto swim the river. His journey blatantly bridges North and South, turning political enterprise into the melodramatic incident of the heroic crossing. *Diarios* describes a political voyage fully embracing a dramatic convention that overshadows nuanced and idiosyncratic development. In the film itself, politics disappears into the conflation of revolutionary text with consumer culture.

In *Diarios*, however, the political aspects are far more complex. Produced, directed, made, and acted by a Latin American team, for the most part in Latin America, and about a truly Latin American figure, the film represents a political act. The self-awareness of its making reflects the socialist thinking of Guevara's time, in which Leftist influence from outside Latin America had to slot into local thought and experience; Guevara served as the embodiment of the local for South America. *Diarios* could be said to be the equivalent local symbol for Latin American film, or even media, given García Bernal's personal extension of the project through different vehicles and for a range of audiences across the globe. Part of what the production and García Bernal work on, consciously or unconsciously, is a sense of remembrance for the revolutionary era. Nostalgia acknowledges the passage of time, creating distance from the original object or experience, transforming the memory into a longing. Ernesto Guevara's "life-changing" journey is at a safe distance from its historical moment and insurrectional power. Or is it? Ironically, there are more democratic socialist governments in Latin America today than during Guevara's period of insurgency, adding political currency to the now not so insurrectional force of the emblematic image of the figure. Instead, the nostalgia of *Diarios* contributes to the cultural significance of Guevara throughout the world; a cultural significance that is a safe commodity (movies, t-shirts, caps, bikinis, posters, magnets, etc.), which the narrative constrains in the film as always *becoming* politicized. Such commercialization, nevertheless, does not dilute the achievement of the larger project of *Diarios* as a political act, an intentional appropriation on the part of a tiny media subset concerned with its own identity and community.

Latin American scholar Jean Franco has rightly posited the complexity of the political Left in Latin America, suggesting that, "communist parties and their sympathizers . . . cannot be easily fitted into the U.S. State Department's kit for profiling communists. For in addition to witnessing the indignity, not to mention the injustices, of U.S. interventions in the region, they were faced with constant abuses of power in their own countries, parodic elections, corruption and capital flight."[7] The communist party had exerted a significant influence over intellectuals and culture in general so that the emergence of Ernesto Guevara occurs within the context of the cold war and differing positions on Marxism, either old-school or reformist, that had been debated since the 1920s and 30s.

In a sense, *Motorcycle Diaries* answers one of Birri's questions: "Who was Che Guevara?" The answer comes in the form of an early biography of the man. It is an adaptation of parts of Guevara's and Alberto Granado's personal diaries of the same journey through South America between 1951 and 1952. The telling of this part of the life story focuses on transformation. It points to the prospect of a not-yet-revolutionary Che. It is about his awakening and answering a call to action. The film lures viewers through adventure and exploration, just as Guevara and Granado were seduced by the challenges of the road. Taking dramatic liberties, the biopic expands on small events, as seen, for example, in the exaggerated heroics of the night swim across the Amazon River. The wheezing sound of an asthmatic swimming against the strong river current is set in contrast to chanting from the leper colony residents waiting on the other side. Guevara becomes their hero in a type of aggrandizement that creates a virtuous character. The real-life energy is displaced onto Granado, who is far from perfect. Critics of Salles accuse him of "selling out" to Hollywood by creating a timid perspective of Guevara. Others oppose the glorification of an authoritarian "murderer." Latin American reviewers, on the other hand, hailed the film for depicting an important historical figure, and for drawing interest to this aspect of historical record through an elegant and successful film. What *Diarios* does is reenergize the icon by adding a backstory and a body. This makes it appear three-dimensional. As opposed to setting the icon free from the limitations still exercised by a previous time, Salles defines it with a conventional narrative bound to the physicality of García Bernal.

The icon has thus traveled from its original fixation in the guerrillero's body, which was perceived as a powerful threat to American interests in the region. The response by states to the insurrectional political project invested in the man was to go after the body, to secure its utter destruction. This is seen in the treatment of the hands, the mask, and the corpse. What has proven indestructible, however, is the myth. Guevara's martyrdom is

Street poster in Bogotá, Colombia.
Photo Cristina Venegas.

premised on the perception of Guevara as an indestructible instrument of discipline and moral certitude. The evocation of pleasure by the memory of a "good" Guevara in its connotations of strength, endurance, and ultimately immortality appears to underlie the sustained generation of Che texts from the point of burial to the ascendance of cinema's charmed revolutionary.

The resulting Che icon travels through different appropriations from a range of perspectives. Guevara's death as a physical and political reality sees the man, the corpse, and the icon defined by political accomplishments and failures.

Most of the resulting images and symbolization, however, derive not from achievements but from the dismembered corpse, the fetish of hands, the retrieval of bones, venerated images of the revolutionary's body, his final ragged semblance, and intense gaze. These corporeal elements are symbols of revolution in Latin America. The dismembered body signaled the metaphorical fracturing and weakening of the Left; a symbolic end to the armed struggle, which preceded the bitter disappointment of the Nicaraguan Revolution in 1979. Bodies circulate as images in the popular imagination, through the arts, the press, and fashion magazines to be appropriated in consumer culture. Guevara's image now circulates also as the image of García Bernal. His description of himself as "only a man" is a counterpoint to those who wanted to destroy him. Reducing his own stature to that of an ordinary man bridged the distance between his exceptional life and that of his followers. It bestowed heroic status on the common man, echoing one of the central themes in his ideas: the common man shall make the Revolution; he shall become a *new* man. The photograph of the corpse captures the striking expression of martyrdom and redemption exacerbated by the brutality of how the corpse was mutilated, hands and face, suggesting that in the hysteria of the execution there was greater fear for the dead than the living guerrillero. The struggle over the hands and death mask by the generals and their eventual return to Cuba by a sympathizer reiterates that bodies and images acquire different status when consumed as icons. Viewing the body as the repository of power was the utterly ignorant motivation behind the attempt to destroy it, as if this act could lead to the end of revolutionary ideas. In contrast, the reenactment by media is a conscious appropriation of the persistence of vision after the destruction of the body. This is where García Bernal's actions have potential as possible impetus for a new political force. Such potential derives from harnessing what persists, and magnifying its power with the additional ingredient of pleasure.

Embedded in celebrity culture, the literary document brings the famous person closer to its admiring public. Guevara's diaries and other texts describe the phases of development of his persona: the young man in South America, the guerillero in the Sierra Maestra of Cuba, and the seasoned revolutionary in Congo and Bolivia. The documents make the experience concrete, material, inspiring, associating the image with the subjectivity of the man, his biases, and aspirations. Guevara forges a personal example of strong leadership, a quality that resonates with multiple generations. Uruguayan writer Eduardo Galeano attributes Guevara's greatness to this quality: "he said what he thought, and did what he preached." Whichever means Guevara used to communicate his message he transgressed by collapsing the distance between a celebrity and their public, allowing his public an atypical but authentic and appealing closeness. Typically, shaped by a religious discipline based on a self-assigned moral obligation, those who followed Guevara felt a strong affinity for him. His egalitarian, straightforward morality became a principal enduring attribute of the man, and a trait strongly attached to the abstract desire to carry out a utopian project.

Guevara's political resolve not only brought him closer to the people, but also made his image synonymous with the idea of revolution. Major revolutionary concepts emerged from the mid-twentieth century socialist political project that encompassed an international field of struggles. Guevara's persona contributes to the rendering of the geopolitical "South" as a site of anti-imperialist and anti-colonial resistance, socialist triumph and failure, and capitalist and neoliberal exploitation. *Diarios* extrapolates these qualities both playfully and soberly. For instance, the "reel" Ernesto promises his girlfriend he will buy a bathing suit for her with the dollars she gave him. Instead, he gives the money to a poor Chilean couple in the Atacama Desert. This act anticipates Guevara's real focus on the idea of sacrifice of personal gain and desires as a building block for the construction of solidarity among people. Solidarity as a social project gained strength from Guevara's politicization of Latin American identity as part of a larger struggle; the film captures the spirit here, if not the struggle, at a key moment in *Diarios* when Ernesto pauses gracefully at an impromptu birthday celebration; in an improvised moment of gratitude, Ernesto makes a toast to the common mestizo heritage of Latin Americans from Mexico to the Straits of Magallanes and to the strength of its people. As he speaks, a reaction shot of Granado punctuates the scene with solemnity. The moment emboldens Ernesto, who moments later jumps into the currents of the Amazon to continue the birthday celebration on the other side of the river with the other leper patients. What drives him to the other side of the river is solidarity with the most marginalized patients. Upon his departure the following day, a long, slow, and warmly lit tracking shot of the goodbye feels more like a collective farewell to the corpse that is missing from the narrative. The film brings together proto-revolutionary concepts and the pre-revolutionary Che, only anticipating the person and personality that some, but not all, of the audience knows he will become. *Diarios*, then, reenacts the incipient dreams of a middle-class medical student moved and challenged to action by his own discovery of a cruel and incongruent world lying just beyond the confines of a comfortable life. This appropriation by media cloaks Ernesto's revolutionary appeal in the immature utopian vision of a romantic, individualistic adventure far from the puritanical imagining of regional political unity by the guerrillero of the original texts.

## Revolutionary Chic?

According to press interviews, the filmmakers of *Diarios* stated that their intention was to make a film about a young medical student, not about politics. This seems a valid and important choice and distinction. However, it constitutes almost a disavowal of the politics that characterize older Leftists struggles. The new revolutionary politics borrows from the symbols, not the revolutionary concepts, substituting for insurrectional charge. The new generation of Latin American filmmakers thus seizes opportunities to tell the stories of their own heroes, rather than their heroes' politics.

As a commodity, Guevara's image is appropriated to signal revolutionary, chic fashion instead of political perspective. García Bernal's image, too, is associated with style. His provocative and sensuous look is the perfect conduit for pared down and expensive hip design. Bernal's fashion spreads in magazines are usually accompanied by pithy essays about his emerging global presence, his politics, and his independent-minded spirit. One piece characterizes him as an actor-activist.[8] Converging in commerce, the two images sit uncomfortably with the underlying capitalist impulse that promotes them. While Bernal described *Déficit* (2007), his directorial debut, as a story about the inequities of social classes in Mexico, the high price tag of the clothes he modeled for *Angeleno* magazine spoke to an elite audience.[9] Most of all, the popular press appears to cast García Bernal as a different type of star not only due to his status among the most famous Latin stars of his time, but because he possesses a clear sense of self. He continually avoids Hollywood, its lifestyle, and work ethic, and this entices the media to enhance his currency as a rebel, an individual thinker.

What is to be made of Guevara's famous revolutionary face stenciled on a pair of jeans? Beyond the dissonance of Leftist political ideology being portrayed and marketed through fashion and gadgets, Guevara's and García Bernal's individual personas also converge in the role assigned by each to

Che jeans.
Photo Cristina Venegas.

Latin American culture. For Guevara, culture is political, a field for social change; for García Bernal it is personal beliefs, and home, a platform for individual achievement. Both advocate resistance to the status quo, however, thus appealing on both emotional and moral levels. Ernesto of *Diarios* and Bernal are both young men discovering the limits of their knowledge and experience. The viewer witnesses a handsome revolutionary subjectivity-in-the-making as the filmmakers offer pride in presence, position, and personal beliefs. In *Diarios*, these come wrapped in voyeuristic and affective pleasure as the viewer watches the hero encounter an astonishing landscape, its extremes of weather, altitude, and class privilege. The journey of Ernesto's political stance reaches only the invented climactic gesture of the river crossing. Politics are really not just missing in the film, they are submerged beneath heroic iconicity and the weight of consumption of García Bernal's celebrity around the picture and the actor's life.

*Diarios* secured García Bernal's position, box-office clout, and global appeal. The number of Bernal magazine covers and fashion spreads indicate a high celebrity quotient. With every new film, magazines capitalize on the appetites of fans for the viscerally cool image. Even while speaking about a new role in *Babel* (González Iñárritu, 2006), only a short distance from his portrayal of Che, the aura of Guevara continues to define García Bernal's public persona. He speaks of global human rights issues and the importance of working within his own country to bring about social change. This has won him an interesting cross-platform popularity. Emerging on the international scene in *Amores Perros* (González Iñárritu, 2000), he was immediately taken up and associated with renewal, bold attitude, and beauty; a beauty that appeals to both men and women as in Pedro Almodóvar's *La mala educación* (2004). His earlier role in *Y tu mamá también* (Cuarón, 2001) had also codified this actor with a fluid sexuality. His style is messy and individual; indeed, he appears as comfortable in a tux at the Cannes Film Festival as he does in an olive green army jacket. He has a hard masculine edge and a feminine softness. Interviews repeatedly establish his authenticity. As an actor, he states his interest in projects that relate to his sense of self and to socially relevant issues that articulate the actor as a point between the social and the personal. The fact that he only bears a slight youthful resemblance to the not-yet-Che of 1951 in *Diarios* or in the earlier *Fidel* (Atwood, 2002) appears not to be important because his presentation of himself as an artist evokes the type of discipline and conviction that resonate with the qualities of the real Che Guevara.

The power assigned to García Bernal's expressive eyes immediately recalls earlier descriptions of the martyred Che. Julia Cortés, the schoolteacher who, at age 19, spoke to Guevara when he was held captive by the Bolivian government in 1967, was interviewed by the BBC World as it marked the 2004 inauguration of *Ruta del Che*. Cortés recalled Che as "someone very attractive, with a strong presence and penetrating eyes." Alberto Korda, the Cuban photographer who captured the face in the most famous Che photograph in March of 1960, said that it was a piercing expression of rage, a look that penetrated.[10] At the time, *Revolución*, the magazine that Korda worked for, published a different photo. The now famous photo was first published seven years later, when Guevara died, setting it free from terrestrial anchors. While there are hundreds of photographs of Che Guevara, the resurrected 1960 image endured, becoming imbued with the political significance of an era. The famous eyes talked about by Korda and the schoolteacher retain their power in the photograph of the corpse taken by Freddy Alberto in the village laundry in Vallegrande. This image of a dead Che was later immortalized at the end of part one of Fernando Solanas and Octavio Getino's *La hora de los hornos* (*Hour of the Furnaces*, 1969), a film essay and political act typical of another era. Controversy over the use of the image of Che in death, a cadaver that stared back at viewers, led to the reediting of this portion of the film. The length of the image onscreen was shortened and recontextualized amid other revolutionary figures that the filmmakers felt better represented ideas of liberation.[11] In *Diarios*, the eyes of the dead hero are transferred to García Bernal's soft, seductive, piercing, green eyes, linking them to the charisma, visceral pleasure, and emotion of the original gaze.

In *Diarios*, Che, as played by García Bernal, is honest, charming, adventurous, smart, vulnerable, and quietly sexual; the latter, a quality that stems from García Bernal's own essence as an actor rather than from Guevara's actual character—contrary to this rendering, biographies of Che Guevara point to his great sexual appetite. *Diarios* brings the cultural significance of landscape together with idealism and adventure, which make for inspiring travel companions. The journey is one of the many that Guevara made: he embarked on a second trip through South and Central America after receiving his medical degree, and then went to Cuba, Africa, and finally Bolivia. The writing style of the motorcycle journal is analytical, linking his observation of capital production and exploitation of resources to the impoverished condition of peasants and indigenous groups. His analysis compares the geopolitical relations of Latin America with the type of exploitation that occurs as a result of colonial power structures. His observations of the Inca site of Machu Pichu key onto the strategic advantages of the location for the creation of defensible positions from potential enemies, even though the structure is not a military garrison. This apparently provides license to the filmmakers for Ernesto's aforementioned fictional embrace of militarism; obviously, the development of the fighter had, in fact, already begun. The film's distortion, then, is greater than first appears since its portrayal of Guevara at this point relies more on the appealing immaturity of its star than on the intelligence and acuity of the actual author of the diaries. However, the film does document the journey as a quest for knowledge, an aspect given weight specifically in the final parting between Granado and Ernesto. García Bernal's Guevara appears to have acquired an introspective distance as expressed in his reaction to Granado's invitation to study in Caracas: he responds that there are many things he has to think about at length, but the late shift to a portrayal of the deliberative character of Che

Guevara still leaves the balance of the film invested more in the actor than the acted.

The repeated conflation of Guevara with Bernal's own persona can be read as the manner in which a star's celebrity constitutes what Chris Rojek has called a "market of sentiments." In this case, the sentiments revolve around utopian ideals and the emotive significance of the revolutionary project.[12] García Bernal's achieved celebrity is doubled in the representation of an already famous person. This increases consumer desire for Bernal, due not merely to his attractive characteristics but also to their association with the appealing moral principles of a hero.

Displacing the political onto the sensual ironically forms the film's most political aspect. It projects onto Bernal's softer masculinity and soulfulness the revolutionary imagination embodied by Che Guevara. This presents an opportunity to rethink Che's image of ultra-masculinity—which is reiterated in Soderbergh's *Che*—as media products transform his significance. Any doubts about the potential of García Bernal's look are easily put to rest with his portrayal of Ángel/Juan/Zahara in *La mala educación*. Here, Bernal is remarkably attractive as a transvestite. The feminization of Guevara is persuasive even when burdened by the patriarchal definitions already embedded in ideas of masculine and feminine relations. The construction of the New Man, which became Guevara's enduring crusade in Cuba, is thus built on power relations involved in gender. Alongside come contradictions of patriarchal societies, developmentalist ideas, and the moral ethics of worn-out humanism. Overlaying the malleable sexuality of Bernal may provoke renewed assessment of Guevara's means of influence, but in postmodern consumer culture it risks serving more to distract from the weight of Che Guevara as a real man—for all the ambiguity of that phrase itself.

The circulation and construction of the dramatic personalities of Gael García Bernal, the vulnerable, sexy, and smart global Latin American, and of the rough, unpolished, wildly commanding revolutionary, Ernesto Guevara, in *Diarios* are important social integration functions. Aside from the obvious connection between the two "celebrities" around the film, it is their iconic status that encourages inquiry beyond the historical record of Guevara's life story, either as a young man or a seasoned revolutionary. Blending the reproduced, desirable image with ideas of revolution offers the pleasure of utopian longings while consuming the experience of global stardom.

But while the film focuses on Ernesto discovering an expanded set of emotions beyond the experience of his bourgeois class, the scope of his emerging enlightened perceptions is limited to notions of injustice, eschewing the broader influence of contemporary regional Leftist politics on his formation. In other words, the film positions Guevara within a narrow and romantic, more pleasurable politics as the would-be hero, replacing political depth with the physical sensuousness of García Bernal and the visceral power that this adds to the consumption of the film. Bernal's Ernesto is so gentle as to conjure only the sweetness of a pleasant memory. It abstains from strong emotions except for principled stubbornness. Strong feelings are confined to the audience, seduced by a vulnerable hero, and enthralled by Bernal's beauty. Franco's poignant question about political legacies reverberates: "Why must Marxism, which had such a profound influence on generations of Latin American intellectuals, be sweetened this way?"[13] The original political events and players are communicated across time and space by and through those vesting interest and becoming stakeholders in subsequent cultural dramas and markets. The rise of consumerism may provide an answer for the loss of the grit of Guevara: postmodern markets mine profit from pleasure. And yet, consuming an icon that steadfastly stood against capitalist endeavors and individualism produces real enjoyment dispersed through its multiple iterations.

García Bernal as the young Ernesto and as the star maps a geography of desire for the consumption of Latin America. Ernesto Che Guevara, the most famous Latin American in the world, is, in the words of *Back Stage* magazine, "brought down to earth by Bernal's tender and inspiring performance."[14] When Bernal talks about playing Che he reveals a personal affinity for the character. "Before I played Che, I asked the spirit of Che for permission." He then considers his own transformation, "*me conocí a mi mismo* / I learned more about myself," echoing the movie's simple slogan, "Let the world change you and you can change the world." His affinity for Guevara appears genuine, and has led him to portray the revolutionary leader more than once. His first portrayal was in Showtime Network's miniseries *Fidel*, a performance that although critically praised, did not achieve the same notoriety. Lacking the Latin American cultural clout of the latter *Diarios*, the role was much more utilitarian. According to the actor, "The only thing it did was pay the rent and make me want to play the character again."[15] Becoming the *heroic* guerrillero has its financial upside.

In *Diarios*, revolution in acting and Revolution are joined. García Bernal is influential in his native Mexico, considered the central *cabrón* of a brash and hip new generation of celebrities who are global in their lifestyle and taste.[16] The U.S. media hype alludes to revolutionary concepts associated with Guevara. He is "the face of a revolution."[17]

The promotional machine behind the *Diarios* campaign certainly took advantage of the excitement integral to hints of revolution. The Mexican weekly *Proceso* says he goes against the formula of Hollywood.[18] Bernal used the media hype concurrently to underscore his own views on the media market by refuting the importance of English in international films, asking calmly in a television interview: "Why should a film that takes place in Mexico be spoken in English?"[19] His importance at the box-office internationally is explained in *InStyle* magazine, which called him the "hottest male import," and assessed his importance in terms of Free Trade Agreements.[20] And yet García Bernal defines himself as a Latin American actor, specifically a Mexican actor from Guadalajara. He has been described for the market, as was Che Guevara, as the Latin James Dean, another instance in which the market of emotions erases ideological differences that may exist between these three obviously crucial symbols of rebellion and ambiguous sexuality. He is said to be at the forefront of a Latin American new wave of talent. *Back Stage* magazine writes that, "his onscreen portrayals are viscerally hot, coolly meditative, and fiercely political, while at the same time grounded in proper talent"; he is found not to be interested in selling out, "a new breed: an acting activist!"[21] Cultural location clearly plays an important part in packaging for the consumer. In the case of Bernal, this entails not only revolutionary politics, but also the presentation of the actor as a revolutionary figure, if only as a leader of the new generation of filmmaking that is transforming Latin American cinema into a more marketable industry. If the aura of revolution once defined Latin America as a political, social, and cultural project in the post–World War II era, it now serves as a promotional moniker, a citation of a symbolic imagination transformed by the market into profitable cultural capital.

New economic ventures can thus capitalize on the nostalgia of revolution and the pleasure of consuming the often contradictory association of politics and pop icons. *Diarios* exemplifies the privileging of a culture of consumerism over one of political community. As such, it represents a pragmatic response by and to a region seeking to reestablish its identity in the era of globalization. Similar motivation has led to the development of *Ruta del Che*,

**BACK STAGE WEST**

Sept. 30–Oct. 6, 2004

THE ACTOR'S RESOURCE

Face of a Revolution

**Gael García Bernal** has

by Cassie Carpenter

n a mere four years Mexican actor Gael García Bernal has risen to the forefront of the modern Latin American cinematic

He is a new breed of actor: an acting activist. He is only interested in films that pertain to his personal quest, and that has turned out to be his greatest strength. He loves to take risks and relishes being in the eye of the storm, but he remains committed to his cultural roots. His last film, *El*

Cover of Back Stage magazine 2004.
Photo Cristina Venegas.

"Che's Route," a tourism venture supervised by Bolivia Care, producing cultural tourism as a trip along the key places visited by Guevara on his expedition throughout Bolivia. The local venture purports to promote economic development via local tourism, which benefits the indigenous population in the area of La Higuera. Guevara's daughter, who lives in Cuba, gave her blessing to the Bolivia Care enterprise, which is partly financed by the British Department of International Development.[22] State investment, media, and pure commerce combine to make a very different project than *Diarios*. But "Che's Route" exhibits the same confused mix of historic and postmodern concepts and icons as new iterations that rise or fall at the whim of the market in which politics are buried. It has yet to be seen if such projects can generate a fresh politics geared to influence beyond the market. Whatever goals it serves, the icon corners the market in persistence, propelled by the weight of its source. Guevara's eyes even in death had a major impact despite the fact that he died physically spent, dirty, and wounded. Aware perhaps of the possibility of a reduction of political significance of Guevara's revolutionary ideas, Cortés, the schoolteacher witness, viewed the economic endeavor with trepidation despite the speculated benefits. The irony of the Bolivian government embracing an international tourist venture around the legend of Latin America's most famous revolutionary could not be possible without a redefinition of the political terms, a softening of language just as in *Diarios*. In this case, Che Guevara's Bolivian campaign, once described by the military as "armed insurgency," is transformed by the distance from its insurgent roots to become "Che's Route" as tourism welcomes the uneasy marriage of political memory and global economics. In many ways, *Diarios de motocicleta* and *Ruta del Che* are the same product, as they both re-purpose cultural and political memory into a politically correct, capitalist enterprise. The commercial and cultural value of the Che Guevara narrative reinforces the notion of memory and place as repositories of sentiment, and redefines revolution as pleasurable within the arena of consumption. Appropriation of the narrative text, whether by the state, by commerce, or by media, produces the same result in a global consumer world. If *Diarios* and the actions and rhetoric of its star exhibit new political beginnings, these have still to be realized beyond the consumerist hype. Ultimately, the film *Diarios de motocicleta* imagines revolution as heroic gesture and journey, a chronicle of a death as a postscript in which the man is a glimmer, the corpse is absent, and the icon is everywhere.

# 9

# SAUDADES ON THE AMAZON

## TOWARD A SOFT SWEET NAME
## FOR INVOLUTION

CRAIG SAPER

*The only things in life*
*I am not sure of*
*Are established names,*
*Recognized words . . . .*
　　　　—Bob Brown, from "A Soft Sweet Name" *Tahiti*, 1915

*Becoming is involutionary, involution is creative. To regress is*
*to move in the direction of something less differentiated. But to*
*involve is to form a block that runs its own line "between" the*
*terms in play and beneath assignable relations.*
　　　　—Deleuze and Guattari, *A Thousand Plateaus*, 1987

In 1942, with Carmen Miranda's *The Gang's All Here* in production and promising to be a big hit, Hollywood producers were eager to make more movies with Brazilian characters or settings. They were talking with Orson Welles about his never-completed film about a Rio carnival celebration and they decided to send Bob and Rose Brown down the Amazon to generate ideas for movies. About a decade before, in the late 1920s and early 1930s, the Browns were expatriate surrealists living in France. Bob had created a sensation among the avant-garde with his "reading machine," including praise from Gertrude Stein, Marcel Duchamp, Stuart Davis, Marsden Hartley, Kay Boyle, and F. W. Marinetti.[1] The machine sought to change the habituated assignable relations among readers, texts, and technologies; a fuller explanation of the machine is beyond the scope of this chapter, but a number of detailed descriptions and discussions of the implications of the machine now exist.[2]

When the Depression began, the Browns left France, moved to London for less than a year, and arrived in the States practically broke and tried to put together new sources of income by publishing cookbooks, travel memoirs, and Hollywood movie treatments.

Eventually, they returned to Brazil, where they had lived from 1919 to 1927, and arranged to travel along the Amazon River in a deal with movie studios and as good will ambassadors for the U.S. government, resulting in the publication of the *Amazing Amazon* in 1942. This chapter focuses on that book in the context of their previous work as radical teachers, publishers, curators, and surrealist poets. Most of the discussions of Bob Brown's avant-garde publications cite, in passing, his previous career as a bestselling writer for pulp magazines, but none of the studies mention his later work.[3] Did the Browns simply drop their dedication to surrealism and what Deleuze and Guattari call involutionary art, or does surrealist involution appear in the Browns' later work in nuanced formations? In answering that question, this chapter looks at Deleuze's and Guattari's discussions of masks, involution, deterritorialization, and alternatives to faciality, because those seemingly abstract theoretical terms seem to have a concrete link to the findings in the Browns' book.

The story of Bob and Rose Brown's life together, lush and overgrown, reads like an epic novel; one cannot believe the scope of their interests, accomplishments, and travels. The sheer volume of their writings while they traveled (Rose alone published at least seven detailed volumes and many articles either alone or with her collaborators in the early 1940s) staggers the imagination. As a novel, it might have the title, "Brown Family Robinson," the name Bob gave to his never-completed autobiography. Rose and Bob wrote millions of words, and with Cora Lovisa Brown (1860–1939), Bob's mother, they produced cookbooks and party guides. The list includes *The European Cookbook for American Homes*, *10,000 Snacks*, *Salads and Herbs*, *America Cooks*, *The Complete Book of Cheese*, and many more.[4] Cora also wrote guides to cooking, had earlier written stories for the pulps, and had coached Bob in how to crank out the word counts. By the time they published the cookbook on American cuisine in 1940, they were able to claim that they "put in twenty years of culinary adventuring in as many countries and wrote a dozen books about it."[5] Rose published five single-authored books on Brazil, all in the early 1940s, including three chapter books, *Two Children of Brazil*, *Two Children and their Jungle Zoo*, and *Amazon Adventures of Two Children*; one social geography, *Land and People of Brazil*; and one biographical history, *American Emperor: Dom Pedro II of Brazil* (an Honor List Book from *Horn Book Magazine*).

Bob Brown published about eight volumes of experimental writing and poetry as an expatriate from 1929 until 1931, five in 1931 alone, including four volumes in which the visual design played crucial roles in the meaning of the texts. Most of the volumes he published with his own press, Roving Eye Press. In 1929, Harry and Caresse Crosby's Black Sun Press, in Paris, had published Brown's *1430-1930*, a book of hand-drawn visual poetry. One of those poems, "Eyes on the Half-Shell," previously appeared in Duchamp's *Blindman*, in 1917, and its free-hand style and visual puns impressed many avant-garde artists and writers including Nancy Cunard, who published Brown's *Words* in 1931 with her Hours Press. In 1930, Bob Brown published *The Readies* manifesto with his own fine press, Roving Eye Press. He includes plans for an electric reading machine, strategies for preparing the eye for mechanized reading, and instructions for preparing texts as readies. His discussion of reading machines seems prescient in light of text messaging with abbreviated language, electronic text readers, and even online books and databases. The expatriate modernists in Paris embraced *The Readies* project, especially those associated with the modernist magazine, *transition*, which advocated a "revolution of the word." After returning to the United States he continued to publish avant-garde works, advocated Surrealist writing, traveled to the Soviet Union, and simultaneously published tracts advocating communes and pro-laborer positions, wrote Hollywood B-movie story-treatments, and co-authored numerous cookbooks. One could argue that the Browns took the details of the avant-garde's fun and parties, which they helped invent (e.g., Bob had staged some of the famous Webster Hall decadent costume balls in Greenwich Village), and spent the rest of their lives popularizing those recipes of a spirited and engaged life.

They described food in ways that embedded social economy and literal practices of its consumption, as well as lush detailed descriptions. They did not simply describe the food, but showed how it appears in a web of relations, practices, and economies, rather than as distinct entities riven from their sociopoetic connections. Here is a passage from *Amazing Amazon*:

> A humble barefoot employee of the miracle tree's owner lops off a ripe
> healthy jocá bigger than our two heads and with a green hide as rough
> and tough as an alligator's. Like the fruit of the cacao, these jacás that

look like gigantic breadfruit thrust straight out from the trunk on very short stems; and as we look up the fat tree stem we see that it's studded with fruit in different degrees of ripeness.[6]

The anecdote starts with this description of picking the fruit and then moves to a description of its consumption. "A single jacá goes a long way, for it's eaten raw, seed by pulpy seed. Usually it's sold in portions of a few seeds covered with the slippery yellowish white pulp that's sickeningly sweet to our Northern palates. Deathly sweet!"[7] They connect the fruit to other tropical fruits. "It somewhat resembles the smaller chirimoya or fruta de Conde; only stickier and not nearly so parfumé, but the fruity pulp is sucked off the black shiny seeds in the same way."[8] Finally, they place the fruit at the center of a mercantile exchange, an economics lesson, and a social geography:

> If you should fall heir to a jacá weighing around fifty pounds, as we did, you could go to the nearest marketplace, sit down and sell it off three or four seeds to a clutch and end up after half a day with a pocketful of coppers. It's as popular throughout Brazil as chewing gum at home. Once in Rio we saw a sweet shop opened on a corner with one enormous jacá for its entire stock. Kids and oldsters flocked around like flies and we estimated that the take was a couple of dollars, which is a lot of money for just one fruit.[9]

Traditional travel guides might describe the look of a fruit, and cookbooks its taste, but the description of how to make money selling off parts of the fruit makes the Browns' efforts something very different from a guide for the idle rich.

Rather than assuming their avant-garde and radical work as a reaction against their commercial works, like the cookbooks, one can appreciate how their radicalism took place in the cultural context of "years of tossing up snacks and tossing down drinks in cafés and home kitchens of all foreign capitals."[10] Yet, the Browns' travels and cosmopolitan life around the world set the stage for their particular diasporic avant-garde way of working, or what Brown calls nomadism (decades before the publication of *A Thousand Pleateaus*).

Working collectively as they traveled, they also created a collective identity, called CoRoBo (created from the first two letters of each of their names) in keeping with their fascination with reinventing their identities through pseudonyms, collaborative work, parties, and travel. The corporate name almost looks and sounds like a Concrete poem with its repeating o's and its poetic assonance: even their names become the locus for fun and a marker of a social economy of production.

The Browns represent a modernist generation that defined itself, in large part, by its interests in travel and diasporas as well as the cosmopolitans' resistance to nationalist hysteria. For the modernist generation, cosmopolitanism implied being a citizen of the world, unmoored from a single place (provincialism) or national identity (nativism). This nomadism often wanted to use literary and artistic experimentation as a wedge to break open provincialism, nativism, and Puritanism. Often artists, as travelers and bricoleurs, created an ethnocentric and Occidental Orientalism. These travelers did not participate in the cultures from which they borrowed ideas and designs. The Browns, however, complicate this impression of the nomadic modernists. For they explain that the effort to assuage or (in their phrase, *matar saudades*, literally) to kill the indefinable longing, motivates their trip to the Amazon region. Instead of setting out to experience the exotic, primitive, or Otherness, they long for "our old home away from home."[11] Their journey was a diasporic return because the Browns had settled in Brazil in 1919 for about 7 years, before traveling the world, living as expatriates in France, and returning to the United States in the 1930s, before returning to Brazil.

The Browns left the States as self-described "defunct rebels" when Cora died in 1939. In a typical twist in their radical *and* pop-culture making lives, they funded their travels down the Amazon, in part, with profits from a Hollywood movie treatment for the situation comedy (with plenty of slapstick) *Nobody's Baby* (1937). The Hal Roach production illuminated aspects of the Browns' lives that exceed the scope of this chapter, but that I describe in my biography of the Browns.

During their research for the Amazon trip, the Browns discovered that Brazil was a destination for emigrants from a less civilized country: the United States. The defeated Confederate rebels fled to Brazil in the tens of thousands after the Civil War, not to create a new Confederacy, but to flee for their lives (displaced people in a diaspora that complicates the term); Union soldiers also went to Brazil. Zora Neale Hurston recounts how a colonel who had initially fled to Brazil, only to return a few years later, founded her town, Eatonville, Florida. The Browns adopt a poem written by one of these "Defunct Rebels" as their theme song for their trip through the Amazonian region. While it is common to think of the Amazon as untouched by travelers from the outside, including the United States, before the turn of the century (and even until the last decades of the twentieth century), North Americans had, in a forgotten diaspora, arrived in the nineteenth century. The Rebels' descendents, now multiracial Afro-Brazilians, still live in Brazil. They stage festivals in which the men dress as Confederate soldiers and the women dress in Southern Belle gowns (surreal for outsiders from the United States). The Rebel battle flag, soldiers' uniforms, and women's dresses have meanings, in these celebrations, unrelated to those in the United States except to memorialize a diaspora.

In the context of leaving the United States because of frustrations with the lack of a continuation of progressive social change, they see themselves as the new "defunct rebels." They flee another lost cause. The notion of defunct rebels, losers in history (whether deserving or not), complicates the usual celebration of displaced persons. Sometimes displaced persons engage in war, genocide, or oppression in the places they flee to or the homelands they return to conquer. Sometimes they leave so that they can practice a more repressive absolutist politics on their own communities. In addition to this mythology of the displaced as necessarily victims, histories of diasporas often portray the U.S. as the safe haven, the rescuer and protector (see for example the main exhibit at the Smithsonian Holocaust Museum), and the welcoming melting pot, rather than the nation that displaces people to other territories. Do we have names for those displaced to other lands? Is the word expatriates adequate to describe refugees from the States? Can we even imagine a moment in history when people illegally fled from the United States over the Mexican border and toward South America?

The Browns, who had in 1917 fled the United States as blacklisted writers and war resisters, saw Brazil as a safe haven of civilization and not as an escape to a primitive, simpler past. It was a return to civilization, not a vacation from civilization. Rose, in her study of Dom Pedro II, describes the Philadelphia exhibit, where Dom Pedro II visited in the late spring and summer of 1876. Instead of the Brazilian Ruler merely seeing the technological advances and cultural achievements, he also observed "how blind was the North American system of jails and penitentiaries, how cruel was their treatment of caring for the insane, and how forbidding were the half-measures taken to protect and educate freed slaves."[12]

They comment that "it's easy to see how much more civilized they are than we."[13] Comparing themselves to the indigenous people now seems in keeping with a multicultural attitude, but they wrote these comments in the early 1940s, at a time when both Axis and Allied forces aggressively pursued imperialist goals, often under the modern guise of a civilizing force. Their writings and adventures have some of the elements of the tourist's drive for collecting the exotic, but always with an appreciation of the unique and continuing history of the people and ecology they deal with on their journey. They are self-aware and read the sociopolitical history back into their poetic reflections. Here is an earlier poem by Bob about Brazil from his *Nomadness* collection:

> *"Saudades for Carioca"*
> Tender tendrils of thought
> fond fondling of words
> lithe living of life
> Color
> rainbows dancing
> across lacy waves
> [. . .]
> native raw-eyed rum
> shrimps and cod-fish
> mangoes and Antarctica beer.[14]

Instead of the conquering heroes, the Browns exemplify visitors' *becoming-native.* This new type of traveler appears in a magical-realist-like description they recount from mythic stories they hear about apocryphal travelers. A young woman who graciously lends a hand to her hosts and sleeps near them, finds herself protected by "fireflies tied by their antennae to her hair; so any movement of her head during the night, would illuminate her and anyone in the hammocks around her." To illuminate the traveler's every move instead of making her invisible seeks to reorient tourism, not as a punishment, but as a poetic opening. This other type of guide unveils something known well, but, nevertheless, usually missing from tourist destinations: an invitation to celebrate with those you meet.

The Browns, still the life of the party, told stories, joked with the men on the boat, ate, took siestas, and wrote. Their journey memoir includes the expected anecdotes about characters they meet on their travels, but is mixed unexpectedly with cultural history not of the kind of systematic boredom found in more standard travel guides. Here is the Browns' description in *Amazing Amazon* of one lunch. "Lunch at twelve consists of real meat soup with plenty of vegetables, then fish maybe caught through a hotel window, or a humpbacked turtle, although this is a rare food."[15] Of course, the image of catching lunch through the hotel window gives pause and once again suggests the Browns strategy to include the social situation of a meal's production and consumption.[16] Then they go on to describe the actual meal. In one course, "*Capivara*, venison, wild duck and other occasional game come to the table, but we have chicken only two or three times a week, because the price is prohibitive [. . .] you can eat half a dozen cackle-berries if you like, for 'cackle and come again' is the motto of this bounteous board where individual portions are unknown."[17] Again, personal economics, and social customs of communal eating, enter the conversation. The description of the last few courses connects the food to other customs. "Dessert consists of candied bananas, whipped up abacates or graviola, that heavenly fruit which our English cousins dub custard apple because it is otherwise unclassifiable to palates accustomed to Bird's custard and watery fruit salad to finish off a meal. There's other fruit, too, the best tasting mamão, papaya, in all the tropics, and that special green-skin banana you're supposed to cry for."[18]

After the meal, "having finished with fruit, coffee and toothpicks," the Browns explain how "you flop into the old string hammock for a couple of hours." They go on to explain that "Amazon travelers usually carry two different kinds of hammocks, a big cloth one from Ceara for all-night work and a lighter, cooler one for siestas. At three PM precisely, Monica, the first maid, wakes you with another demitasse."[19]

The stories meander, dense with detail, flowering into allusions and comparisons, erudite without pretension, evoking the feeling of amazing cocktail talk with multiple voices in the form of quotes from newspapers, books, songs, and passengers on their journey. It captures the lushness of the Amazon—not just the literal agricultural and biological diversity—but the cultural and racial complexity. Brazil has a long history of interracial and multiracial people: its creed, mixed as a nation. The tropical ecology described by the Browns includes encounters with howling monkeys, saracura water birds, parrots, porpoises, egret birds (garças), mosquitoes, and scorpions; one practical joke involves the crew putting a live scorpion on Bob Brown's back and then rushing to get it off him before it fatally strikes. The crew and the Browns see these parodic performances of the exotic and dangerous jungle as more about the encounter of tourists with those that stage the show. In this version, the crew made tourists and tourism the butt of the joke.

The Browns collect stuff like baby anteater skin ("we put andiroba oil on it to keep it from mildewing until we can get it tanned"[20]), or "straw covered bottles and bird-nest baskets."[21] They also recognize the exotic wonders of the place. "Parrots come in all sizes, colors and noises, from the great gaudy shrieking macaw through medium-size royal purple, manuve, and golden-headed louros who are terrific talkers."[22] They eat "salted capivara . . . plus tapir, jaboti, alligator tail, both turtle and sea cow mixira, parrot and smoked monkey, never did sink tooth in that mythical guanaco meat. Might as well ask for a unicorn steak . . . ".[23] At one point, a boat captain suggests a party. The menu includes "a five gallon tin full of rich mixira—the kind made of sea cow, naturally, since turtle put up in toothsome mixira style is almost prohibitive in price these days."[24] Another passenger requests "a plate of toucan tongues." The captain concurs, adding how useful the tongues are "to suck up the turtle eggs." They describe eating koro, a "pale-colored grub" found in "rotting tree-trunks."[25] The grub is "a fat, cream colored creature, rather like a silkworm [and] the body spurted a whitish, fatty substance which I [Bob or Rose?] managed to taste after some hesitation; it has the consistency and delicacy of butter, and the flavor of coconut milk."[26] They never act too squeamish, but eat with the enjoyment of learning a new name, a new word, a new pleasure, a delicacy one longs for (i.e., *saudade*).

The Browns lived in a hundred cities, and stressed that they did not simply visit (they ate and thought of themselves as involved in "becoming other"). Instead of the traveler as spectator positioned as a transcendental consumer by the tourism apparatus (with guides, sites, and tours), the Browns operate in a different mode, and never suggest how the reader could visit. Their descriptions resemble one plateau in *A Thousand Plateaus* about the face and of facializing objects, including landscapes. The face mechanism situated at the intersection of significance and subjectification appears not only on human heads, but also in the treatment of bodies and things.[27] In the traditional tourist scenario, the face and facialized objects function as windows onto subjective intention and assemblages of meaningful looks: the tourists look at the natives and seek to see everything as a face onto the primitive soul. We not only say, for example, "he had a sad face," suggesting significance, but also imply that "he is sad" precisely because he had a sad face. Kuleshov's (perhaps apocryphal) experiment (the Kuleshov effect) illustrates the intersection of subjectivity and significance in a face, and demonstrates how objects become facialized. He showed an audience clips of film with the famous actor Ivan Mozzhukhin—in each clip Kuleshov used the exact same shot—intercut with shots of a bowl of soup, a funeral procession, a springtime scene, etc. The participants raved about the amazing acting skills of the actor; that is, they imputed subjective qualities to him from what they saw in his face. After all, what's a face for, anyway? Likewise, the objects became charged with intention as well; they spoke to the actor's face; they said, hungry? sad? happy? Deleuze explains, in *Cinema I*, that "the close-up is by itself face."[28]

Essential attributes do not define the face. Instead of defining objects as geometrically static, this plateau suggests that "differential speeds" lead to the always changing relationships among supposedly well defined territories. So, for example, the movable hand and a use object join in a deterritorialized relationship; likewise, the maps of the Amazon do not illuminate the cognitive maps described by the Browns. This "block" shifts the body's hand from its territory, or proper place, and sets it in relation to the use object; another example, the upright head deterritorializes the human away from the animal kingdom toward wanderings on a steppe. The Browns wander, meander, and seek a different non-snapshot of the native's faces or the facialized objects. They seek much more involvement with what they eat, smell, and experience in their journey. Involution describes the process of "becoming" among nodes in a network; the connected nodes are involved with each other so much to suggest a becoming-something besides the individuated identity one might usually associate with one object, territory, or person. The Browns' cognitive map, visceral connections, hostility to the tourist's gaze, and thirstiness for otherness, leads to a different way to map and understand their journey. The crucial example, for this plateau, concerns the relationship between the face and the landscape. Everything becomes facialized, ready for someone to fill it with significance and subjective intentions. Italo Calvino's "The First Sign" in *Cosmi-Comics* wonderfully illustrates facialities preexisting any tracing of sign systems back to any deeply rooted origin.

In Calvino's story, some faceless entity makes a mark in some undefined space, and soon the mark returns with another mark on top of it. This infuriates the faceless entity, but soon the entire universe is filled completely with marks. The first mark is built upon embryonic narcissism—once the entity makes the mark, s/he/it hits the fan: the entity has to *face* the cluttered landscape. The overtones of a godlike entity also suggest the importance of a Christ figure who faces and facializes the world. Christian morality demands that we face our sins. Psychoanalysis demands that we face up to our subjectivity. Information theory demands that we interface with the facialized world around us. Face-ness always demands a proportionate response: subjectivity is always in a proper proportion to a transcendent signifying godlike system. If the subject moves too close to the god, or the god overwhelms the subject, then the facialization breaks down into a glossolalia of potentialities: the face becomes a mask. Against trying to capture the faces of the natives, the Browns try on the mask themselves.

Deleuze and Guattari explain that "The black hole/white wall system must already have gridded all of space and outlined its arborescences or dichotomies for those of signifier and subjectification even to be conceivable." Understanding the optics of fascination only in terms of the lures of the exotic, the indigenous as Other, ignores a crucial aspect of optics of fascination. In the second understanding of the gaze, it functions as a shock to the consciousness. The double meaning of the gaze depends on understanding the lure or spell. The gaze is not the look (of the tourist) but the lure of the inanimate that looks at the Browns. This second notion of the optics of fascination suggests something that *disrupts,* rather than reinforces, the tourist's unobstructed view:

*"Guides"*
Guides with pimply faces
uncouth unbuttoned mouths and
leering lecherous slobbery eyes;
guides who spew upon the
beauty of everything seen
in their company.
Wordy, mouthy, mumbling guides:
"This is the great stone now
made of rock
right here
very historic
the great stone what they used then
for that.
This is it
famous for centuries.
This is it, right here, sir!"
Guides with shifty dribbly glances
pointing smudgy fingers at
crystalline alabasters

nearly wearing out decrepit jokes
violating hallowed historic spots
sway-backed, bow-legged
sag-bellied, knock-kneed
coaxing, pleading
brow-beating, bullying
Guides
casting their bloated
hideous, besmirching shadows
over all the
most beautiful places of the world.[29]

This nasty description seems more contemporary with our cynical post-modern era rather than from a time when mass tourism for the middle class was still considered romantic and relatively rare. One would expect a travel poem to unapologetically embrace and celebrate the important monument while cropping the image of the guide out of sight. Bob's poem gives a different view in the conventions and style of the form it parodies.

The Browns described the politics of a situation usually left invisible in both scientific and travelers' accounts. The experiments in poetry and art led quickly, profoundly, and lastingly to a generation of poets and artists conceiving of their lives in terms of a diasporic search for a cosmopolitanist everyday life beyond internationalism. The Browns' writings, from the cookbooks to the visual poetry, were guides to popularize a way to eat, travel, and party: not as outsiders fascinated by quaint primitive customs, but as participants; not as taxonomists, but as poets. Not as tour guides, but as hosts and guests. They traveled up the Amazon longingly looking for the poetic juxtapositions including the embedded social and political history, and potential futures, in the present moment. Every recipe and journey was an encounter with *saudade*. Their travels were literally about trying on the masks rather than emulating the tourist's gaze.

Those "primitive" cultures use masks in ways that do *not* suggest the subjectivity of a face. Rather the mask ensures that the head belongs to the body as becoming-animal. The face deterritorializes the head away from the body, and reterritorializes it with subjectivity and meaning. Precisely because the mask's evil eye suggests neither approval nor disapproval, the "gotcha" is not an interpolation. It knocks your face off. Understanding the optics of fascination in terms of the *fascinum*, allows for a cultural and media plateau that does not merely confront the paternalizing tourist by locating its power in the "tourist's gaze," but instead works at a different level. Rather than an instrument of a patriarchal law or symbolic order, the evil eye interrupts and sways the tourist's drive. In this sense, an optics of fascination offers an alternative to hermeneutic cultural theories of tourism. How or where does this fascination (read as the *fascinum*—the evil eye—a spell cast) appear? The answer: on masks. The Browns do not taxonomically capture the sights, but allow the sightings to fascinate and sway them.

Regarding the way a mask operates as an evil-eye, Johan Huizinga writes, "The terrors of childhood, open-hearted gaiety, mystic fantasy, and sacred awe are all inextricably entangled in this strange business of masks and disguises." This play activity (related to a different notion of representation; a re-presentation rather than an identification) functions neither to imitate some existing reality nor to normalize activities by legitimating smiles or dismissive frowns. Instead this type of masked rite, a dance of the mask-as-evil-eye, as Huizinga explains, "causes the worshippers to participate in the sacred happening itself." The effects on the participant include seizure, thrill, and enrapture. A key factor in this optics of fascination is that "whether one is sorcerer or sorcerized one is always knower and dupe at once. But one chooses to be the dupe . . . a good spectator who can be frightened to death" by something imaginary.

Understanding optics of fascination as a dance of the masks stresses ludic disruption instead of the lures of a spectacle coordinated for social control. The Browns were on a journey of ludic disruption, not social control of the people. Deleuze and Guattari explain this figurative navigation by alluding to "primitive" mapping strategies. Navigation maps from, for example, the Marshall Islands (made with palm ribs, cowrie shells, and string) suggest important differences to modern facialized maps. The islanders' navigation charts have more detail and closer scale for areas closer to the mapmaker's home. Looking at these charts, one might say that the elements do not appear in proportion to each other. Again, the crucial factor in facialized objects is a proper proportion between subjective perception and meaning systems: if you hold the map too close, or in this case, build the map out of proportion, then the organizing or ordering system no longer has transcendent power. You and your map are too close. European globes made in the middle of the sixteenth century also had a mixed sense of scale: pictures of particular fish, gods blowing winds, strange monsters and animals, pictures of boats as if scale were relative and simultaneous.

The nonliterate maps were precisely the type one might associate with the indigenous peoples the Browns encountered on their journey up the Amazon, but these multiperspectival maps were the Browns' illuminations of their own fascinations.

These examples use non-equidistant notions of scale as in Western contemporary maps; all of these modern maps function on the same hermeneutic plane, or on the same scale, as if the reader of the map was in a transcendent vanishing point and each and every point in the map was an equal distance from the objective perceiver: no point is closer than any other, and the map is organized on how far points are from each other. The reader can then imagine him- or herself at a particular point, and the distance to be traveled to the next point; these contemporary maps function like screens, and similarly spectators take up transcendental positions in relation to these screens. The Browns went with the flow; they did not seek to map the journey with a single scale, but chose a mixed scale system. When the navigation uses a mixed scale, then certain details will appear in different sizes. "Primitive" mapping baffles a single point of view: no longer an interface, no longer in proportion to the point where a face studies it. Both primitive mappings and modern maps demonstrate interconnectedness of many elements along a surface. The equidistance scale of modern mapmaking limits the connections to a hierarchical tree-like structure: things of equal scale are in relation (e.g., countries), and within these units are smaller units in relation to each other (e.g., cities). Even if they did appear on a modern map, neither a big fish nor a path behind the house, for examples, would appear in relation to, or in proper proportion to, elements higher up the hierarchy. A mixed scale changes the hierarchy: a rhizomatic scale allows elements out of proportion to each other to find a relation, a common intensity.

On the one hand, Bob saw the adventure in terms of his research for Hollywood movies. For example, he thought about ways to consider turtle eggs, the size of ping-pong balls, as a weapon to stop villains, with an egg fight, in his potential action-adventure slapstick movie treatment. He did write treatments for silly slapstick movies at the very same time that he was involved with radical progressive movements in the United States, like founding the Museum of Social Change; so the juxtaposition makes sense in that context. Stuck there in the descriptions of the peoples living in the Amazon basin, the Browns might describe the "defunct rebels," or the pretext, and funding, for this trip as it related to U.S. foreign policy at the time.

The Browns did not see their radical efforts as anathema to either writing slapstick for Hollywood or serving as Goodwill Ambassadors in Brazil for the U.S. government. Although even they rarely mention the usually distinct aspects of their lives—vanguardist poets and revelers, pop culture producers, and defunct rebels—and when they do, they see the avant-garde, in particular, as a reaction against popular culture. But they did not see the avant-garde as completely opposed to either the popular front or popular culture. Likewise, they did not see their voracious collecting in Brazil as in conflict with wanting to tell the sociopolitical history of the indigenous people's forced labor, diasporas, and genocides.

The Amazon River begins far inland, at the city of Manaus, where the Rio Negro and Rio Solimoes meet. It is a place called the "meeting of the waters," and it is a famous natural wonder of the world. The two rivers have different colors that do not seem to mix for seven kilometers. At the mouth of the Amazon, the Browns describe another mixing area where the "gray-brown Amazon pushes the blue Atlantic back in one place, and the blue rushes in to attack a charge of gray in another."[30] It is an allegorical, or at least socio-poetic, image of the way that the Browns lived and visited Brazil and the Amazon. They flowed alongside their hosts. As if the river could talk and illustrate a sociopoetics, the river's route traced a way of traveling next to, beside, and together in very slowly giving up difference. In one of her children's books on the Amazon, Rose describes how the children wait for the blue river before swimming. Instead of vainly trying to change the flow, they go with the flow.

The Browns see the Amazonian folk not as the primitive Other but as a model of diasporic civilizations and as involutionary potential. They join in the cultures: becoming, rather than romanticizing, a simpler life. Claude Lévi-Strauss confesses, "I hate traveling and explorers,"[31] and explains that "Amazonia, Tibet, Africa fill the bookshops in the form of travelogues, accounts of expeditions and collections of photographs, in all of which the desire to impress is so dominant as to make it impossible for the reader to assess the value of the evidence put before him. Instead of having his critical faculties stimulated, he asks for more such pabulum and swallows prodigious quantities of it."[32] Bob's poetry, similarly, often skewers the guides, visitors, and travelers just as Lévi-Strauss realizes that the sought-after pure encounter with the supposedly primitive folk was always already compromised. A certain type of mainstream guide, like *Baedeker's*, is now what needs demythologizing. Here is another earlier poem by Bob. In their cookbook on South American cuisine, they include the following recipe:

*Saudades (Brazilian Longings)*

Lightly beat 5 egg yolks with 1 cup sugar and knead in enough sifted *polvinho* to mold into small balls. Place these on an oiled board and bake until dry in a cool oven.

They explain, "Saudades is a word often heard in Brazil. It covers a whole lot of emotions, all the way from homesickness to a vague longing for sweets like these."[33] They offer a model of travel that allows for the longings usually effaced by the tour guide and happy tourists. The Browns' surrealist approach to the river inflected their desire to illuminate the river's life as an involution, a web of linking practices, and masks.

# 10
# STATES OF DISTRACTION
## MEDIA ART STRATEGIES
## WITHIN PUBLIC CONDITIONS

MAT RAPPAPORT

In recent years, medium and large-scale video screens have proliferated in public contexts. Digital billboards, video displays mounted to the sides of busses, and myriad interior screens inhabit our landscape, resembling the ever-present media environment of futuristic dystopic fantasies. Traditionally, the scale of these screens paralleled what was available for home consumption. However, as technologies developed for larger and brighter screens, they have been applied to domestic interior and outdoor applications. The larger-scale screens compete in public spaces with the surrounding architecture and signage for a fragment of our attention.

As with any new technology aimed at a mass audience, there has been an engagement by artists who seek to comment on, critique, and enhance its social and cultural impact. At first glance, the large screens on which videos are presented look like big televisions mounted to the sides of buildings. However, it's the fusion of "publicness" and artist-created content that facilitates an alternate voice in commercial spaces and extends the intervention to engage the viewer's experience of architecture and the built environment. In an era marked by the rapid expansion, diffusion, and integration of media, the artist's intervention in ostensibly nonmediated spaces reintroduces classic question of media scholarship. This chapter presents several such interventions and assesses their impact on explicit and implicit practices of worldmaking.

In 2004, I co-initiated *v1b3* ("video in the built environment") with Conrad Gleber and John Marshall of the art collective rootoftwo. *v1b3* set out to explore the impact of media arts on the experience of public space and simultaneously developed a network of artists engaged in conceptual art practice that converged in thematic and formal ways. The *v1b3* projects take the form of curatorial partnerships that select video-based works created for large-scale public presentations as site-specific media installations, performances, and interventions. The public space provides a vehicle to interpret and map architectural and social contexts.

The early days of television saw fast adoption by the American public. Television broadcasting represented a model in which a small number of content distributors, the networks, pushed content to a wide audience. Yet as the medium of television permeated private spaces of the home, artists and activists developed strategies for critiquing the medium and inserting alternative positions onto the sanctioned airwaves. By the 1960s, artists began to create works that utilized video and television to question its influence and cultural significance.

In his book *Feedback, Television Against Democracy*, David Joselit traces 1960s and 1970s artists' and activists' strategies to formulate counter positions to network television's principal function: to produce audiences for advertisers. Joselit discusses how early video artists and activists utilized the shared television ecology to open its closed circuit as acts of resistance.[1] He argues that in the early days of video art, artists like Nam Jun Paik, Richard Serra, Joan Jonas, Frank Gillete, Dan Graham, and collectives like Ant Farm and TVTV (top value television) created work that manipulated and critiqued the television device and signal. Often the work created was intended for an elite art gallery context. However, collectives like TVTV and Ant Farm created media spectacles that garnered mainstream media attention. The broadcast of news segments about or by these collectives represented an appropriation of the airwaves. Similarly, activists like the Diggers and the Yippies, under the charismatic leadership of Abbie Hoffman, developed staged political street theater with the purpose of having it reported and broadcast. These strategies aimed to produce the effect of *feedback* by coopting the program and inserting alternate voices into the network.

In television, the *program* refers to the shows that a network broadcasts, but, as in the use of the term in architecture, it has a sanctioning role. The boundary of the *program* or programming can be thought to include the interstitial commercials (and products represented within) as they represent a system of intra-validations. The commercial product has its identity intentionally constructed in relationship to the "show" and vice versa. And the show, which is how the program is traditionally defined, produces an audience comprised of affinities that can be quantified for marketing strategies. Television programming is thus a system of sanctions.

In architecture, the *program* usually refers to a document created early in a project that defines overarching goals. Interestingly, it commonly refers to the objectives for human movement and use of a building or built space. It is through the implementation of the program that use becomes defined either in accordance with the program or in reaction to it. The program is a regulatory device that directs intentional use. However, as additional buildings and spaces are added, subtracted, or modified, the use of the designed spaces change.

Art presented on public large-scale video screens can function like oversized television sets. Like television, the screens often combine mixed content like news, sports, and arts programming. Typically, the screens are applied to the sides of buildings without consideration or formal integration with the building's surface. However both large public screens and ephemeral media works set in urban environments differ from television in that they are consumed by a distracted public within a fragmented built environment. This experience, which extends the ubiquity of mediation into unexpected spaces, revives questions that have accompanied each moment of dramatic change in media and technology.

## Distraction

*Architecture has always represented the prototype of a work of art the reception of which is consummated by a collectivity in a state of distraction.*
                                        —Walter Benjamin

Horns sound, traffic signals blink, myriad conversations shift as one navigates one's way down the street toward a destination. The city street is nothing if not a complex and fragmented environment consisting of many stimuli vying for our attention. Given the scale and complexity of most urban architectural environments, sensory overload sends us to seek methods to curb the flow of stimulation and information. Ear buds and iPods shut out the noise of the street, the glow held against the side of a head gripping the voice on the other end of the cellular connection and the telltale elevation of voices talking to no one apparent; media is isolation against negotiating the city. Human beings nonetheless have the ability to filter much of this information. With repetition, habituation sets in and relieves us from recognizing the pressure of the ear buds against our ears as well as the specifics of the route from points a to b. Simultaneously, the media we consciously integrate into our daily routine exists amid a wider media world that includes the built environment. So, while the state of distraction itself is not a new observation, the negotiation of distraction through intensely mediated life represents a qualitative change in the nature of distraction.

In his essay "The Work of Art in the Age of Mechanical Reproduction," Walter Benjamin likens the experience of film to that of architecture. He argues that film, as a widely reproducible art form, facilitates a mass audience. One of the core distinctions of how film functions differently from painting, for example, is that it is received by a mass audience in a state of distraction. Extending his critique to broader cultural space, Benjamin emphasizes that we experience buildings in at least two ways: "use and perception or rather, by touch and sight."[2] And he goes on to say, "Tactile appropriation is accomplished not so much by attention but by habit . . . habit determines to a large extent even optical reception. [Optical reception] occurs much less through rapt attention than by noticing the object in incidental fashion."[3] In other words, the optical reception of a building is tempered by the manner in which we move through space. As the viewer navigates space, the building is viewed in fragments that are seamed together as a quasi-narrative amalgamation of the building. This optical experience is shaped by the affordances and constraints that the building presents to the viewer, who now assumes the position of user.

Benjamin's argument clearly puts a positive (or at the very least optimistic) spin on a situation in which the viewer consumes the work of art/film/architecture in a state of distraction. What he doesn't address is the regulating influence of the architectural program and, in our contemporary context, the potential for the radical integration of media, architecture, and space, of which the projection of moving pictures into and onto the building's surface is one, iconoclastic, instance. In our contemporary media environment, audience distraction and the consumption of an architectural space laden with moving pictures becomes a marketing opportunity for advertisers and corporate sponsors. However, it also offers an opportunity for artists to comment on and shape these environments. As artists project and overlay their works into public spaces and insert nonprogrammatic messages, they produce *feedback* within multiple viewing contexts.

Media-based projects implemented in the built environment rely on attributes of film, television, and architecture including the fragment, temporality, and program. The habitual use of these spaces is the key to pursuing a disruption and to inserting feedback into the system. If the viewer experiences the built environment through the known and practiced, then the insertion of modification and augmentations signals alternate fragments requiring integration. Likewise, the perceived ubiquity of media is distorted through unexpected lines of convergence with the built environment. Hence, media based art implemented in public allows for the habitual distraction that seems very much like active scanning as a new model for seeing and knowing. In my work, these models emerge through creative media interventions in the built environment.

### *v1b3* [video in the built environment]

In 2004, *v1b3* was organized around the question of how video and media art could be implemented within and shape the experience of the built environment. *v1b3* is a hybrid curatorial and production project with the goal of fostering an expanded network of artists while providing a Web-based archive (http://www.v1b3.com) of the works presented. To date over sixty artists from five countries have participated in *v1b3* activities. Since 2005, *v1b3* has developed collections of video art in conjunction with British- and Australian-based "big screens." The screens are operated with a commitment to noncommercial and art-based programming. The collections have an overarching goal of addressing broad themes related to the built environment and transitory viewership.

The first screen that *v1b3* partnered with is located in Exchange Square, in Manchester, England. Exchange Square is the commercial center of the city and in 1996 was heavily damaged by an IRA bombing. After 1996, there was a major initiative to redevelop Exchange Square and in 2003, the BBC, Philips, and the City Council partnered to bring the first large-scale public screen to the United Kingdom. The Manchester screen is 25 square meters (269 sq ft) in size and has an estimated 50,000 people walking by it per day. For comparison purposes, Manchester proper has a population of 450,000 people and greater Manchester 2,240,000. While the screen was initially operated exclusively by the BBC, in 2005 the BBC partnered with Cornerhouse Gallery to curate original art programming. By the time *v1b3* became involved, art programming ran between 2-4 times daily

Exchange Square. Manchester, UK.
Photo Credit John Marshall.

within half-hour slots.[4] In 2009, there were nine big screens in the United Kingdom.

When considering arts programming for large urban screens, it is important to underscore a double sense of Benjamin's concept of distraction. The built environment, as context, is an architectural space that is experienced by an audience in a state of distraction. Into this environment, often grafted onto its surface, is a screen that contains material that also presents a structurally fragmented series of messages. Video presented on discrete screens both caption and are captioned by the built environment that surrounds them. Figure and ground loop in priority as these relationships are negotiated. Consequently, the video programs push feedback both within the context of the screen content and extending out into the reception of the architectural space itself.

The temporal and temporary nature of the majority of the programming on the large screen/s presents a significant variable. Given their habitual use of the space, viewers are often traveling from points a to b and usually interact with the screen content for very short periods of time. They function as passersby, not stopping along their path while still collecting and assembling fragmentary experiences of the space. And yet, one of the interesting conditions of the Manchester screen is that, within Exchange Square, public seating actually faces the screen. While the screen is not a television per se, the combination of community seating with popular programming (such as sporting events and live-broadcast music performance) does have the effect of transforming the square into a community TV-viewing room. Viewers are thus invited to participate in a durational, communal, and social experience.

In response to these conditions, *v1b3* has over time shortened the works presented for the large screens from over five minutes in the first collection to an emphasis on one-minute or shorter works. The intent of the shorter works is to incorporate a structure in which the piece can be accessed by the transitory viewer, and where it can create feedback within the larger field of programming within the architectural space.

In an attempt to broaden the exploration of hybrid architecture and media art works in other ways, *v1b3* has initiated a number of site-specific, non-big-screen projects. In 2005, the University Film and Video Association, with the support of Columbia College, sponsored four independent works by four artists in Chicago's South Loop. Each piece ran for one night and sought to interact with the local residents and conference attendees. The pieces represented distinct approaches to site specificity and video-based media work within architectural space.

The projected image merges the surface and the projected content, thereby creating an optical field that integrates both elements. The result is an ephemeral illusion that can transform the reading of both image and object. This is in contrast to the Big Screens that function as architectural elements and transform the built environment as they relate to the other built elements: buildings, streets, bridges. The projection-object is transformative in that it has the potential for changing the viewer's perception of the object. In effect, the work creates an afterimage that is remembered once the media component has disappeared.

In *Escape*, Annette Barbier created animations of people walking down a fire escape and jumping from the final platform. The geometry of the stairs was taken from the building onto which it was projected, completing the illusion of silhouettes walking and then jumping off the building. She explains:

> The first in a series of works reflecting on the life of buildings—what has happened in their past, what lies within, and how they relate to the natural environment. This work uses the evocative potential of the fire escape to speak about flight, disappearance and leave-taking.[5]

*Building Id*, Conrad Gleber. Video projection.
Photo Credit Conrad Gleber and Gail Rubini.

The second piece using projection was Conrad Gleber's *Building Id*. *Building Id* is "a sequence of projected video images about the place buildings have in our social life and their role as witnesses over time. The images, all subjects about movement, seen projected on and with the building suggest a dream state and create an entity, a character, out of the relationship between the juxtaposition of what the building is and how we see it."[6] One of the most provocative aspects of this piece was the image of the windows of the building shimmering over the "real" windows. The juxtaposition destabilized the solidity of the building and reduced both building and video to image.

The second mode of media intervention was an interactive performance. In the work *Preserving Disorder*, Drew Browning shifted the viewer into the position of performer. As one approached a group of floating images on the ground, one's bodily movement directed the motion of the images to reveal text. Browning explains his intervention in this way: "Based on the social unrest of 1968 in the area of the conference (Chicago's South Loop), this piece looks at issues of dissent and disorder. A person walking on the

———————————— View of stationary screen and truck outfitted ————————————
with mobile screen. *rove*, Mat Rappaport.
Photo Credit Conrad Gleber and Gail Rubini.

sidewalk will interact with images from the summer of '68, triggering behavior in virtual agents that reflects that of the protestors and police."[7] What is remarkable in this piece is that the viewer transforms into performer. The animation requires the activation of the viewer's body in space, thus linking body to place and place to the past. The setting of the sidewalk, often experienced through habit, has been overlaid and activated by a presentation of and interaction with historic context.

My own contribution to the project was entitled *rove* and it aimed to explore notions of alertness and distraction through an examination of local architecture and travel patterns. *rove* was comprised of two video screens. The first video screen was mobile and mounted in the back of a moving truck that traced a four block loop. A second screen was located at one of the street corners along the path that the mobile unit traced. Once every eight minutes the mobile screen pulled up to the stationary screen and rested for four minutes. During this time the two screens combine and are read as one larger surface.

The two screens shared similar imagery. Both presented video clips of the L train passing overhead, L infrastructure, and escalators with and without people. The video on the two screens was differentiated in that images that included people were relegated to the stationary screen. The video was shot on site and was clearly recognizable as such. The positioning of the screen in relation to the street orientation allowed for a view of the real L tracks and trains a block to the east. This allowed for somewhat randomly rotating instances of both screens showing the L with the physical "real" L appearing in the distance as a mirror.

Like *Preserving Disorder*, *rove* can be read as a performance in which three elements—mobile screen, stationary screen, and the built environment in the form of the L—move in and out of coherent relationship. The work is predicated on fragmentation and is coalesced imperfectly by the moving unit and the unpredictability of the L. As *rove* exists as distributed fragments, it resists the notion of a work of art requiring the concentration of the viewer and instead feeds into the state of distraction in which Benjamin's public exists. Like the viewer, the piece shifts between states of fragmentation/distraction and coalescence/attention.

Truck-mounted mobile screen travelling through the neighborhood. *rove*, Mat Rappaport. Photo Credit Conrad Gleber and Gail Rubini.

Within my own practice I have continued to develop other mobile video works in the vein of *rove*. I have been fascinated by the manner and frequency with which threats to social and national security have been depicted in the news media as well as dramatized on television and film. The relationship between the factual and dramatic has become blurred as one feeds off the other. In 2006 there was a significant media focus on ports as potential security risks precipitated by the announced sale of six American port operations to a company based in the United Arab Emirates (UAE). In response to this controversy, I developed a multichannel video installation and public performance titled *span*.[8] This installation draws attention to the Port of Milwaukee and the Milwaukee Art Museum, two sites of import and distribution in the city of Milwaukee. By using two box trucks to repeatedly trace the route between the port and the Milwaukee Art Museum, *span* links these sites literally and symbolically. One of my goals with *span* was to confound the timeline between the event, the reenactment, and the performance. The gallery presentation was both a reenactment and a dramatization of the symbolism of the truck performance. In this case, however, the reenactment preceded the dramatization.

The intersection of architecture, television, and film remakes a world whose audience is conditioned to a state of distracted consumption. The architectural program and the treatment of the public as an audience configures a new condition of viewing, a process of worldmaking in which the audience is both habitual and transient. Populating urban built environments with televisual media infrastructure and programming presents opportunities for artists to insert *feedback* into the system, whether sanctioned or unsanctioned. The *v1b3* projects and associated works that I have discussed here address the viewer as part of a system of distractions, aimed at providing feedback into the existing messages that are often passed by. The truck is no longer a truck but a carrier of images; the sidewalk is no longer for passing but evokes its own history; an old fire escape becomes the armature for images evacuating the picture plane and the building breathes and contorts as a reminder if its vitality. As an artist and as one of the distracted masses, I attempt to make connections between the fragments of my experience: an image, some text, a clip, the façade. Together they have me wondering about these sites of consumption and the possibility of pushing back at the signal.

# 11
# Bio Art

## EDUARDO KAC

In 1998, I introduced the concept and the phrase "bio art," originally in relation to my artwork "Time Capsule" (1997). This work approached the problem of wet interfaces and human hosting of digital memory through the
implantation of a microchip. The work consisted of a microchip implant,
seven sepia-toned photographs, a live television broadcast, a Webcast, interactive telerobotic Webscanning of the implant, a remote database intervention, and additional display elements, including an X-ray of the implant.
While "bio art" is applicable to a large gamut of in-vivo works that employ
biological media, made by myself and others, already in 1998, I started to
employ the more focused term "transgenic art" to describe a new art form
based on the use of genetic engineering to create unique living beings. Art
that manipulates or creates life must be pursued with great care, with
acknowledgment of the complex issues it raises and, above all, with a commitment to respect, nurture, and love the life created. I have been creating
and exhibiting a series of transgenic artworks since 1999. I have also been
creating bio art that is not transgenic. The implications of this ongoing body
of work have particular aesthetic and social ramifications, crossing several
disciplines and providing material for further reflection and dialogue. What
follows is an overview of these works, the issues they evoke, and the debates
they have elicited.

For almost two decades my work has explored the boundaries between
humans, animals, and robots.[1] Thus, transgenic art can be seen as a natural
development of my previous work. In my telepresence art, developed since
1986, humans coexist with other humans and nonhuman animals through
telerobotic bodies. In my biotelematic art, developed since 1994, biology and
networking are no longer co-present but coupled so as to produce a hybrid of

the living and the telematic. With transgenic art, developed since 1998, the animate and the technological can no longer be distinguished.

The presence of biotechnology will increasingly change from agricultural and pharmaceutical practices to a larger role in popular culture, just as the perception of the computer changed historically from an industrial device and military weapon to a communication, entertainment, and education tool. Terms formerly perceived as "technical," such as *megabytes* and *ram*, for example, have entered the vernacular. Likewise, jargon that today may seem out of place in ordinary discourse, such as *marker* and *protein*, will simply be incorporated into the larger verbal landscape of everyday language. This is made clear by the fact that high school students in the United States already create transgenic bacteria routinely in classroom school labs through affordable kits. The popularization of aspects of technical discourse inevitably brings with it the risk of dissemination of a reductive and instrumental ideological view of the world. Without ever relinquishing its right to formal experimentation and subjective inventiveness, art can and should contribute to the development of alternative views of the world that resist dominant ideologies. As both utopian and dystopian artists such as Moholy-Nagy and Jean Tinguely have done before, in my work I appropriate and subvert contemporary technologies—not to make detached comments on social change, but to *enact* critical views, to make present in the physical world invented new entities (artworks that include transgenic organisms) that seek to open a new space for both emotional and intellectual aesthetic experience.

I have been employing the phrase "bio art" since 1997, in reference to my own works that involved biological agency (as opposed to biological objecthood), such as "Time Capsule"[2] and "A-positive,"[3] both presented in 1997. The difference between biological agency and biological objecthood is that the former involves an active principle, while the latter implies material self-containment. In 1998 I introduced the phrase "transgenic art" in a paper-manifesto of the same title[4] and proposed the creation (and social integration) of a dog expressing green fluorescent protein. This protein is commonly used as a biomarker in genetic research; however, my goal was to use it primarily for its visual properties as a symbolic gesture, a social marker. The initial public response to the paper was curiosity laced with incredulity. The proposal was perfectly viable, but it seemed that few believed that the project could or would be realized. While I struggled to find venues that could assist me in creating the aforementioned project, entitled "GFP K-9," I, too, realized that canine reproductive technology was not developed enough at the time to enable me to create a dog expressing green fluorescent protein.[5] In the meantime, I started to develop a new transgenic art work, entitled "Genesis," which premiered at Ars Electronica '99.[6]

## Genesis

"Genesis" is a transgenic art work that explores the intricate relationship between biology, belief systems, information technology, dialogical inter-action, ethics, and the internet. The key element of the work is an "artist's gene," a synthetic gene that was created by translating a sentence from the biblical book of "Genesis" into Morse Code, and converting the Morse Code into DNA base pairs according to a conversion principle I specially developed for this work. The sentence reads: "Let man have dominion over the fish of the sea, and over the fowl of the air, and over every living thing that moves upon the earth." It was chosen for what it implies about the dubious—yet divinely sanctioned—notion of humanity's supremacy over nature. Morse Code was chosen because, as the first example of the use of radiotelegraphy, it represents the dawn of the information age—the genesis of global commu-nication. The "Genesis" gene was incorporated into bacteria, which were

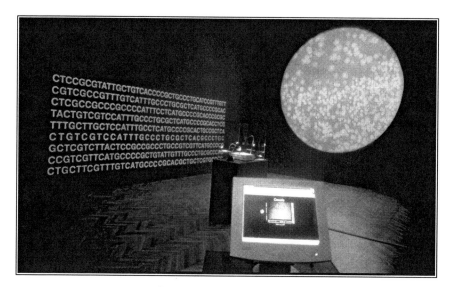

———————— Eduardo Kac, "Genesis," 1999. ————————
Transgenic work with artist-created bacteria, ultraviolet light,
internet, video (detail), edition of 2, dimensions variable.
Collection Instituto Valenciano de Arte Moderno (IVAM), Valencia, Spain.

shown in the gallery. Participants on the Web could turn on an ultraviolet light in the gallery, causing real, biological mutations in the bacteria. This changed the biblical sentence in the bacteria. After the show, the DNA of the bacteria was translated back into Morse Code, and then back into English. The mutation that took place in the DNA had changed the original sentence from the Bible. The mutated sentence was posted on the "Genesis" Web site. In the context of the work, the ability to change the sentence is a symbolic gesture: it means that we do not accept its meaning in the form we inherited, and that new meanings emerge as we seek to alter it.

While presenting "Genesis," I also gave a public lecture at the symposium "Life Science," presented by Ars Electronica '99. My lecture focused on the "GFP K-9" proposal. To contextualize my presentation, I reviewed the long history of human-dog domestication and partnership, and pointed out the direct and strong human influence on the evolution of the dog up to the present day. Emphasizing that there are no packs of Poodles and Chihuahuas running in the wild and that the creation of the dog out of the wolf was a technology—a fact that we have lost awareness of over the centuries—I proceeded to point out the complex relationship between dogs and humans throughout their long history together, going back to at least fourteen thousand years, according to archeological records. While some showed support and appreciation for the work, others reacted against the project and voiced their opposition. The stage was set for a very productive dialogue, which was one of my original intentions. As I see it, a useful debate must go beyond official policy-making and academic research to encompass the general public, including artists. "GFP K-9" was discussed in art magazines and books and science journals. Daily newspapers and general magazines also discussed the work in progress. While specialized publications showed greater appreciation for "GFP K-9," the response in the general media covered the gamut, from forthright rejection to consideration of multiple implications to unequivocal support. The shock generated by the proposal curiously caused one critic to declare "the end of art."[7] As I see it, there's no reason to see the beginning of a new art as the end of anything.

**GFP Bunny**

This pattern of response repeated itself, on a truly global scale, when I announced in 2000 the realization of my second transgenic work. Entitled "GFP Bunny," the work consisted of the creation of a green fluorescent rabbit

Eduardo Kac, "GFP Bunny," 2000, transgenic artwork. ——————
Alba, the fluorescent rabbit.

(named Alba), the public dialogue generated by the project, and the social integration of the rabbit. This work was realized with the assistance of Louis Bec and Louis-Marie Houdebine. Louis Bec worked as the producer, coordinating the activities in France. Bec and I met at Ars Electronica (September 1999) and soon afterward he contacted Houdebine on my behalf to propose the project. Months later, in 2000, Alba, a gentle and healthy rabbit, was born. As I stated in my paper entitled "GFP Bunny,"[8] "transgenic art is a new art form based on the use of genetic engineering to create unique living beings. This must be done with great care, with acknowledgment of the complex issues thus raised and, above all, with a commitment to respect, nurture, and love the life thus created."

"GFP Bunny" attracted local media in the south of France in June 2000 when the former director of the French institute where Alba was born used his authority to overrule the scientists who worked on the project and refused to let Alba go to Avignon and then come to my family in Chicago. This was an arbitrary decision and was privately made by one individual (the former director of the institute). He never explained his reason for the refusal, so it remains unknown to this day. Bec and I denounced the censorship through the internet and through interviews with the press.[9] If the objective was to silence the media, the result backfired. "GFP Bunny" became a global media scandal after a front-page article appeared in the *Boston Globe*,[10] sharing headlines with articles about the 2000 Olympics and U.S. presidential debates. Articles about Alba were published in all major countries, with wire services further spreading the news worldwide.[11] Alba was also on the cover of *Le Monde*, the *San Francisco Chronicle*, and *L'Espresso*, among others. *Der Spiegel* and the *Chicago Tribune* dedicated full pages to "GFP Bunny." She also appeared on the front page of the Arts section of the *New York Times*. Broadcasts by ABC TV, BBC Radio, and Radio France also took the Alba story to the whole planet. From mid-2000 to early 2003, the relentless response to "GFP Bunny" was equally intense and fascinating, with fruitful debate consisting of both strong opposition and support. Since October 15, 2000, the "Alba Guestbook" has been collecting general opinions about the work and expressions of support to bring Alba home.[12] Through lectures and symposia, internet postings, and e-mail correspondence, the debate intensified and became richer, more subtle and nuanced, as I had hoped. The response to "GFP Bunny" constitutes extremely rich material, which I hope to revisit in the near future.

As part of my intercontinental custody battle to obtain Alba's release, between December 3 and December 13, 2000, I staged a public campaign in Paris, which included lectures, broadcasts, public and private meetings, and the public placement of a series of seven posters. I placed individual posters in several neighborhoods, including: Le Marais, Quartier Latin, Saint Germain, Champs de Mars, Bastille, Montparnasse, and Montmartre. The posters reflect some of the readings afforded by "GFP Bunny." They show the same image of Alba and me together, each with a heading using a different French word: Art, Médias, Science, Éthique, Religion, Nature, Famille.[13] During those ten days, in conjunction with radio (Radio France and Radio France Internationale), print (*Le Monde*, *Libération*, *Transfert*, *Ça M'intéresse*, *Nova*), and television (Canal+, Paris Première) interviews and debates, I posted these images on the streets in an effort to intervene in the context of French public opinion and gather support for my cause to bring Alba home. I also engaged the public directly through a series of lectures (Sorbonne, École Normale Superior, École Superior des Beaux Arts, Forum des Images) and through face-to-face conversations on the street sparked by the public's interest. In total, I reached approximately 1.5 million people (about half of the population of Paris). This was an important step, as it allowed me to address the Parisian public directly. In 2001, I created "The Alba Flag," a white flag with the green rabbit silhouette, and started to fly it in front of my Chicago-area house. The flag not only publicly signals the green bunny's home, but, most important, stands as a social marker, a beacon of her absence.

Continuing my efforts to raise awareness about Alba's plight and to obtain her freedom, in 2002 I presented a solo exhibition entitled "Free Alba!"[14] at Julia Friedman Gallery, in Chicago (May 3–June 15, 2002). "Free Alba!" included a large body of new work comprised of large-scale color photographs, drawings, prints, Alba flags, and Alba t-shirts. Seen together for the first time were the posters from my public interventions in Paris (2000), an Alba flag flying outside the Gallery (2001), photographs that reclaim green bunny narratives circulated by global media (2001–2002), drawings that reflect on our closeness to the "animal other" (2001–2002), and Alba t-shirts that extend Alba's cause beyond gallery walls (2002). Through the leitmotif of the green bunny, this exhibition explored the poetics of life and evolution. The story of "GFP Bunny" was adapted and customized by news organizations worldwide, often generating new narratives that, both intentionally and unintentionally, reinstated or overlooked the facts. My "Free Alba!" exhibition featured photographs in which I reappropriated and recontextualized this vast coverage, exhibiting the productive tension that is generated when contemporary art enters the realm of daily news. The photographs in this series dramatize the fact that the reception of "GFP Bunny" was complex, taking place across cultures and in diverse locations. I will continue to develop new strategies to make Alba's case public and to pursue her liberation.

Parallel to this effort, transgenic art evolves. One new direction involves the creation of nanoscale three-dimensional structures built of amino acids. This "proteic art," or "protein art," can be experienced in many forms, including in vivo, in vitro, and expanded into other settings, such as rapid-prototype models and online navigational spaces. All of these forms, and many others, can be combined through new bio-interfaces. A prominent aspect of this path is the fact that these three-dimensional structures are assembled according to combinatory rules that follow strict biological principles (otherwise it is not possible to produce them), even if one invents and synthesizes a new protein. This constraint imposes a biomorphology that offers a new and fascinating creative challenge. A second new direction involves complex interactive transgenic environments with multiple organisms and biobots, biological robots partially regulated by internal transgenic microorganisms.

## Sculpting New Proteins

While the first phase of "Genesis" focused on the creation and the mutation of a synthetic gene through Web participation, the second phase, carried out in 2000/2001, focused on the protein produced by the synthetic gene, the "Genesis" protein,[15] and on new works that examine the cultural implications of proteins as fetish objects. The "Genesis" protein is another step in the translation of the original Biblical text, this time from the "Genesis" gene (itself encoding the English sentence) to a three-dimensional form made up of discrete parts (aminoacids). The transmogrification of a verbal text into a sculptural form is laden with intersemiotic resonances that contribute to expand the historically rich intertextuality between word, image, and spatial form. The process of biological mutation extends it into time.

A critical stance is manifested throughout the "Genesis" project by following scientifically accurate methods in the real production and visualization of a gene and a protein that I have invented and that have absolutely no function or value in biology. Rather than explicating or illustrating scientific principles, the "Genesis" project complicates and obfuscates the extreme simplification and reduction of standard molecular biology descriptions of life processes, reinstating social and historical contextualization at the core of the debate. I appropriate the techniques of biotechnology to critique the language of science and its inherent ideologies, while developing transgenic art as an alternative means for individual expression. In its genomic and proteomic manifestations, the "Genesis" project continues to reveal new readings and possibilities.

Protein production is a fundamental aspect of life. Multiple research centers around the world are currently focusing their initiatives on sequencing, organizing, and analyzing the genomes of both simple and complex organisms, from bacteria to human beings. After genomics (the study of genes and their function) comes proteomics (the study of proteins and their function). Proteomics, the dominant research agenda in molecular biology in the postgenomic world, focuses on the visualization of the three-dimensional structure of proteins produced by sequenced genes.[16] It is also concerned with the study of the structure and functionality of these proteins, among many other important aspects, such as similarities among proteins found in different organisms. The second phase of "Genesis" critically investigates the logic, the methods, and the symbolism of proteomics, as well as its potential as a domain of artmaking.

In order to arrive at the visualization of the "Genesis" protein, I first explored aspects of its two-dimensional structure.[17] The next step was to compare the predicted folding pattern of the "Genesis" protein to another known protein to which it is similar: Chorion. With the goal of producing a tangible rendition of the nanostructure of the "Genesis" protein, I researched protein fold homology using the Protein Data Bank, operated by the Research Collaboratory for Structural Bioinformatics (RCSB). I then produced a digital visualization of the "Genesis" protein's three-dimensional structure.[18] This three-dimensional dataset was used to produce both digital and physical versions of the protein. The digital version is a fully navigable Web object rendered both as VRML (Virtual Reality Modeling Language) and PDB (Protein Data Bank) formats, to enable close inspection of its complex volumetric structure. The physical rendition is a small solid object produced via rapid-prototyping, to convey in tangible form the fragility of this molecular object.[19] This object was used as a mold for casting the final form of the protein used in the creation of the "Transcription Jewels."

"Transcription Jewels" is a set of two objects encased in a custom-made round wooden box. The word "transcription" is the term employed in biology to name the process during which the genetic information is "transcribed" from DNA into RNA.[20] One "jewel" is a two-inch genie bottle in clear glass with gold ornaments and 65mg of purified "Genesis" DNA inside. "Purified DNA" means that countless copies of the DNA have been isolated from the bacteria in which they were produced and accumulated and filtrated in a vial. The gene is seen here out of the context of the body, its meaning intentionally reduced to a formal entity to reveal that without acknowledgment of the vital roles played by organism and environment, the "priceless" gene can become "worthless." The other "jewel" is an equally small gold cast of the three-dimensional structure of the "Genesis" protein. By displaying the emblematic elements of the biotech revolution (the gene and the protein) as coveted valuables, "Transcription Jewels" makes an ironic commentary on the process of commodification of the most minute aspects of life. Neither the purified gene in "Transcription Jewels" nor its protein were derived from a natural organism; rather, they were created specifically for the artwork "Genesis." Instead of a "genie" inside the bottle one finds the new panacea, the gene. There are no wishes of immortality, beauty, or intelligence granted by the inert and isolated gene sealed inside the miniature bottle. As a result, the irony gains a critical and humorous twist by the fact that the "precious commodity" is devoid of any real, practical application in biology.

All pieces described and discussed above, including the net installation with live bacteria, were presented together in my solo exhibition "Genesis," realized at Julia Friedman Gallery, in Chicago, between May 4 and June 2, 2001. The multiple mutations experienced biologically by the bacteria and graphically by the images, texts, and systems that compose the exhibition reveal that the alleged supremacy of the so-called master molecule must be questioned. The "Genesis" series challenges the genetic hype and opposes the dominant bio-deterministic interpretation, stating that we must continue to consider life as a complex assemblage at the crossroads between belief systems, economic principles, legal parameters, political directives, scientific laws, and cultural constructs.

## The Eighth Day: A Transgenic Net Installation

"The Eighth Day" is a transgenic artwork that investigates the new ecology of fluorescent creatures that is evolving worldwide. It was shown from October 25 to November 2, 2001 at the Institute for Studies in the Arts, Arizona State University, Tempe.[21] While fluorescent creatures are being developed in isolation in laboratories, seen collectively in this work for the first time they form the nucleus of a new and emerging synthetic bioluminescent ecosystem. The piece brings together living transgenic life forms and a biological robot (biobot) in an environment enclosed under a clear Plexiglas dome, thus making visible what it would be like if these creatures would in fact coexist in the world at large.

As the viewer walks into the gallery, she first sees a blue-glowing hemisphere against a dark background. This hemisphere is a four-foot dome, aglow with an internal blue light. Our viewer also hears the recurring sounds of water washing ashore. This evokes the image of the Earth as seen from space. The sounds of water function as a metaphor for life on Earth (reinforced by the spherical blue image) and resonate with the video of moving water projected on the floor. In order to see "The Eighth Day" the viewer is invited to "walk on water."

In the gallery, visitors are able to see the terrarium with transgenic creatures both from inside and outside the dome. As they stand outside the dome looking in, someone online sees the space from the perspective of the biobot looking out, perceiving the transgenic environment as well as faces or bodies of local viewers. An online computer in the gallery also gives local visitors an exact sense of what the experience is like remotely on the internet.

Local viewers may temporarily believe that their gaze is the only human gaze contemplating the organisms in the dome. However, once they navigate the Web interface they realize that remote viewers can also experience the environment from a bird's eye point of view, looking down through a camera mounted above the dome. They can pan, tilt, and zoom, seeing humans, mice, plants, fish, and the biobot up close. Thus, from the point of view of the online participant, local viewers become part of the ecology of living creatures featured in the work, as if enclosed in a Websphere.

"The Eighth Day" presents an expansion of biodiversity beyond wildtype life forms. As a self-contained artificial ecology, it resonates with its title, which adds one day to the period of creation of the world as narrated in the Judeo-Christian Scriptures. All of the transgenic creatures in "The Eighth Day" are created with the same gene I used previously in "GFP Bunny" to create Alba, a gene that allows all creatures to glow green under harmless blue light. The transgenic creatures in "The Eighth Day" are GFP plants, GFP amoeba, GFP fish, and GFP mice. Selective breeding and mutation are two key evolutionary forces. "The Eighth Day" literally raises the question of transgenic evolution, since all organisms in the piece are mutations of their respective wildtype species and all were selected and bred for their GFP mutations.

"The Eighth Day" also includes a biological robot. A biobot is a robot with an active biological element within its body that is responsible for aspects of its behavior. The biobot created for "The Eighth Day" has a colony of GFP amoeba called Dyctiostelium discoideum as its "brain cells." These "brain cells" form a network within a bioreactor that constitutes the "brain structure" of the biobot. When amoebas divide, the biobot exhibits dynamic behavior inside the enclosed environment. Changes in the amoebal colony (the "brain cells") of the biobot are monitored and cause it to move about throughout the exhibition. The biobot also functions as the avatar of Web participants inside the environment. Independent of the ascent and descent of the biobot, Web participants are able to control its audio-visual system with a pan-tilt actuator. The autonomous motion, which often causes the biobot to lean forward in different directions, provides Web participants with new perspectives of the environment.

The biobot's "amoebal brain" is visible through the transparent bioreactor body. In the gallery, visitors are able to see the terrarium with transgenic creatures from outside and inside the dome, as a computer in the gallery gives local visitors an exact sense of what the experience is like on the internet. By enabling participants to experience the environment inside the dome from the point of view of the biobot, "The Eighth Day" creates a context in which participants can reflect on the meaning of a transgenic ecology from a first-person perspective.

## Move 36

"Move 36" makes reference to the dramatic move made by the computer called Deep Blue against chess world champion Gary Kasparov in 1997, which culminated in the computer's win after a series of six games.[22] This competition pitted the greatest chess player who ever lived against the greatest chess player who never lived. The installation—presented for the first time at the Exploratorium, in San Francisco, from February 26 to May 31, 2004— sheds light on the limits of the human mind and the increasing capabilities developed by computers and robots, inanimate beings whose actions often acquire a force comparable to subjective human agency.

According to Kasparov, Deep Blue's quintessential moment in Game Two came at Move 36. Rather than making a move that was expected by viewers and commentators—a sound move that would have afforded immediate gratification—Deep Blue made a move that was subtle and conceptual and, in the long run, better. Kasparov could not believe that a machine had made such a keen move. The game, in his mind, was lost.

The installation presents a chessboard made of earth (dark squares) and white sand (light squares) in the middle of the room. There are no chess pieces on the board. Positioned exactly where Deep Blue made its Move 36 is a plant whose genome incorporates a new gene that I created specifically for this work. The gene uses ASCII (the universal computer code for representing binary numbers as Roman characters) to translate Descartes' statement: "Cogito ergo sum" (I think therefore I am) to the four bases of genetics, ACGT.

Through genetic modification, the leaves of the plants grow multiple plantlets. In the wild, these leaves would be smooth. The "Cartesian gene" was coupled with a gene for the expression of the plantlets, so that the public can easily see with the naked eye that the "Cartesian gene" is expressed precisely where the plantlets grow.

The "Cartesian gene" was produced according to a new code I created especially for the work. In 8-bit ASCII, the letter C, for example, is: 01000011. Thus, the gene is created by the following association between genetic bases and binary digits:

A = 00
C = 01
G = 10
T = 11

The result is the following gene with 52 bases:

CAATCATTCACTCAGCCCCACATTCACCCCAGCACTCATTCCATCCCCCATC

The creation of this gene is a critical and ironic gesture, since Descartes considered the human mind a "ghost in the machine" (for him the body was a "machine"). His rationalist philosophy gave new impetus both to the mind-body split (Cartesian Dualism) and to the mathematical foundations of current computer technology.

The presence of this "Cartesian gene" in the plant, rooted precisely where the human lost to the machine, reveals the tenuous border between humanity, inanimate objects endowed with lifelike qualities, and living organisms that encode digital information. A single focused light shines in a delicate luminous cone over the plant. On two opposing walls, silent, square-formatted video projections contextualize the work, evoking two chess opponents in absentia. Each video projection is composed of a grid of small squares, resembling a chessboard. Each square shows short animated loops cycling at different intervals, thus creating a complex and carefully choreographed thread of movements. The cognitive engagement of the viewer with the multiple visual possibilities presented on both projected boards subtly emulates the mapping of multiple paths on the board involved in a chess match.

This work encompasses a game for phantasmic players, a philosophical statement uttered by a plant, a sculptural process that explores the poetics of real life and evolution, and gives continuity to my ongoing interventions at the boundaries between the living and the non-living. Checkmating traditional notions, nature is revealed as an arena for the production of ideological conflict, and the physical sciences as a locus for the creation of science fictions.

## Specimen of Secrecy about Marvelous Discoveries

"Specimen of Secrecy about Marvelous Discoveries" is a series of works comprised of what I call "biotopes," which are living pieces that change during the exhibition in response to internal metabolism and environmental conditions, including temperature, relative humidity, airflow, and light levels in the exhibition space.[23] Each of my biotopes is literally a self-sustaining ecology comprised of thousands of very small living beings in a medium of earth, water, and other material. I orchestrate the metabolism of this diverse microbial life in order to produce the constantly evolving, living works.

My biotopes expand on ecological and evolutionary issues I previously explored in transgenic works such as "The Eighth Day." At the same time, the biotopes further develop dialogical principles that have been central to my work for over two decades. The biotopes are a discrete ecology because within their world the microorganisms interact with and support each other (that is, the activities of one organism enable another to grow, and vice versa). However, they are not entirely secluded from the outside world: the aerobic organisms within the biotope absorb oxygen from outside (while the anaerobic ones comfortably migrate to regions where air cannot reach). A complex set of relationships emerge as the work unfolds, bringing together the internal dialogical interactions among the microorganisms in the biotope and the interaction of the biotope as a discrete unit with the external world.

The biotope is what I refer to as a "nomad ecology," that is, an ecological system that interacts with its surroundings as it travels around the world. Every time a biotope migrates from one location to another, the very act of transporting it causes an unpredictable redistribution of the microorganisms inside it (due to the constant physical agitation inherent in the course of a trip). Once in place, the biotope self-regulates with internal migrations, metabolic exchanges, and material settling. Extended presence in a single location might yield a different behavior, possibly resulting in regions of settlement and color concentration.

The biotope is affected by several factors, including the very presence of viewers, which can increase the temperature in the room (warm bodies) and release other microorganisms in the air (breathing, sneezing). I consider the exhibition opening as the birth of a given biotope. Once an exhibition begins, I allow the microorganisms in suspended animation to become active again. From that point on, I no longer intervene. The work becomes progressively different, changing every day, every week, every month. When the viewer looks at a biotope, she sees what could be described as an "image." However, since this "image" is always evolving into its next transformative state, the perceived "stillness" is more a consequence of the conditions of observation (limits of the human perception, ephemeral presence of the viewer in the gallery) than an internal material property of the biotope. Viewers looking at the biotope on another day will see a different "image." Given the cyclical nature of this "image," each "image" seen at a given time is but a moment in the evolution of the work, an ephemeral snapshot of the biotope metabolic state, a scopic interface for human intimacy.

Each of my "biotopes" explores what I call "biological time," which is time manifested throughout the life cycle of a being itself, in vivo (contrary to, say, the frozen time of painting or photography, the montaged time of film or video, or the real time of a telecommunications event). This open process continuously transforms the image and may, depending upon factors such as lighting conditions and exhibition length, result in its effacement—until the cycle begins again. The biotope's cycle starts when I produce the self-contained body by integrating microorganisms and nutrient-rich media. In the next step, I control the amount of energy the microorganisms receive in order to keep some of them active and others in suspended animation. This results in what the viewer may momentarily perceive as a still image. However, even if the image seems "still," the work is constantly evolving and is never physically the same. Only timelapse video could reveal the transformation undergone by a given biotope in the course of its slow change and evolution.

To think of a biotope only in terms of microscopic living beings is extremely limiting. While it is also possible to describe a human being in terms of cells, a person is much more than an agglomerate of cells. A person is a whole, not the sum of parts. We shall not confuse our ability to describe a living entity in a given manner and the phenomenological consideration of what it is like to be that entity, for that entity. The biotope is a whole. Its presence and overall behavior is that of a new entity that is at once an art work and a new living being. It is with this bioambiguity that it manifests itself. It is as a whole that the biotope behaves and seeks to satisfy its needs. The biotope asks for light and, occasionally, water. In this sense, it is an art work that asks for the participation of the viewer in the form of personal care. Like a pet, it will keep company and will produce more colors in response to the care it receives. Like a plant, it will respond to light. Like a machine, it is pro-grammed to function according to a specific feedback principle (e.g., expose it to more heat and it will grow more). Like an object, it can be boxed and transported. Like an animal with an exoskeleton, it is multicellular, has fixed bodily structure, and is singular. What is the biotope? It is its plural ontolog-ical condition that makes it unique.

## Conclusion

Quite clearly, genetic engineering will continue to have profound conse-quences in art as well as in the social, medical, political, and economic spheres of life. As an artist, I am interested in reflecting on the multiple social implications of genetics, from unacceptable abuse to its hopeful prom-ises, from the notion of "code" to the question of translation, from the syn-thesis of genes to the process of mutation, from the metaphors employed by biotechnology to the fetishization of genes and proteins, from simple reduc-tive narratives to complex views that account for environmental influences. The urgent task is to unpack the implicit meanings of the biotechnology rev-olution and contribute to the creation of alternative views, thus changing genetics into a critically aware new art medium.

The tangible and symbolic coexistence of the human and the transgenic, which I have developed in several of my aforementioned works, shows that humans and other species are evolving in new ways. It dramatizes the urgent need to develop new models with which to understand this change, and calls for the interrogation of difference, taking into account clones, transgenics, and chimeras.

The Human Genome Project (HGP) has made it clear that all humans have in their genome sequences that came from viruses,[24] acquired through a long evolutionary history. This shows that we have in our bodies DNA from organ-isms other than human. Ultimately, this means that we too are transgenic. Before deciding that all transgenics are "monstrous," humans must look inside and come to terms with our own "monstrosity," with our own trans-genic condition.

The common perception that transgenics are not "natural" is incorrect. It is important to understand that the process of moving genes from one species to another is part of wild life (without human participation). The most common example is the bacterium called "agrobacterium," which enters the root of plants and communicates its genes to it. Agrobacterium has the ability to transfer DNA into plant cells and integrate the DNA into the plant chromosome.[25] Transgenic art suggests that romantic notions of what is "natural" have to be questioned and the human role in the evolutionary history of other species (and vice versa) has to be acknowledged, while at the same time respectfully and humbly marveling at this amazing phenomenon we call "life."

# NOTES

## INTRODUCTION

1  Daniel Nettle and Suzanne Romaine, *Vanishing Voices: the Extinction of the World's Languages* (New York: Oxford University Press, 2000).

2  See Arjun Appadurai for problems with the homogenization argument; he brings to attention new disjunctures in the global cultural economy. Arjun Appadurai, *Modernity at Large: Cultural Dimensions of Globalization* (Minneapolis: University of Minnesota Press, 1996).

3  George Ritzer, *The McDonaldization of Society: An Investigation into the Changing Character of Contemporary Social Life* (Newbury Park, Calif.: Pine Forge Press, 1993); James Watson, *Golden Arches East: McDonald's in East Asia* (Stanford, Calif.: Stanford University Press, 1997).

4  Ludwig Wittgenstein, *Philosophical Investigations* (New York: Macmillan, 1953); Niklas Luhmann, *Social Systems* (Stanford, Calif.: Stanford University Press, 1984); Gilles Deleuze, *Difference and Repetition* (New York: Columbia University Press, 1994).

5  Peter L. Berger and Thomas Luckmann, *The Social Construction of Reality: A Treatise in the Sociology of Knowledge* (New York: Anchor Books, 1990).

6  Berger and Luckmann, *The Social Construction of Reality*, 52.

7  John R. Searle, *The Construction of Social Reality* (New York: Free Press, 1995).

8  Ian Hacking, *The Social Construction of What?* (Cambridge, Mass.: Harvard University Press, 1999).

9  Berger and Luckmann, *The Social Construction of Reality*, 52.

10  Appadurai, *Modernity at Large*, 31.

11  Benedict Anderson, *Imagined Communities: Reflections on the Origin and Spread of Nationalism* (New York: Verso, 1991).

12  Appadurai, *Modernity at Large*.

13  James G. Ferguson and Akhil Gupta, "Beyond 'Culture': Space, Identity, and the Politics of Difference," *Cultural Anthropology* 7:1 (1992): 6–23.

14  A. Aneesh, "Imperial Neutrality: Clashes of the Future in India's Call Centers," *global-e* 2:1 (2008).

## CHAPTER 1

1  See for example the important volume by Pheng Cheah and Bruce Robbins, Pheng Cheah and Bruce Robbins, eds., *Cosmopolitics: Thinking and Feeling Beyond the Nation* (Minneapolis: University of Minnesota Press, 1998).

**2** David Held for example begins his discussion of cosmopolitan political theory by turning to Kant, in *Democracy and the Global Order: From the Modern State to Cosmopolitan Governance* (Palo Alto, Calif.: Stanford University Press, 1995).

**3** Jacques Derrida, *Cosmopolites de Tous les Pays, Encore un Effort!* (Paris: Galilée, 1997); Cheah and Robbins, *Cosmopolitics*; Ulrich Beck and Patrick Camiller, trans., *What is Globalization?* (Malden, Mass.: Blackwell, 2000); Mike Featherstone and Scott Lash, *Recognition and Difference: Politics, Identity, Multiculture* (London: Sage, 2002).

**4** Immanuel Kant and Lewis White Beck, trans., *Idea for a Universal History from a Cosmopolitan Point of View (1784). From "On History"* (Indianapolis: The Bobbs-Merrill Co., 1963), 16.

**5** For a recent example of theorizing the universal see Judith Butler, Ernesto Laclau, Slavoj Zizek, *Contingency, Hegemony, Universality: Contemporary Dialogues on the Left* (New York: Verso, 2000).

**6** The Robbins/Cheah collection contains not a single essay on media. Only the Gayatri Spivak essay mentions the question of media and does so briefly. Yet another collection of essays on "cosmopolitics" has no essay on media and does not mention media theorists or raise the question of media at all. See Daneile Archibugi, *Debating Cosmopolitics* (Verso: London, 2003).

**7** John Fiske and John Hartley, *Reading Television* (London: Methuen, 1978); Henry Jenkins, *Textual Poachers: Television Fans & Participatory Culture* (New York: Routledge, 1992), 180.

**8** Manuel Castells, *The Internet Galaxy: Reflections on the Internet, Business, and Society* (New York: Oxford University Press, 2001).

**9** Martin Hand and Barry Sandywell, "E-Topia as Cosmopolis or Citadel: On the Democratizing and De-Democratizing Logics of the Internet, or, Toward a Critique of the New Technological Fetishism," *Theory, Culture & Society* 19:1–2 (2002): 202.

**10** Hand and Sandywell, "E-Topia," 202.

**11** Hand and Sandywell, "E-Topia," 198.

**12** Hand and Sandywell, "E-Topia," 202.

**13** Lisa Parks, *Cultures in Orbit: Satellites and the Televisual* (Durham, N.C.: Duke University Press, 2005), 2.

**14** Wendy Hui Kyong Chun, *Control and Freedom: Power and Paranoia in the Age of Fiber Optics* (Cambridge, Mass.: MIT Press, 2006).

**15** Gary Hall, *Digitize This!* (Minneapolis: University of Minnesota Press, 2008).

**16** Theodor Adorno and Max Horkheimer, *Dialectic of Enlightenment* (New York: Continuum, 1972).

**17** Walter Benjamin, "The Work of Art in the Age of Mechanical Reproduction," in *Illuminations* (New York: Schocken, 1969), 217–251.

**18** Benedict Anderson, *Imagined Communities: Reflections on the Origin and Spread of Nationalism* (New York: Verso, 1983).

**19** Michael Warner, *The Letters of the Republic: Publication and the Public Sphere in Eighteenth-Century America* (Cambridge, Mass.: Harvard University Press, 1992).

**20** Marshall McLuhan, *Understanding Media: The Extensions of Man* (New York: McGraw-Hill. 1964).

**21** Roland Barthes, *S/Z* (New York: Hill and Wang, 1974).

**22** Katherine Hayles, *Writing Machines* (Cambridge, Mass.: MIT Press, 2002).

**23** Fiske and Hartley, *Reading Television*.

**24** Adrian Johns, "The Identity Engine: Print and Publication in the Age of the Knowledge Economy," in *The Mindful Hand: Inquiry and Invention from the Late Renaissance to Early Industrialization*, eds. L. Roberts, S. Schaffer and P. Dear (Chicago: University of Chicago Press, 2007).

**25** Lev Manovich, *The Language of New Media* (Cambridge, Mass.: MIT Press. 2001).

**26** Alexander Galloway, *Protocol: How Control Exists After Decentralization* (Cambridge, Mass.: MIT Press, 2004).

**27** David Morley, "Where the Global Meets the Local: Notes From the Sitting Room," in *Planet TV: A Global Television Reader*, eds. L. Parks and S. Kumar (New York: New York University Press, 2003), 286–302.

**28** Manuel Castells, *The Rise of the Network Society* (Cambridge: Blackwell Publishers, 1996).

**29** George Yúdice, "We Are *Not* the World," *Social Text* 31/32 (1992): 202–216.

**30** Walter Benjamin, "The Task of the Translator," in *Walter Benjamin: Selected Writings, Volume 1*, eds. M. Bullock and M. Jennings (Cambridge, Mass.: Harvard University Press, 1996), 253–263.

**31** Rey Chow, *Primitive Passions: Visuality, Sexuality, Ethnography, and Contemporary Chinese Cinema* (New York: Columbia University Press, 1996).

**32** Rey Chow, *Writing Diaspora* (Bloomington: Indiana University Press, 1993).

**33** Chow, *Primitive Passions*, 180.

**34** Chow, *Primitive Passions*, 194.

**35** Kevin Robins, "Transnational Cultural Policy and European Cosmopolitanism," *Cultural Politics* 3:2 (2007): 147–174.

**36** Aihwa Ong, *Flexible Citizenship: The Cultural Logics of Transnationality* (Durham, N.C.: Duke University Press, 1999); Nestor Garcia Canclini, *Consumers and Citizens: Globalization and Multicultural Conflicts* (Minneapolis: University of Minnesota Press, 2001).

**37** Robins, "Transnational Cultural Policy," 158.

**38** John Tomlinson, *Globalization and Culture* (Chicago: Chicago University Press, 1999).

**39** For an excellent discussion of media concentration from its inception see Edward Herman and Robert McChesney, "The Rise of Global Media," in Parks and Kumar, *Planet TV*, 21–39.

**40** Rosemary Coombe, *The Cultural Life of Intellectual Properties: Authorship, Appropriation, and the Law* (Durham, N.C.: Duke University Press, 1998); Lawrence Lessig, *The Future of Ideas: The Fate of the Commons in a Connected World* (New York: Vintage, 2001).

**41** Laura Gurak, *Persuasion and Privacy in Cyberspace: The Online Protests over Lotus Marketplace and the Clipper Chip* (New Haven, Conn.: Yale University Press, 1997).

**42** Manuel Castells, *The Power of Identity* (Malden, Mass.: Blackwell, 1997).

**43** Graeme Turner, "Shrinking the Borders: Globalization, Culture and Belonging," *Cultural Politics* 3:1 (2007): 5–19.

**44** Lisa Parks, *Cultures in Orbit: Satellites and the Televisual* (Durham, N.C.: Duke University Press, 2005), 73.

45 Ramesh Srinivasan, "Indigenous, Ethnic and Cultural Articulations of New Media," *International Journal of Cultural Studies* 9:4 (2006): 497–518.

46 Ien Ang, "Culture and Communication: Toward an Ethnographic Critique of Media Consumption in the Transnational Media System," in *Planet TV*, 363–375.

CHAPTER 2

Fred Turner, "Burning Man at Google: A Cultural Infrastructure for New Media Production," *New Media & Society* 11:1–2, 73–94, copyright© 2009 by SAGE Publications. Reprinted by Permission of SAGE.

1 "AfterBurn Report 2005" (Burning Man Organization, 2005a): http://afterburn. burningman.com/05/ (URL consulted Jan. 2007).

2 Robert V. Kozinets, "Can Consumers Escape the Market? Emancipatory Illuminations from Burning Man," *Journal of Consumer Research* 29 (2002): 21; Lee Gilmore, "Theater in a Crowded Fire: Spirituality, Ritualization and Cultural Performativity at the Burning Man Festival" (Ph.D. Dissertation, Graduate Theological Union, 2005): 308; "What is Burning Man? 2005 Theme Camps and Villages" (Burning Man Organization, 2005b): http://www.burningman.com/whatis burningman/2005/05_camp_vill_1.html (URL consulted Jan. 2007).

3 Kozinets, "Can Consumers Escape the Market?"; Katherine K.Chen, "The Burning Man Organization Grows Up: Blending Bureaucratic and Alternative Structures" (Ph.D. Dissertation, Harvard University, 2004); Gilmore, "Theater in a Crowded Fire"; Lee Gilmore and Mark Van Proyen, eds., *AfterBurn: Reflections on Burning Man* (Albuquerque: University of New Mexico Press, 2005). See also: Fred Turner, *From Counterculture to Cyberculture: Stewart Brand, the Whole Earth Network, and the Rise of Digital Utopianism* (Chicago: University of Chicago Press, 2006); Lynne Hume and Kathleen McPhillips, *Popular Spiritualities: The Politics of Contemporary Enchantment* (Aldershot, England; Burlington, Vt.: Ashgate, 2006).

4 Vanessa Hua, "Burning Man," *San Francisco Examiner* (August 20, 2000): http:// www.sfgate.com/cgi-bin/article.cgi?file=/examiner/archive/2000/08/20/ NEWS14692.dtl (URL consulted Jan. 2007); Kozinets, "Can Consumers Escape the Market?"; Valleywag (2007): http://valleywag.com/search/burning%20man/ (URL consulted Sept. 2007).

5 Doc Searls, "Bigger Bang," *Doc Searls Weblog* (December 10, 2002): http://doc-weblogs.com/2002/12/10 (URL consulted Sept. 2007).

6 Google, "Untitled video," (2007): http://video.google.com/videoplay?docid=-634 0495833736475157 (URL consulted Sept. 2007).

7 Richard L. Florida, *The Rise of the Creative Class: And How It's Transforming Work, Leisure, Community and Everyday Life* (New York: Basic Books, 2002); Gina Neff, "The Changing Place of Cultural Production: The Location of Social Networks in a Digital Media Industry," *The Annals of the American Academy of Political and Social Science* 597 (2005): 134–152; Fred Turner, "Where the Counterculture Met the New Economy: The Well and the Origins of Virtual Community," *Technology and Culture* 46:3 (2005); Turner, *From Counterculture to Cyberculture*.

8 Florida, *The Rise of the Creative Class*, 235–248.

9 Over the last year, I have done extensive research in the Burning Man Organization's online archives (http://www.burningman.com) and in individual participants' collections. I have conducted formal interviews with twenty-five longtime

participants, including leaders of the Burning Man Organization, participants in three Burning Man groups with strong links to Silicon Valley (the Mad Scientists, Burning Silicon, and Fast Furnishings), and participants who worked for Google, IDEO, and other Silicon Valley information and design firms. Finally, I attended Burning Man for four days each in 2006 and 2007, and had perhaps twice as many informal conversations with participants there.

10  Tiziana Terranova, "Free Labor: Producing Culture for the Digital Economy," *Social Text* 18:2 (2000): 33–58; Andrew Ross, *No-Collar: The Humane Workplace and Its Hidden Costs* (New York: Basic Books, 2003); Gina S. Neff, "Organizing Uncertainty: Individual, Organizational and Institutional Risk in New York's Internet Industry, 1995–2003" (Ph.D. Dissertation, Columbia University, 2004); Neff, "The Changing Place of Cultural Production"; Steven Weber, *The Success of Open Source* (Cambridge, Mass.: Harvard University Press, 2004); Michael Hardt and Antonio Negri, *Multitude: War and Democracy in the Age of Empire* (New York: Penguin Press, 2004); Yochai Benkler, *The Wealth of Networks: How Social Production Transforms Markets and Freedom* (New Haven, Conn.: Yale University Press. 2006); Henry Jenkins, *Convergence Culture: Where Old and New Media Collide* (New York: New York University Press, 2006).

11  Terranova, "Free Labor"; Weber, *The Success of Open Source*; Hardt and Negri, *Multitude*; Jenkins, *Convergence Culture*.

12  Benkler, *The Wealth of Networks*, 63.

13  Weber, *The Success of Open Source*, 135–136.

14  Weber, *The Success of Open Source*, 135–136.

15  Turner, "Where the Counterculture Met the New Economy."

16  Walter W. Powell, "The Capitalist Firm in the Twenty-First Century: Emerging Patterns in Western Enterprise," in *The Twenty-First Century Firm: Changing Economic Organization in International Perspective*, ed. Paul DiMaggio (Princeton, N.J.: Princeton University Press, 2001), 33–68.

17  Annalee Saxenian, *Regional Advantage: Culture and Competition in Silicon Valley and Route 128* (Cambridge, Mass.: Harvard University Press, 1994), 37; Neff, "The Changing Place of Cultural Production."

18  Robert P. Vecchio, *Organizational Behavior* (New York: Harcourt Brace, 1995), 20; Harrison M. Trice and Janice M. Beyer, *The Cultures of Work Organizations* (Englewood Cliffs, N.J.: Prentice-Hall, 1993), 29–32.

19  Tom J. Peters and Robert H. Waterman, *In Search of Excellence: Lessons from America's Best-Run Companies* (New York: Harper & Row, 1982); William G. Ouchi, *Theory Z: How American Business Can Meet the Japanese Challenge* (Reading, Mass.: Addison-Wesley. 1981).

20  Po Bronson, *The Nudist on the Late Shift* (New York: Random House, 1999); Ross, *No-Collar*; Michael Indergaard, *Silicon Alley: The Rise and Fall of a New Media District* (New York: Routledge, 2004); Neff, "Organizing Uncertainty."

21  David Vise and Mark Malsee, *The Google Story* (New York: Delacorte, 2005), 20–57; John Battelle, *The Search: How Google and Its Rivals Rewrote the Rules of Business and Transformed Our Culture* (New York: Portfolio. 2005), 65–93.

22  Dan Farber, "A View into Google's Inner Workings," ZDNet.com (October 25, 2005): http://blogs.zdnet.com/BTL/?p=2065 (URL consulted Jan. 2007).

23  Quoted in Farber, "A View into Google's Inner Workings."

**24** Marissa Mayer, "Speech to Stanford Technology Ventures Program" (Stanford University: May 17, 2006a): http://edcorner.stanford.edu/IndivRec?author=205 (URL consulted Jan. 2007).

**25** Mayer, "Speech to Stanford Technology Ventures Program."

**26** Mayer, "Speech to Stanford Technology Ventures Program."

**27** Battelle, *The Search*, 143–144; Vise and Malsee, *The Google Story*, 133–136.

**28** "100 Best Companies to Work For 2007," *Fortune Magazine* (2007): http://money.cnn.com/magazines/fortune/bestcompanies/2007/snapshots/1.html (URL consulted Jan. 2007).

**29** Bruce Fallick, Charles A. Fleischman, and James B. Rebitzer, "Job-Hopping in Silicon Valley: Some Evidence Concerning the Microfoundations of a High-Technology Cluster," *Review of Economics and Statistics* 88:3 (2006): 472–481.

**30** Gilmore, *Theater in a Crowded Fire*; Gilmore and Van Proyen, *AfterBurn*.

**31** Jess Baron, "Founder on Event's Past, Present, Future," posted on WildWeb.com (1999), reposted on Poprocks: http://www.poprocks.com/journal/burn/larry.html (URL consulted Jan. 2007).

**32** Gilmore, *Theater in a Crowded Fire*, 11.

**33** Matt Wray, "Burning Man and the Rituals of Capitalism," *Bad Subjects* 21 (1995): http://bad.eserver.org/issues/1995/21/wray.html (URL consulted Jan. 2007); quoted in Kozinets, "Can Consumers Escape the Market?"

**34** Robert Kozinets and John F. Sherry, "Welcome to the Black Rock Café," in Gilmore and Van Proyen, *AfterBurn*, 90.

**35** Kozinets, "Can Consumers Escape the Market?" 31.

**36** Baron, "Founder on Event's Past, Present, Future."

**37** Gilmore, *Theater in a Crowded Fire*, 264; Hua, "Burning Man."

**38** Hua, "Burning Man."

**39** Burning Man Organization, "2004 Census Report" (2004): http://afterburn.burningman.com/04/census/census_incspend.html (URL consulted Jan. 2007); Gilmore, *Theater in a Crowded Fire*, 295–308.

**40** Leslie Fulbright, "Burning Man Already a Hot Ticket" *San Francisco Chronicle* (January 6, 2005): B3.

**41** Burning Man Organization, "What is Burning Man? 10 Principles" (2007a): http://www.burningman.com/whatisburningman/about_burningman/principles.html (URL consulted Jan. 2007).

**42** Turner, "Where the Counterculture Met the New Economy."

**43** Tim Black, "Interview with the author" (September 21, 2006).

**44** Larry Harvey, "Interview with the author" (August 30, 2006).

**45** Émile Durkheim and Karen E. Fields, trans., *The Elementary Forms of Religious Life* (New York: Free Press, 1995), 217–221.

**46** Burning Man Organization, "Tales from the Playa" (2007b): http://www.burningman.com/blackrockcity_yearround/tales/index_tales.html (URL consulted Jan. 2007).

**47** Greg MacNicol, "Interview with the author" (October 6. 2006).

**48** Tom Gruber, "Interview with the author" (August 24. 2006).

**49** Waldemar Horwat, "Interview with the author" (August 23. 2006).

**50** MacNicol, "Interview with the author."

**51** Quoted in Katherine K. Chen, "Incendiary Incentives: How the Burning Man Organization Motivates and Manages Volunteers," in Gilmore and Van Proyen, *AfterBurn*, 116–117.

**52** Andie Grace, "Interview with the author" (August 30, 2006); Burning Man Organization, "Regionals" (2007c): http://regionals.burningman.com (URL consulted Jan. 2007).

**53** Burning Man Organization, "Burning Man Earth" (2007d): http://bmearth. burningman.com (URL consulted Jan. 2007).

**54** Rod Garrett, "Interview with the author" (October 6. 2006).

**55** Michael Favor, "Interview with the author" (August 31. 2006).

**56** Andy Johnstone, "Interview with the author" (September 27. 2006).

**57** Paul J. DiMaggio, "Cultural Entrepreneurship in Nineteenth-Century Boston," in *Nonprofit Enterprise in the Arts*, ed. Paul J. DiMaggio (New York: Oxford University Press, 1986), 41–61.

**58** Florida, *The Rise of the Creative Class*.

**59** Lilly Irani, "Interview with the author" (July 27, 2006).

**CHAPTER 3**

**1** Bill Willingham (writer), and Mark Buckingham, Craig Hamilton, Steve Leialoha, P. Craig Russell (artists), *Fables: March of the Wooden Soldiers* (New York: DC Comics, 2004).

**2** Bill Willingham, Mark Buckingham, David Hahn, and Steve Leialoha, *Fables: Homelands* (New York: DC Comics, 2005).

**3** William Appleman Williams, *The Tragedy of American Diplomacy* (New York: W. W. Norton, 2009), 32.

**4** Williams, *The Tragedy of American Diplomacy*, 36.

**5** Quoted in William Appleman Williams, *Empire as a Way of Life* (New York: Oxford University Press, 1980), 95.

**6** Williams, *The Tragedy of American Diplomacy*, 43.

**7** Williams, *Empire as a Way of Life*, 51.

**8** Williams, *Empire as a Way of Life*, 51.

**9** Williams, *Empire as a Way of Life*, 160.

**10** Andrew Bacevich, *The Limits of Power: The End of American Exceptionalism* (New York: Holt, 2009), 27.

**11** Morris Berman, *Dark Ages America: The Final Phase of Empire* (New York: Holton, 2006), 247.

**12** Williams, *Empire as a Way of Life*, 159.

**13** Williams, *Empire as a Way of Life*, 50.

**14** Bacevich, *The Limits of Power*, 12.

**15** Bacevich, *The Limits of Power*, 66.

**16** Williams, *Empire as a Way of Life*, 31.

**17** Cormac McCarthy, *The Road* (New York: Alfred A. Knopf, 2006), 152.

**18** McCarthy, *The Road*, 7.

**19** Tadeusz Borowski, *This Way for the Gas, Ladies and Gentlemen*, trans. Barbara Vedder (New York: Penguin, 1976), 155.

**20** Borowski, *This Way for the Gas*, 156.

**21** Williams, *Empire as a Way of Life*, 149.

**22** George Kennan, *Memoirs 1950–1963* (New York: Pantheon, 1972), 83.

**23** Kennan, *Memoirs*, 85.

**24** Michael T. Klare, *Rising Powers, Shrinking Planet: The New Geopolitics of Energy* (New York: Metropolitan, 2008), 11.

**25** John Gray, "The New Wars of Scarcity," *Heresies: Against Progress and Other Illusions* (London: Granta, 2004), 119.

**26** Imre Szeman, "System Failure: Oil, Futurity, and the Anticipation of Disaster," *South Atlantic Quarterly* 106:4 (Fall 2007): 817.

**27** Szeman, "System Failure."

**28** José Saramago, *Blindness*, trans. Giovanni Pontiero (New York: Harcourt Brace, 1997), 39.

**29** Saramago, *Blindness*, 118–119, 121.

**30** Saramago, *Blindness*, 124.

**31** Alain Joxe, *Empire of Disorder*, trans. Ames Hodges (Los Angeles: Semiotext(e), 2002), 81.

**32** Joxe, *Empire of Disorder*, 13, 81.

**33** Saramago, *Blindness*, 264–265.

**34** Saramago, *Blindness*, 221.

**35** John Gray, review of *The Neoliberal State* by Raymond Plant. *New Statesman* (Jan. 7, 2010): http://www.newstatesman.com/non-fiction/2010/01/neoliberal-state-market-social.

**36** John Gray, *Straw Dogs: Thoughts on Humans and Other Animals* (London: Granta, 2002), 29.

**37** Quoted in Tasha Robinson, "Interview: Bill Willingham." *The A.V. Club* 6 (August 2007): http://www.avclub.com/articles/bill-willingham,14134.

**38** Bill Willingham, Mark Buckingham, and Steve Leialoha, *Fables: Animal Farm* (New York: DC Comics, 2003), 104.

**39** Gray, "The New Wars of Scarcity," 115.

### CHAPTER 4

**1** Michel de Certeau, *The Practice of Everyday Life*, Steven Rendall, trans. (Berkeley: University of California Press, 1984), 40.

**2** Catherine de Zegher and Mark Wigley, eds., *The Activist Drawing: Retracing Situationist Architectures from Constant's New Babylon to Beyond* (Cambridge, Mass.: MIT Press, 2001), 10.

**3** de Zegher and Wigley, *The Activist Drawing*, 27.

**4** de Zegher and Wigley, *The Activist Drawing*.

**5** See especially Iain Borden and Sandy McCreery, eds., *New Babylonians: Contemporary Visions of a Situationist City* (London: Academy Press/John Wiley &Sons, 2001).

**6** Borden and McCreery, *New Babylonians*, 10.

7 Borden and McCreery, *New Babylonians*, 50.

8 Borden and McCreery, *New Babylonians*, 27.

9 Borden and McCreery, *New Babylonians*, 24–25.

10 Mark Wigley, "Paper, Scissors, Blur," in Zegher and Wigley, *The Activist Drawing*, 34–36.

11 Mark Wigley, "Paper, Scissors, Blur," in Zegher and Wigley, *The Activist Drawing*, 15.

12 Mark Wigley, "Paper, Scissors, Blur," in Zegher and Wigley, *The Activist Drawing*, 25.

13 Mark Wigley, "Paper, Scissors, Blur," in Zegher and Wigley, *The Activist Drawing*, 46.

14 Mark Wigley, "Paper, Scissors, Blur," in Zegher and Wigley, *The Activist Drawing*, 31.

15 Zegher and Wigley, *The Activist Drawing*, 10.

16 Tracy Kidder, *The Soul of a New Machine* (Boston: Little, Brown, 1981); Michael A. Hiltzik, *Dealers of Lightning: Xerox PARC and the Dawn of the Computer Age* (New York: Harper Collins, 2000); M. Mitchell Waldrop, *The Dream Machine: J.C.R. Licklider and the Revolution that Made Computing Personal* (New York: Viking Adult, 2001); John Markoff, *What the Dormouse Said: How the 60s Counterculture Shaped the Personal Computer* (New York: Viking Adult, 2005).

17 Douglas Thomas, *Hacker Culture* (Minneapolis: University of Minnesota Press, 2003); Fred Turner, *From Counterculture to Cyberculture: Stewart Brand, the Whole Earth Network, and the Rise of Digital Utopianism* (Chicago: University of Chicago Press, 2006).

18 Gabriella Coleman, "The Political Agnosticism of Free and Open Source Software and the Inadvertent Politics of Contrast," *Anthropological Quarterly* 77:3 (2004): 511–512.

19 Turner, *From Counterculture to Cyberculture*.

20 Turner, *From Counterculture to Cyberculture*, 21.

21 For an extended discussion of the influence of Jacobs's ideas on Linden Lab, see Thomas M. Malaby, *Making Virtual Worlds: Linden Lab and Second Life* (Ithaca, N.Y.: Cornell University Press, 2009).

22 Turner, *From Counterculture to Cyberculture*, 65.

23 William James, *The Varieties of Religious Experience: A Study in Human Nature* (New York: The Modern Library, 1902).

## CHAPTER 5

1 For these, see Albert Moran, "Television Formats in the World/The World of Television Formats," in *Television Across Asia: Television Industries, Programme Formats and Globalization*, eds. Albert Moran and Michael Keane (Abingdon: Routledge-Curzon, 2004); Silvio Waisbord, "McTV: Understanding the Global Popularity of Television Formats," *Television & New Media* 5:4 (2004); and Tasha Oren and Sharon Shahaf, eds., *Global Formats: Understanding Television Across Borders* (New York: Routledge, 2010).

2 Graeme Turner, "Television and the Nation," in *Television Studies After Television*, eds. Graeme Turner and Jinna Tay (New York: Routledge, 2009).

3 Turner, "Television and the Nation," 57.

4 Jean Chalaby, ed., *Transnational Television Worldwide: Towards a New Media Order* (London: I.B. Tauris, 2005), 8.

5 Albert Moran and Justin Malbon, *Understanding the Global TV Format* (Bristol: Intellect Press, 2006), 39.

6 Moran and Malbon, *Understanding the Global TV Format*, 38.

7 Moran and Malbon, *Understanding the Global TV Format*, 39.

8 Albert Moran, *Copycat TV: Globalisation, Program Formats and Cultural Identity* (Luton: University of Luton Press, 1998), 20.

9 The format package may also include an actual consultant who will travel to the production site to provide on-hand help. For reasons I will enumerate in this chapter, this form of on-site production guidance is increasingly rare.

10 Moran and Malbon, *Understanding the Global TV Format*, 15, 20.

11 Kevin Robins and Asu Aksoy, "Whoever Looks Always Finds: Transnational Viewing and Knowledge Experience," in *Transnational Television Worldwide*, ed. Chalaby.

12 Robins and Aksoy, "Whoever Looks Always Finds: Transnational Viewing and Knowledge Experience," 18.

13 Minna Aslama and Mervi Pantti, "Flagging Finnishness: Reproducing National Identity in Reality TV," *Television & New Media* 8:1 (2007) and Sharon Sharp, "Global Franchising, Gender, and Genre: The Case of Domestic Reality Television" in *Global Formats*, eds. Oren and Shahaf (New York: Routledge, 2010).

14 *Global Public Opinion In the Bush Years (2001–2008)*, a Pew Global Attitudes Project report (Washington, DC: The Pew Reserach Project, 2008).

15 Zygmunt Bauman, *Globalization: The Human Consequences* (New York: Columbia University Press, 1998).

16 Albert Moran and Michael Keane, "Cultural Power in International TV Format Markets," *Continuum: Journal of Media & Cultural Studies* 20:1 (2006): 71–86.

17 Silvio Waisbord, "McTV: Understanding the Global Popularity of Television Formats," *Television & New Media* 5:4 (2004).

18 See Moran and Keane, "Cultural Power in International TV Format Markets."

19 Timothy Havens, *Global Television Marketplace* (New York: Palgrave Macmillan, 2008).

20 Waisbord, "McTV: Understanding the Global Popularity of Television Formats," 363.

21 Graeme Turner, "Cultural Identity, Soap Narrative, and Reality TV," *Television & New Media* 6:4 (2005).

22 See also Toby Miller's discussion of the planet Hollywood phenomena and the international division of cultural labor in Toby Miller (with Nitlin Govil, John McMurria and Richard Maxwell) *Global Hollywood* (London: BFI, 2001).

23 Albert Moran, *Copycat TV*.

24 Koichi Iwabuchi, "Feeling Glocal; Japan in the Global Television Format Business," in *Television Across Asia*, 34.

25 Moran, "Distantly European? Australia in the Global Television Business," in *Television Across Asia*, 170.

26 I borrow the term from Charles Liebman and Eliezer Don Yehiya, who contrast it with a functionary "state without vision" (a "service state") in Charles Liebman and Don Yehiya Eliezer, *Civil Religion in Israel* (Berkeley: University of California Press, 1983).

CHAPTER 6

1   See Omar Rincón, "La TelePasión de los Gavilanes: En busca de la telenovela neutra que no puede existir," *Chasqui* (forthcoming); and "Colombia: Cuando la Ficción Cuenta Más que los Informativos," in *Culturas y mercados de la ficción en Iberoamérica, Anuario Obitel 2007,* Lorenzo Vilches, ed. (Barcelona: Gedisa, 2007), 133–158.

2   Rincón, "La TelePasión de los Gavilanes."

3   For information on programming flows across the region, see Maria Immacolata Vasallo de Lopes and Lorenzo Vilches, eds., *Mercados Globais, Histórias Nacionais* (Rio de Janeiro: Globo Universidade, 2008).

4   See Arlene Dávila, *Latinos, Inc.: The Marketing and Making of a People* (Los Angeles: University of California Press, 2001).

5   I have been influenced by Natalie Karagiannis and Peter Wagner's call for scholars to move beyond the narrative on homogenizing global forces and pay attention to the plurality of worldmaking, that is, how people understand their diverse situations in political, philosophical, and cultural terms. Natalie Karagiannis and Peter Wagner, "Introduction: Globalization or World-Making?," in *Varieties of World-Making: Beyond Globalization,* Natalie Karagiannis and Peter Wagner, eds. (Liverpool: Liverpool University Press, 2007), 1–9.

6   For an analysis on the marginalization of blacks and indigenous people in Latin American, Spanish Caribbean, and U.S. Spanish-language media, see Dávila, *Latinos, Inc.*; Yeidy M. Rivero, *Tuning Out Blackness: Race and Nation in the History of Puerto Rican Television* (Durham, N.C.: Duke University Press, 2005); and Ella Shohat and Robert Stam, *Unthinking Eurocentrism: Multiculturalism and the Media* (London: Routledge, 1994).

7   I am drawing from Diana Taylor's concepts of the archives and the repertoire. Although Taylor makes a distinction between the archives ("enduring material," which includes film) and the repertoire ("performances, gestures, orality, movement, dance, [and] singing, . . . which require presence"), the progressive absence of particular bodily, verbal, and cultural enactments from commercial media allow us to re-think these films as mediated representations of the repertoire. As Taylor writes, "A video of a performance is not a performance though it often comes to replace the performance as a *thing* in itself (the video is part of the archive; what it represents is part of the repertoire)." Diana Taylor, *The Archive and the Repertoire: Performing Cultural Memory in the Americas* (Durham, N.C.: Duke University Press, 2004), 19–20.

8   For a broad interpretation of Doreen Massey's work, see David Morley, *Home Territories: Media, Mobility and Identity* (London: Routledge, 2000); and Jayne Rodgers, "Doreen Massey: Space, Relations, and Communication," *Information, Communication & Society* 7:2 (June 2004): 273–291.

9   Doreen Massey, "Imagining Globalization: Power Geometries of Time-Space," in *Global Futures: Migration, Environment and Globalization,* Mary J. Mickman and Máirtín Mac an Ghaill, eds. (London: Macmillan Press Ltd., 1999), 27–44.

10  Doreen Massey in Hans Gebhardt and Peter Meusburger, eds., *Power-Geometries and the Politics of Space Time, Hettner-Lectures 2* (Heidelberg: Department of Geography, University of Heidelberg, 1998), 28.

11  Massey, "Imagining Globalization," 41.

12  Massey, "Imagining Globalization," 41.

13  Massey, "Imagining Globalization," 41.

14  Doreen Massey, "A Place Called Home?," *New Formations* 17 (Summer 1992): 3–15.

15  Richard Bauman, *Verbal Art as Performance* (Prospect Heights, Ill.: Waveland Press, 1977), 5.

16  Richard Bauman, *A World of Others' Words: Cross-Cultural Perspectives on Intertextuality* (Oxford: Blackwell Publishing, 2004), 9.

17  Massey, *Power-Geometries*, 40.

18  Massey, "Imagining Globalization," 38; Morley, *Home Territories*, 196.

19  Doreen Massey, *Space, Place, and Gender* (Minneapolis: University of Minnesota Press, 1994), cited in Morley, *Home Territories*, 201.

20  Newyorican is the term generally used in Puerto Rico for Puerto Ricans born and raised in the United States, even though some of these first- and second-generation members were not necessarily born in New York City.

21  The Spanish influence that is part of the constructed Puerto Rican ethnic family is also included in the narrative through a priest character. On the airplane and in several flashbacks, he is portrayed as a respected individual not only because of his position within the Catholic Church but also because he has immersed himself within the community.

22  As I discussed elsewhere, humor and satire have been used extensively in Puerto Rico's mediascape as ideological weapons to transgress, to a certain extent, the political and social order. Even in the most politically repressive moments in Puerto Rican history, suppressed ideological positions disguised through humor were able to enter the official public stage and criticize U.S. interventions on the island as well as the local pre- and post-commonwealth authorities. See Rivero, *Tuning Out Blackness*.

23  It is important to note that three of the characters' motivations for traveling are elaborated through a series of flashbacks.

24  It is worth mentioning that Frances Negrón-Muntaner's 1994 film *Brincando el charco: Portrait of a Puerto Rican*, questions issues of colonialism, homophobia, machismo, migration, and identity in Puerto Rico's local and translocal communities. For an analysis of *Brincando el Charco*, see Gilberto Blasini, "Exiled Desire as a Desired Exile: Puerto Rican Identities in Frances Negrón-Muntaner's 'Brincando El Charco'" (American Studies Association Conference, Kansas City, Missouri, 1996); and Yeidy M. Rivero, "Diasporic and Marginal Crossroads: The Films of Frances Negrón-Muntaner," *Latino Studies Journal* 7:3 (September 2009): 336–356.

25  Bauman, *Verbal Art as Performance*, 22.

26  I am referring to what Richard Bauman and Charles L. Briggs call 'indexical grounding.' According to the authors, indexical grounding includes "deictic markers of a person, spatial location, [and] time" among other contextual elements. Richard Bauman and Charles L. Briggs, "Poetics and Performance as Critical Perspectives on Language and Social Life," *Annual Review of Anthropology* 19: 59–88.

27  See Samuel Juni and Bernard Katz, "Self-Effacing Wit as a Response to Oppression: Dynamics of Ethnic Humor," *Journal of General Psychology* 128:2 (April 2001): 119–143.

28  Massey, "A Place Called Home?," 152.

29 For information of Dominican migrations to the United States, see Sherri Grasmuck and Patricia R. Pessar, *Between Two Islands: Dominican International Migration* (Los Angeles: University of California Press, 1991).

30 Agustín Laó-Montes, "Introduction" to *Mambo Montage: The Latinization of New York City*, Agustín Laó-Montes and Arlene Dávila, eds. (New York: Columbia University Press, 2000), 4.

31 Aníbal Quijano, "The Colonial Nature of Power and Latin America's Cultural Experience," in *Sociology in Latin America*, Roberto Briceño-León and Heinz Sonntag, eds. (Colonia Tovar, Venezuela: ISA, 1997), 27–38.

32 As the sequel of *Nueba Yol* (*Nueba Yol 3: Bajo La Nueva Ley*) demonstrates, that was not the real end of Balbuena's immigrant ordeal. After being assaulted (a sequence included in *Nueba Yol*) and spending months in a hospital, he lost all his savings and could not return to the Dominican Republic.

33 Arlene Dávila, *Barrio Dreams: Puerto Ricans, Latinos, and the Neoliberal City* (Los Angeles: University of California Press, 2004), 171.

34 Dávila, *Barrio Dreams*, 171.

35 For an analysis of Cuban American films, see Ana López, "Greater Cuba," in *The Ethnic Eye: Latino Media Arts*, Chon A. Noriega and Ana López, eds. (Minneapolis: University of Minnesota Press, 1996), 38–58.

36 See Dávila, *Barrio Dreams*; Laó-Montes, "Introduction"; and Ramón Grosfoguel and Chloé S. Georas, "Latino Caribbean Diasporas in New York," in *Mambo Montage*, 97–118.

37 For information on the Dominican migrations to Puerto Rico, see Jorge Duany, "Caribbean Migration to Puerto Rico: A Comparison of Cubans and Dominicans," *International Migration Review* 26:1 (1992): 46–66; and *Los Dominicanos en Puerto Rico: Migración en la Semi-periferia* (Río Piedras, Puerto Rico: Huracán, 1990).

38 For a broad examination of Puerto Rico's anti-Dominican sentiment in relation to nationalism, see Jorge Duany, *The Puerto Rican Nation on the Move: Identities on the Island and in the United States* (Chapel Hill: The University of North Carolina Press, 2002).

39 Dávila, *Barrio Dreams*.

40 Dávila, *Latinos, Inc.*, 115.

41 My reading has been influenced by what Roman Jakobson labels as "intersemiotic translation," which he defines as "an interpretation of verbal signs by means of signs of nonverbal sign systems." Roman Jacobson, "On Linguistic Aspects of Translation," in *The Translation Studies Reader*, Lawrence Venuti, ed. (London: Routledge, 2000), 113–118.

42 As several scholars have argued, these areas are then gentrified to attract upscale (white) residents. See Philippe Bourgois, *In Search of Respect: Selling Crack in el Barrio* (New York: Cambridge University Press, 1995); and Dávila, *Barrio Dreams*.

43 An important aspect of these Afro-diasporic connections relates to the pre-1898 Cuban and Puerto Rican migrations to New York City. For an analysis of late-nineteenth-century and twentieth-century Puerto Rican migrations, see Virginia Sanchez-Korrol, *From Colonia to Community: The History of Puerto Ricans in New York City* (Berkeley: University of California Press, 1994). For an examination of Cuban migrations pre-1959, see Nancy Raquel Mirabal, "'No Country But the One We Must Fight For': The Emergence of an Antillean Nation and Community in

New York City, 1860–1901," in *Mambo Montage*, 57–72; "Scripting Race, Finding Place: African Americans, Afro-Cubans, and the Diasporic Imaginary in the United States," in *Neither Enemies nor Friends: Latinos, Blacks, Afro-Latinos*, Anani Dzidzienyo and Suzanne Oboler, eds. (New York: Palgrave MacMillan, 2005), 189–208; and Lisa Maya Knauer, "Eating in Cuban," in *Mambo Montage*, 425–448. For an ethnographic analysis of Garifuna immigrants in New York City, see Sarah England, "Negotiating Race and Place in the Garifuna Diaspora: Identity Formation and Transnational Grassroots Politics in New York City and Honduras," *Identities* 6:1: 5–53. See also Grosfoguel and Georas, "Latino Caribbean Diasporas in New York."

44 My analysis is based on Ramón Grosfoguel's and Chloé S. Georas's interpretation of Aníbal Quijano's concept of "coloniality of power." "Colonialidad y modernidad/racionalidad," *Perú Indígena* 29 (1992): 11–22, cited and interpreted in Grosfoguel and Georas, "Latino Caribbean Diasporas in New York," 102.

45 Richard Bauman and Charles L. Briggs, "Poetics and Performance," 76.

46 As Paul Gilroy notes regarding black music and communal performance of the African diaspora, "In the black Atlantic context, they [musical performances] produce the imaginary effect of an internal racial core or essence by acting on the body through the specific mechanisms of identification and recognition that are produced in the intimate interaction of performer and crowd." Paul Gilroy, *The Black Atlantic: Modernity and Double Consciousness* (Cambridge, Mass.: Harvard University Press), 102.

47 Laó-Montes, "Introduction," 18–19.

48 Rivero, *Tuning Out Blackness*.

## CHAPTER 7

1 Roy Armes, *Third World Filmmaking and the West* (Berkeley: University of California Press, 1987), 88.

2 Robert Stam, *Tropical Multiculturalism: A Comparative History of Race in Brazilian Cinema and Culture* (Durham, N.C.: Duke University Press, 1997), 287.

3 Paul Willemen, "The Third Cinema Question: Notes and Reflections," in *Questions of Third Cinema*, Jim Pines and Paul Willemen, eds. (London: BFI Publishing, 1989), 3.

4 Willemen, "The Third Cinema Question," 2.

5 Franz Fanon, *The Wretched of the Earth* (New York: Grove Press, 1968), 227.

6 Fanon, *Wretched of the Earth*, 233.

7 Gayatri Chakravorty Spivak, "Megacity," *Grey Room* 1 (Autumn, 2000): 13.

8 Lisa Shaw and Stephanie Dennison, *Brazilian National Cinema* (London: Routledge, 2007), 87.

9 Carlos Diegues, "The Cinema That Brazil Deserves," in *The New Brazilian Cinema*, ed. Lúcia Nagib (London and New York: I.B. Tauris, 2003), 24.

10 Edward Dimendberg, *Film Noir and the Spaces of Modernity* (Cambridge, Mass.: Harvard University Press, 2004); James Donald, *Imagining the Modern City* (Minneapolis: University of Minnesota Press, 1999); Sabine Hake, *Topographies of Class: Modern Architecture and Mass Society in Weimar Berlin* (Ann Arbor: University of Michigan Press, 2008); Linda Krause and Patrice Petro, *Global Cities: Cinema,*

*Architecture, and Urbanism in a Digital Age* (New Brunswick, N.J.: Rutgers University Press, 2003).

11 John David Rhodes, *Stupendous, Miserable City: Pasolini's Rome* (Minneapolis: University of Minnesota Press, 2007), xv.

12 George Yúdice, *Expediency of Culture* (Durham, N.C.: Duke University Press, 2007), 12-23.

13 Teresa Caldeira, *City of Walls: Crime, Segregation, and Citizenship in São Paulo* (Berkeley: University of California Press, 2001), 299.

14 Quoted in Yúdice, *Expediency*, 138.

15 Iris Marion Young, "City Life and Difference," in her *Justice and the Politics of Difference* (Princeton, N.J.: Princeton University Press, 1990).

16 Caldeira, *City of Walls*.

17 Esther Hamburger, "Politics of Representation: Television in a São Paulo *Favela*," http://www.vibrant.org.br/downloads/a1v1_pr.pdf, (accessed 6/25/09).

18 See "What Color Are You," from the Brazilian Institute of Geography and Statistics, for a list of the one hundred and thirty four racial terms Brazilians use to describe themselves. In Robert M. Levine and John J. Crocitti, eds., *The Brazil Reader* (Durham, N.C.: Duke University Press, 1999), 387–390.

19 A short history comes in James N. Green, "The Gay and Lesbian Movement in Brazil," in Levine and Crocitti, *The Brazil Reader*.

20 Cláudia Milito and Hélio R. S. Silva, "Voices from the Pavement," in *The Brazil Reader*, 422.

21 Giogio Agamben in Vincenzo Binetti and Cesare Casarino, trans., *Means Without End: Notes on Politics* (Minneapolis: University of Minnesota Press, 2000), 35.

## CHAPTER 8

1 Paco Ignacio Taibo II, *Ernesto Guevara también conocido como el Che* (Mexico: Planeta, 1996), 729–761. Taibo's account of the capture, execution, myth, and curse are vividly and dramatically written in this text.

2 Maite Rico y Bertrand de la Grange, "Operación Che," Historia de una mentira de Estado, February 2007, *Letras Libres*, http://www.letraslibres.com/index.php?art =11819, 6/13/09. After an extensive scientific investigation, these two journalists from the Spanish daily El País raised doubts that the remains found in Vallegrande in fact belonged to Che Guevara. Their report challenged forensic conclusions based on the comparison of autopsy reports made in 1967 and 1997. Aleida Guevara, daughter of Guevara, has widely denounced this claim.

3 Larry Rother, "Cuba Buries Che, the Man, but Keeps the Myth Alive," *New York Times* (October 18, 1997), http://www.nytimes.com/1997/10/18/world/cuba-buries-che-the-man-but-keeps-the-myth-alive.html (accessed 6/15/09).

4 Román de la Cámpa, "Postmodernism and Revolution: A Case Study of Central America," *Late Imperial Culture* (London: Verso, 1995), 122–126.

5 Taibo II, "Ernesto," 752–756.

6 Edward Said, "Traveling Theory Reconsidered," *Reflections on Exile and Other Essays* (Cambridge, Mass.: Harvard University Press, 2003), 436–452.

7 Jean Franco, *The Decline and Fall of the Lettered City* (Cambridge, Mass.: Harvard University Press, 2002), 60.

**8** Cassie Carpenter "The Face of a Revolution," *Back Stage West* (September 30–October 6, 2004):1.

**9** *Angeleno*, "Gael Force: Gael García Bernal Takes Hollywood by Storm," cover story, (December 2004).

**10** Alberto Korda took the photograph while Che Guevara attended the funeral in Cuba for the victims of the ship Le Coubre that exploded in the Havana harbor in 1960.

**11** Pablo Russo, "Santiago Álvarez, Fernando 'Pino' Solanas, y La hora de los hornos: no se ha de ver más que luz," Terra en Trance, http://tierraentrance.miradas.net/2008/11/entrevistas/lahoradeloshornos.html (accessed 6/14/09).

**12** Chris Rojek, *Celebrity* (London: Reaktion Books, 2001).

**13** Franco, "Decline," 58.

**14** Carpenter, "Face," 1.

**15** Lexi Feinberg, http://www.joblo.com/index.php?id=5368, accessed 8/14/05.

**16** *Cabrón* here is a playful use of Mexican slang to determine someone who is boldly hip and self-confident.

**17** Carpenter, "Face," 1.

**18** Columba Vértiz, "The Mexican Hollywood," *Proceso* (October 9, 2005): 50.

**19** *The Motorcycle Diaries* DVD Extras, "A Moment With Gael García Bernal—A conversation with the red-hot star of 'Y Tu Mamá También,' 'Amores Perros,' 'El Crimen Del Padre Amaro,' and 'Bad Education,' and Tomo Uno with Gael García Bernal," Universal Studios Home Entertainment (2004).

**20** *InStyle* magazine quoted in Carpenter, "Face," 1.

**21** Carpenter, "Face," 1.

**22** Luis Crespo, "Donde sólo disparen cámaras," *BBC Mundo.com* (October 14, 2004), http://news.bbc.co.uk/hi/spanish/misc/newsid_3744000/3744028.stm (accessed 6/15/09).

### CHAPTER 9

**1** See for example Stein, Davis, Hartley, and Boyle quoted in Bob Brown, *1450–1950* Vol. 31. (Highlands, North Carolina: Jonathan Williams' Jargon Books, 1959), back cover; Marinetti in Bob Brown, *Readies for Bob Brown's Machine* (CagnessurMer: Roving Eye Press, 1931), 47.

**2** Craig Saper, "The Reading Machine," *readies.org*, (May 22, 2009a); Craig Saper, "Book Type Machine: From Bob Brown's Reading Machine to Electronic Simulations, 1930–2010," *The Bonefolder: An e-Journal for the book binder and book artist* 6:1 (2009b); Craig Saper "The Adventures of Bob Brown and His Reading Machine: Abbreviated Texts 50 Years before Txt, Twitter, and WWW," in *The Readies*, ed. Craig Saper (Houston: Rice University Digital Press, 2009c); Craig Saper, "After Words," in *Words*, ed. Craig Saper (Houston: Rice University Press, 2009d); Craig Saper, "Materiality of a Simulation: Scratch Reading Machine, 1931," *Fibreculture*, 15 (2010a); Craig Saper, "Bob Brown's ———," in the Lost Poets Review section, *Paul Revere's Horse, A Literary Journal* 2, no. 2 (Sawkill Press, San Francisco, December 2010): 93-103.

**3** See for example: Michael North, "Words in Motion: The Movies, the Readies, and the 'Revolution of the Word,'" *Modernism/modernity* 9:2 (2002): 205–223; Craig

Douglas Dworkin, *Reading the Illegible—Avant-Garde & Modernism Studies* (Evanston, Ill.: Northwestern University Press, 2003); David M. Earle, *Re-Covering Modernism: Pulps, Paperbacks, and the Prejudice of Form* (Farnham, England; Burlington, VT: Ashgate, 2009); Craig Saper, "Book Type Machine"; Craig Saper, "Adventures of Bob Brown"; Hugh D. Ford, *Published in Paris: American and British Writers, Printers, and Publishers in Paris, 1920–1939* (New York: Macmillan, 1975).

4 The Browns, Cora, Rose, and Bob, *The European Cookbook for American Homes (from Italy, Spain, Portugal and France)* (New York: Farrar & Rinehart, 1936); The Browns, Cora, Rose, and Bob, *10,000 Snacks; a Cookbook of Canapés, Savories, Relishes, Hors D'œuvres, Sandwiches, and Appetizers for Before, After, and Between Meals* (New York: Farrar & Rinehart, 1937); The Browns, Cora, Rose, and Bob, *Salads and Herbs* (Philadelphia: J.B. Lippincott, 1938); The Browns, Cora, Rose, and Bob, *Fish & Sea Food Cook Book* (New York: Grosset & Dunlap, 1940); and Bob Brown, *The Complete Book of Cheese* (New York: Random House, 1955).

5 The Browns, *Fish & Sea Food*, 11.

6 The Browns, *Fish & Sea Food*, 173.

7 The Browns, *Fish & Sea Food*.

8 The Browns, *Fish & Sea Food*.

9 The Browns, *Fish & Sea Food*.

10 The Browns, *10,000 Snacks*, 7.

11 The Browns, *10,000 Snacks*.

12 Rose Brown, *The Land and People of Brazil*, Portraits of the Nations Series (Philadelphia, New York: J.B. Lippincott Company, 1946), 240.

13 Rose Brown, *Land and People*, 10.

14 Rose Brown, *Land and People*, 153.

15 Rose Brown, *Land and People*, 240.

16 Rose Brown, *Land and People*, 240–241.

17 Rose Brown, *Land and People*, 241.

18 Rose Brown, *Land and People*.

19 Rose Brown, *Land and People*.

20 Rose Brown, *Land and People*, 73.

21 Rose Brown, *Land and People*.

22 Rose Brown, *Land and People*, 95.

23 Rose Brown, *Land and People*, 98.

24 Rose Brown, *Land and People*, 116.

25 Rose Brown, *Land and People*, 159.

26 Rose Brown, *Land and People*, 160.

27 Ronald Bogue, *Deleuze and Guattari* (London: Routledge, 1989), 140–142. See also Gilles Deleuze and Félix Guattari, *A Thousand Plateaus: Capitalism and Schizophrenia* (Minneapolis: University of Minnesota Press, 1987), 238–239.

28 Deleuze, Gilles *Cinema I: The Movement—Image* (Minneapolis: University Of Minnesota Press, 1986), 88.

29 Deleuze, *Cinema I*, 50–51.

30 Deleuze, *Cinema I*, 9.

31 Deleuze, *Cinema I*, 17.

**32** Deleuze, *Cinema I*.

**33** Deleuze, *Cinema I*, 258.

## CHAPTER 10

**1** David Joeslit, *Feedback, Television Against Democracy* (Cambridge, Mass.: MIT Press, 2007), 40–41.

**2** Joeslit, *Feedback*, 240.

**3** Walter Benjamin, *The Work of Art in the Age of Mechanical Reproduction* (New York: Shocken Books, 1985), 240.

**4** This is in contrast to Creative Time's the 59th Minute in Times Square. The 59th Minute airs daily in Times Square on the NBC Astrovision by Panasonic on the last minute of every hour from 6:00 a.m. to 1:00 a.m., except between 7:00 and 10:00 a.m. and 6:00 and 7:00 p.m. at 45th Street and the intersection of Broadway and 7th Avenue.

**5** Annette Barbier, "Escape," *IAM: Columbia College Chicago*, 2005, http://iam.colum .edu/abarbier/escape.html.

**6** Conrad Gleber, "Building Id," conradgleber.com, 2005, http://www.conradgleber .com/index.php?load=html/buildingid.htm.

**7** Drew Browning, "Preserving Disorder," *EVL: Electronic Visualization Laboratory*, 2005, http://www.evl.uic.edu/drew/PresDis.50d.mov.

**8** http://www.meme01.com/projects/span.shtml

## CHAPTER 11

**1** See: Eduardo Kac, *Luz & Letra. Ensaios de Arte, Literatura e Comunicação* [Light & Letter. Essays in art, literature and communication] (Rio de Janeiro: Editora Contra Capa, 2004); Eduardo Kac, *Telepresence and Bio Art—Networking Humans, Rabbits and Robots* (Ann Arbor: University of Michigan Press, 2005). See also: <http://www.ekac.org>.

**2** Robert Atkins, "State of the (On-Line) Art," *Art in America* (April 99): 89–95; Mario Cesar Carvalho, "Artista Implanta Hoje Chip no Corpo," *Folha de São Paulo, Cotidiano* 11 (November 1997): 3; Michel Cohen, "The Artificial Horizon: Notes Towards a Digital Aesthetics," in *Luna's Flow. The Second International Media Art Biennale. Media_City Seoul 2002*, ed. Wonil Rhee (Seoul, Korea: Seoul Museum of Art, 2002), 20 and 32–33; Patricia Decia, "Bioarte: Eduardo Kac Tem Obra Polêmica vetada no ICI," *Folha de São Paulo, Ilustrada* (October 10, 1997): 13; Steve Dietz, "Memory_Archive_Database," *Switch* 5:3 (2000), http://switch.sjsu.edu; Steve Dietz, "Hotlist," *Artforum* (October 2000): 41; Luis Esnal, "Un Hombre Llamado 026109532," *La Nacion*, Section 5, Buenos Aires (December 15, 1997): 8; Eduardo Kac, "Time Capsule," *InterCommunication* 26 (Autumn 1998, Tokyo): 13–15; Eduardo Kac, "Time Capsule," in *Database Aesthetics*, eds. Victoria Vesna, Karamjit S. Gill and David Smith, special issue of *AI & Society* 14:2 (2000): 243–249; Eduardo Kac, "Art at the Biological Frontier," in *Reframing Consciousness: Art, Mind and Technology*, ed. Roy Ascott (Exeter: Intellect, 1999), 90–94; Eduardo Kac, "Capsule Temporelle," in *L'Archivage Comme Activité Artistique/Archiving as Art*, ed. Karen O'Rourke (Paris: University of Paris 1, 2000); Arlindo Machado, "A Microchip inside the Body," *Performance Research* 4:2—"On Line" special issue,

London—(1999): 8–12; Christiane Paul, "Time Capsule," *Intelligent Agent* 2:2 (1998): 4–13; Julia Scheeres, "New Body Art: Chip Implants," *Wired News* (March 11, 2002); Maureen P. Sherlock, "Either/Or/Neither/Nor," in *Gallery (Dante) Marino Cettina—Future Perspectives*, ed. Marina Grzinic (Umag, Croatia: Marino Cettina Gallery, 2001), 130–135; Kristine Stiles, "Time Capsule," *Uncorrupted Joy: Art Actions, Art History, and Social Value* (Berkeley: University of California Press, 2003); Stephanie Strickland, "Dalí Clocks: Time Dimensions of Hypermedia," *Electronic Book Review* 11 (2000); Steve Tomasula, "Time Capsule: Self-Capsule," *CIRCA*, 89 (Autumn 1999. Ireland): 23–25.

3 Gisele Beiguelman, "Artista Discute o Pós-Humano," *Folha de São Paulo* (October 10, 1997); Patricia Decia, "Artista Põe a Vida em Risco" e "Bioarte," *Folha de São Paulo* (October 10, 1997); James Geary, *The Body Electric An Anatomy Of The New Bionic Senses* (New Brunswick, N.J.: Rutgers, 2002), 181–185; Eduardo Kac, "A-positive," *ISEA '97— The Eighth International Symposium on Electronic Art* (Chicago: The School of the Art Institute of Chicago, 1997), 62; Eduardo Kac, "A-positive: Art at the Biobotic Frontier," flyer distributed on the occasion of *ISEA '97*; Eduardo Kac, "Art at the Biological Frontier," 90–94; Arlindo Machado, "Expanded Bodies and Minds," in *Eduardo Kac: Teleporting An Unknown State*, eds. Peter Tomaz Dobrila and Aleksandra Kostic (Maribor, Slovenia: KIBLA, 1998), 39–63; Matthew Mirapaul, "An Electronic Artist and His Body of Work," *New York Times* (October 2, 1997); Simome Osthoff, "From Stable Object to Participating Subject: Content, Meaning, and Social Context at ISEA97," *New Art Examiner* (February 1998): 18–23.

4 Eduardo Kac, "Transgenic Art," *Leonardo Electronic Almanac* 6:11 (1998). Also: <http://www.ekac.org/transgenic.html>. Republished in Gerfried Stocker and Christine Schopf, eds., *Ars Electronica '99—Life Science* (Vienna, New York: Springer, 1999), 289–296.

5 In 1998, canine reproductive technology was not developed enough to enable the creation of a transgenic or cloned dog. However, research was already underway to both map the dog genome and to develop canine IVF. In 2005, scientists successfully cloned a dog at Seoul National University, in Korea. Although the lead researcher (Woo Suk Hwang) was proven guilty of falsifying data in the field of stem cell research, the dog-cloning research was proven successful and is internationally accepted. The research is not practical and cannot be easily adapted. This unique research took great effort through an extended period of time, but it stands to demonstrate that "GFP K-9" will be possible in the near future.

6 Eduardo Kac, "Genesis," in *Ars Electronica '99—Life Science*, eds. Gerfried Stocker and Christine Schopf (Vienna, New York: Springer, 1999), 310–313. Also: <http://www.ekac.org/geninfo.html>. "Genesis" was carried out with the assistance of Dr. Charles Strom, formerly Director of Medical Genetics, Illinois Masonic Medical Center, Chicago. Dr. Strom is now Medical Director, Biochemical and Molecular Genetics Laboratories Nichols Institute / Quest Diagnostics, San Juan Capistrano, CA. Original DNA music for "Genesis" was composed by Peter Gena.

7 Charles Mudede, "The End of Art," *The Stranger* 9:15 (Dec. 30, 1999–Jan. 5, 2000, Seattle).

8 Eduardo Kac, "GFP Bunny," in *Eduardo Kac: Telepresence, Biotelematics, and Transgenic Art*, eds. Peter T. Dobrila and Aleksandra Kostic (Maribor, Slovenia: Kibla, 2000), 101–131. Also: <http://www.ekac.org/gfpbunny.html>.

9 I had proposed to live for one week with Alba in the Grenier à Sel, in Avignon, where Louis Bec directed the art festival "Avignon Numérique." In an e-mail

broadcast in Europe on June 16, 2000, Bec wrote: "Contre notre volonté, le programme concernant «Artransgénique», qui devait se dérouler du 19 au 25 juin, se trouve modifié. Une décision injustifiable nous prive de la présence de Bunny GFP, le lapin transgénique fluorescent que nous comptions présenter aux Avignonnais et à l'ensemble des personnes intéressées par les évolutions actuelles des pratiques artistiques. Malgré cette censure déguisée, l'artiste Brésilien Eduardo Kac, auteur de ce projet, sera parmi nous et présentera sa démarche ainsi que l'ensemble de ses travaux. Un débat public permettra d'ouvrir une large réflexion sur les transformations du vivant opérées par les biotechnologies, tant dans les domaines artistiques et juridiques, qu'éthiques et économiques. Nous nous élevons de toute évidence contre le fait qu'il soit interdit aux citoyens d'avoir accès aux développements scientifiques et culturels qui les concernent si directement."

10  Gareth Cook, "Cross Hare: Hop and Glow," *Boston Globe* (9/17/2000): A01.

11  For a bibliography on transgenic art, see: <http://www.ekac.org/transartbiblio. html>.

12  See: http://www.ekac.org/bunnybook.2000_2004.html.

13  These posters have also been shown in gallery exhibitions: *Dystopia + Identity in the Age of Global Communications* (curated by Cristine Wang, Tribes Gallery, New York, 2000); *Under the Skin* (curated by Söke Dinkla, Renate Heidt Heller and Cornelia Brueninghaus-Knubel, Wilhelm Lehmbruck Museum, Duisburg, 2001); "International Container Art Festival" (Kaohsiung Museum of Fine Arts, Taiwan, Dec. 8, 2001, to January 6, 2002); "Portão 2" (Galeria Nara Roesler, São Paulo, Brazil, March 21 to April 27, 2002); "Free Alba!" (Julia Friedman Gallery, Chicago, May 3 to June 15, 2002); "Eurovision—I Biennale d'Arte : DNArt; Transiti: Metamorfosi: Permanenze" (Kunsthaus Merano Arte, Merano, Italy, June 15 to August 15, 2002); "Gene(sis): Contemporary Art Explores Human Genomics" (Henry Art Gallery, Seattle, April 6 to August 25, 2002); "Face/off – Body Fantasies" (Kunst und Kunstgewerbeverein, Pforzheim, Germany, February to May, 2004); "Gene(sis): Contemporary Art Explores Human Genomics" (Frederick Weisman Museum of Art, Minneapolis, January 25 to May 2, 2004). See also the following catalogues: Under the Skin (Ostfildern-Ruit, Germany: Hatje Cantz Verlag, 2001), 60–63; "Eurovision—I Biennale d'Arte : DNArt; Transiti: Metamorfosi: Permanenze" (Milano: Rizzoli, 2002), 104–105; International Container Art Festival (Kaohsiung: Kaohsiung Museum of Fine Arts, 2002), 86–87.

14  Lisa Stein, "New Kac Show Takes a Look at Ethics, Rabbit," *Chicago Tribune* (May 10, 2002), 21.

15  In actuality, genes do not "produce" proteins. As Richard Lewontin clearly explains: "A DNA sequence does not specify protein, but only the amino acid sequence. The protein is one of a number of minimum free-energy foldings of the same amino acid chain, and the cellular milieu together with the translation process influences which of these foldings occurs." See: R. C. Lewontin, "In the Beginning Was the Word," *Science* 291 (February 16, 2001): 1264.

16  In 1985 I purchased an issue of a magazine entitled *High Technology*, whose cover headline read "Protein Engineering: Molecular Creations for Industry and Medicine." Clearly, the desire to "design" new molecular forms has been evolving for approximately two decades. See: Jonathan B. Tucker, "Proteins to Order. Computer graphics and gene splicing are helping researchers create new molecules

for industry and medicine," *High Technology* 5:12 (December 1985): 26–34. A few months before, I had published an article in which I discussed an art of the future, which would "develop a new form of expression in a space minimized to the highest degree." See: "A Arte Eletrônica em Espaço Microscópico" [Electronic Art in Microscopic Space], *Módulo* 87 (September 1985): 49.

**17** Special thanks to Dr. Murray Robinson, Head of Cancer Program, Amgen, Thousand Oaks, CA.

**18** Protein visualization was carried out with the assistance of Charles Kazilek and Laura Eggink, BioImaging Laboratory, Arizona State University, Tempe.

**19** Rapid prototyping was developed with the assistance of Dan Collins and James Stewart, Prism Lab, Arizona State University, Tempe.

**20** Terms like "transcription," as well as "code," "translation," and many others commonly employed in molecular biology, betray an ideological stance, a conflation of linguistic metaphors and biological entities, whose rhetorical goal is to instrumentalize processes of life. In the words of Lily E. Kay, this merger integrates "the notion of the genetic code as relation with that of a DNA code as thing." See: Kay, *Who Wrote the Book of Life: A History of the Genetic Code* (Stanford, Calif.: Stanford University Press, 2000), 309. For a thorough critique of the rhetorical strategies of molecular biology, see: Richard Doyle, *On Beyond Living: Rhetorical Transformations of the Life Sciences* (Stanford, Calif.: Stanford University Press, 1997).

**21** I developed "The Eighth Day" through a two-year residency at the Institute of Studies in the Arts, Arizona State University, Tempe. The exhibition dates: October 25 to November 2, 2001. Exhibition location: Computer Commons Gallery, Arizona State University, Tempe (with the support of the Institute of Studies in the Arts). Documentation can be found at: <http://www.ekac.org/8thday.html>. See: Sheilah Britton and Dan Collins, eds., *The Eighth Day: The Transgenic Art of Eduardo Kac* (New York: ASU / Distributed by DAP, 2003).

**22** See: Elena Giulia Rossi, *Eduardo Kac: Move 36* (Paris: Filigranes Éditions, 2005).

**23** "Specimen of Secrecy About Marvelous Discoveries" premiered at the Singapore Biennale (September 4–November 12, 2006).

**24** See Terence A. Brown, *Genomes* (Oxford: Bios scientific publishers, 1999), 138; and David Baltimore, "Our genome unveiled," *Nature* 409 (February 15, 2001): 814–816. In private e-mail correspondence (January 28, 2002), and as a follow-up to our previous conversation on the topic, Dr. Jens Reich, Division of Genomic Informatics of the Max Delbruck Center in Berlin-Buch, stated: "The explanation for these massive [viral] inserts into our genome (which, incidentally, looks like a garbage bin anyway) is usually that these elements were acquired into germ cells by retrovirus infection and subsequent dispersion over the genome some 10 to 40 million years ago (as we still were early apes)." The HGP also suggests that humans have hundreds of bacterial genes in the genome. See: International Human Genome Sequencing Consortium. "Initial sequencing and analysis of the human genome," *Nature* 409:6822 (February 15, 2001), 860. Of the 223 genes coding for proteins that are also present in bacteria and in vertebrates, 113 cases are believed to be confirmed. See p. 903 of the same issue. In the same correspondence mentioned above, Dr. Reich concluded: "It appears that it is not man, but all vertebrates who are transgenic in the sense that they acquired a gene from a microorganism."

25 This natural ability has made a genetically engineered version of the agro-bacterium a favorite tool of molecular biology. See: Luis Herrera-Estrella, "Transfer and expression of foreign genes in plants," PhD thesis (Ghent University, Belgium: Laboratory of Genetics, 1983); Paul J.J. Hooykaas and R.A., Shilperoort, "Agrobacterium and plant genetic engineering," *Plant Molecular Biology* 19 (1992):15–38; John R. Zupan and Patricia C. Zambryski, "Transfer of T-DNA from Agrobacterium to the plant cell," *Plant Physiology* 107 (1995): 1041–1047.

# ABOUT THE CONTRIBUTORS

**A. ANEESH** is Associate Professor of Sociology and Global Studies at the University of Wisconsin–Milwaukee. His research interests lie at the intersection of technology and work. He is the author of *Virtual Migration: The Programming of Globalization* (2006), which examines how new technologies of globalization affect a break with previous notions of labor migration. He is currently completing a study of international call centers located in India, a research project funded by the MacArthur Foundation.

**LANE HALL** is Professor in the Department of English at the University of Wisconsin–Milwaukee. His books, prints, and installations have been widely exhibited in the United States and Europe. Recent projects include installations at the California Academy of Sciences in San Francisco, Post Gallery in Los Angeles, Monique Meloche Gallery in Chicago, and The Milwaukee Art Museum. His work examines digital art and culture, procedural and experimental literature, and the history of the book.

**EDUARDO KAC** is internationally renowned for his work in telecommunications art, bio art, and transgenic art. His work explores the relationships between biology, media, and digital culture. His written work has been collected in two volumes: *Telepresence and Bio Art: Networking Humans, Rabbits and Robots* (2005) and *Luz & Letra* (2004). His creative work is part of the permanent collection of the Museum of Modern Art in New York, the ZKM Museum in Karlsruhe, Germany, and the Museum of Modern Art in Rio de Janeiro, among others.

**THOMAS M. MALABY** is Associate Professor of Anthropology at the University of Wisconsin–Milwaukee. He has published numerous works on virtual worlds, games, practice theory, and risk. His principal research interest is in the relationships among modernity, unpredictability, and technology, particularly as they are realized through games and game-like processes. He recently published *Making Virtual Worlds: Linden Lab and Second Life* (2009), an ethnography of Linden Lab and its relationship to its creation, Second Life (www.secondlife.com). He is also a featured author at the blog Terra Nova (terranova.blogs.com).

**TASHA G. OREN** is Associate Professor of English at the University of Wisconsin–Milwaukee. She is the author of *Demon in the Box: Jews, Arabs, Politics and Culture in the Making of Israeli Television* (2004), co-editor of *Global Currents: Media and Technology Now* (2004) and *East Main Street: Asian American Popular Culture* (2005), and editor of *Global Television Formats: Circulating Culture, Producing Identity* (2009). She researches and teaches courses in film and media theory, globalization, media history, screenwriting, and popular culture.

**PETER Y. PAIK** is Associate Professor of Comparative Literature at the University of Wisconsin–Milwaukee. He recently published *From Utopia to Apocalypse: Science Fiction and the Politics of Catastrophe* (2010), which is a study of revolutionary change in speculative and science fiction narratives. His articles have appeared in *Theory and Event*, *Postmodern Culture*, *Religion and the Arts*, and the *Yale Broch Symposium*. He is also coeditor (with Marcus Bullock) of *Aftermaths: Exile, Migration, and Diaspora Reconsidered* (2009).

**PATRICE PETRO** is Professor of English and Film Studies at the University of Wisconsin–Milwaukee, where she also serves as Vice Provost for International Education. She is the author, editor, and coeditor of ten books, most recently, *Idols of Modernity: Movie Stars of the 1920s* (2010), *Rethinking Global Security: Media, Popular Culture, and the "War on Terror"* (2006), and *Aftershocks of the New: Feminism and Film History* (2002). She is the former President of the Society for Cinema and Media Studies, the leading professional organization of college and university educators, filmmakers, historians, critics, scholars, and others devoted to the study of the moving image.

**MARK POSTER** is former Chair of the Department of Film and Media Studies and the History Department at the University of California, Irvine. His recent books include *Information Please: Culture and Politics in a Digital Age* (2006); *What's the Matter with the Internet?: A Critical Theory of Cyberspace* (2001); *The Information Subject in Critical Voices Series* (2001); *Cultural History* *and Postmodernity* (1997); *The Second Media Age* (1995); and *The Mode of Information* (1990).

**MAT RAPPAPORT** is Associate Professor of Television at Columbia College in Chicago. His work has been exhibited in the United States and internationally in galleries, film festivals, and public spaces. His current work utilizes mobile video and performance to explore habitation, perception, and power as related to built environments. He is a co-initiator of vɪb3 (www.vɪb3.com), which seeks to shape the experience of urban environments through media-based interventions.

**YEIDY M. RIVERO** is Associate Professor in the Departments of American Culture and Screen Arts and Cultures at the University of Michigan. Her research examines race and media in Latin America and the African diaspora. She is author of *Tuning Out Blackness: Race and Nation in the History of Puerto Rican Television* (2005). Her work has appeared in *Television and New Media*, *Global Media and Communication*, and *Critical Studies in Media Communication*. She is currently working on a manuscript entitled *Broadcasting Modernity: Cuban Commercial TV, 1950–1960*.

**CRAIG SAPER** is Professor and Coordinator of the Texts and Technology PhD program in the English Department at the University of Central Florida. He is author of *Networked Art* (2001) and *Artificial Mythologies* (1997). He has published over fifty articles, which have appeared in journals such as *Rhizomes: Cultural Studies in Emerging Knowledge* and the *Journal of E-Media Studies*. His work focuses primarily on networked art, digital rhetoric, and visual poetry.

**FRED TURNER** is Associate Professor of Communication at Stanford University, and he holds formal affiliations with the programs in Art and Art History, American Studies, Modern Thought, and Literature, Science, Technology, and Society, Symbolic Systems, and Urban Studies. He is author of *From Counterculture to Cyberculture: Stewart Brand, the Whole Earth Network and the Rise of Digital Utopianism* (2006) and *Echoes of Combat: The Vietnam War in American Memory* (2001). His work focuses primarily on media in American cultural history.

**CRISTINA VENEGAS** is Associate Professor of Film and Media Studies at the University of California, Santa Barbara. Her research focuses on international media with an emphasis on "Latin" America, Spanish-language film and television in the United States, and digital technologies. She is author of *Digital Dilemmas: The State, the Individual, and Digital Media in Cuba* (2010). She has curated numerous film programs on Latin American and Indigenous film in the United States and Canada, and is Cofounder and Artistic Director (since 2004) of the Latino CineMedia Film Festival in Santa Barbara that is now co-presented with the Santa Barbara International Film Festival.

**AMY VILLAREJO** is Associate Professor in Film Studies and the Feminist, Gender, & Sexuality Studies program at Cornell University. Her scholarship has focused on documentary cinema, queer politics, and media publics. She is author of *Lesbian Rule: Cultural Criticism and the Value of Desire* (2003), which won the Katherine Singer Kovacs award for best book from the Society for Cinema and Media Studies. She is also author of *Film Studies: The Basics* (2002) and is coeditor, with Jordana Rosenberg, of the anthology *Capital Q: Marxism after Queer Theory* (forthcoming).

# INDEX

CPSIA information can be obt:
Printed in the USA
BVOW030445071111

275443BV00002E

P 94.6 .B48 2012

Beyond globalization